THE VICTORIAN PROPHETS

Peter Keating was born in London in 1939 and educated at the University of Sussex. From 1968 to 1972 he was Lecturer in English at the University of Leicester, and is now Reader in English Literature at the University of Edinburgh. He is the author of *The Working Classes in Victorian Fiction* (1971), *Into Unknown England* (1976) and studies of a number of Victorian writers including George Gissing, Arthur Morrison, Robert Browning and Matthew Arnold. He is at present writing a social history of the late Victorian and early modern novel.

The
Victorian Prophets

A READER FROM CARLYLE
TO WELLS

Edited and with an
Introduction
by Peter Keating

Fontana Paperbacks

This selection first issued in Fontana 1981
Copyright © in the editor's introduction and
this selection Peter Keating 1981

Made and printed in Great Britain by
William Collins Sons and Co. Ltd, Glasgow

Set in Lasercomp Garamond

Contents

Preface

The literature of social prophecy in the nineteenth century is so extensive, and the issues it raises of such continuing interest, that it is tempting in an anthology of this kind either to reprint too much and risk obscuring central concerns or to oversimplify those concerns by reprinting a large number of brief extracts. I have therefore chosen to include only eight major essays or pamphlets and to reproduce them as fully as possible. Most of the items are justly celebrated: each of them makes a distinctive contribution to the complex, many-sided debate on the nature and desirability of change in an emergent democratic society that is so characteristic of the Victorian period.

The only item I have had to abridge is Ruskin's 'The Nature of Gothic'. As Ruskin himself explains in his introductory remarks, this particular chapter of *The Stones of Venice* is divided into two parts, one of which explores the 'mental power or expression' of Gothic architecture, the other its 'material form'. It is the first part that is substantially reprinted here: some necessary further cuts within the extract are indicated by omission marks.

The version of *The Communist Manifesto* I have used differs in one respect from that which is familiar to modern readers. It has become customary to include all of the prefaces which Engels wrote for the various translations of the *Manifesto*, even though these are largely, and inevitably, repetitious. In order to remain consistent with the historical approach of *The Victorian Prophets*, I have reproduced, complete, the standard 1888 English translation which was supervised by Engels; the edition, in effect, that readers of the late-nineteenth and early-twentieth century would have known. The prefaces to the translations into other languages are, therefore, not included.

I have silently deleted a few footnotes where their presence might be confusing, but otherwise all of the original annotation has been retained.

I would like to express my thanks to the estate of the late H.G. Wells for permission to reprint 'The Life-History of Democracy' from *Anticipations* (1901).

Peter Keating

'It is no very good symptom either of nations or individuals, that they deal much in vaticination', Carlyle proclaims in the opening sentence of 'Signs of the Times', establishing immediately as his social ideal a world in which man is completely at one with his age: 'Happy men are full of the present, for its bounty suffices them; and wise men also, for its duties engage them.' Too great a concern with 'vaticination' or prophecy is distrusted by Carlyle because it is seen as characteristic of an age that has lost the will and the power to understand itself, an age given over to what he calls 'frenzies and panics'. But the solution he proposes – an urgent concentration on present tendencies so that the 'signs of the times' can be properly understood – is, by itself, no real alternative as he well realized. Signs are portents: the immediate future lies in the hands of those who control the present as surely as the present has developed from the past, and Carlyle's call is for more, not less, prophecy, providing of course that it is of the right kind:

> The poorest Day that passes over us is the conflux of two Eternities; it is made up of currents that issue from the remotest Past, and flow onwards into the remotest Future. We were wise indeed, could we discern truly the signs of our own time; and by knowledge of its wants and advantages, wisely adjust our own position in it. Let us, instead of gazing idly into the obscure distance, look calmly around us, for a little, on the perplexed scene where we stand.

That kind of insight into the present is not regarded as open to anyone. It takes a truly 'wise' man to interpret the signs of the times and suggest the necessary adjustments to them. It takes a prophet, a Sage, a Vates.

To speak of the prophetic tradition in Victorian literature is not a matter of imposing retrospectively a modern academic label: it is to evoke a mood, tone, and certain kinds of concern with the nature of social change that existed as living realities to the Victorians. One extreme form of the tradition was established by Carlyle. He constantly dramatized himself as a prophet-figure, urged the need for prophetic activity on his contemporaries, and in return received from admirers the appropriate homage. Again and again in his biography of Carlyle, J. A. Froude invokes the prophetic image:

> He was a teacher and a prophet in the Jewish sense of the word. The prophecies of Isaiah and Jeremiah have become a part of the permanent spiritual inheritance of mankind, because events proved that they had interpreted correctly the signs of their own times, and their prophecies were fulfilled. Carlyle, like them, believed that he had a special message to deliver to the present age. Whether he was correct in that belief, and whether his message was a true message, remains to be seen.[1]

In a later passage Froude explains why Carlyle's impact on young men and women of the 1830s and 1840s was so great. At a time, Froude writes, when 'all round us, the intellectual lightships had broken from their moorings', he and many of his contemporaries had been 'saved' by Carlyle: 'Amidst the controversies, the arguments, the doubts, the crowding uncertainties of forty years ago, Carlyle's voice was to the young generation of Englishmen like the sound of "ten thousand trumpets" in their ears.'[2] Carlyle's message – starkly simple and repeated with endless passion – was that the chaos and uncertainty of the age were not merely temporary phenomena which could be safely ignored or left to work themselves out, but the expression of a fundamental shift in the structure of British society. His call was for a true recognition of those

---

[1] *Froude's Life of Carlyle,* edited and abridged by John Clubbe (1979), p. 82.

[2] Ibid., pp. 418–9.

changes and for the dedication and involvement required to make them work for peace rather than conflict. For Carlyle the necessary first step was to reject the debilitating introspective side of romanticism that he saw as infecting the young intellectuals of the time, and to follow, in effect, the example of Goethe who had created the type of the ineffectual romantic in *The Sorrows of Young Werther* (1774) and the anti-type as well in *Wilhelm Meister's Apprenticeship* (1795). Carlyle translated *Wilhelm Meister* so that the important lessons it contained would be available to English readers and he described his own version of the spiritual journey out of 'satanic' romanticism in *Sartor Resartus* (1833–4).

Froude's testimony to Carlyle's influence is valuable because he remained true to Carlyle when many others of his generation were retreating in horror from the wild denunciations that poured from the ageing prophet, or perhaps more precisely, as the implications of his ideas became clearer. But even in reaction there were generous tributes to the important part Carlyle had played in opening the eyes of early Victorians to the forces making for change in society. George Eliot was not exaggerating when, in 1855, she wrote: 'There has hardly been an English book written for the last ten or twelve years that would not have been different if Carlyle had not lived.'[1] All of the writers in this anthology were strongly aware of Carlyle's work. The young Mill was an admirer and personal friend; Arnold was to become severely critical of Carlyle, but he also remembered the days when an article by him seemed to appeal to the heart with 'true pathetic eloquence'; Ruskin, like Froude, did not turn against Carlyle and was moved by the personal encouragement that Carlyle offered during the controversy over *Unto this Last* (1860); in 'How I Became a Socialist' Morris linked Carlyle with Ruskin as the leaders in the 'rebellion against Whiggery'; Marx and Engels acknowledged him as an exception to their usual view of British writers as insular, while Engels wrote an enthusiastic review of *Past and Present* and drew frequently and

[1] *Thomas Carlyle: The Critical Heritage,* edited by J. P. Seigel (1971), p 410.

generally with approval on Carlyle in *The Condition of the Working
Class in England* (1845); and as late as 1885 when H. G. Wells was
a student in South Kensington and increasingly neglecting his
formal studies, Carlyle was one of the authors he slipped away
from lectures to read.[1] Among early- and mid-Victorian
novelists and poets, Charles Kingsley, Mrs Gaskell, Dickens,
Disraeli, Clough, Tennyson, and Browning, in addition to
George Eliot, all reveal their debt to Carlyle.

Carlyle's historical significance has been well described by
Raymond Williams:

> What is important in a thinker like Carlyle is the quality of his
> direct response: the terms, the formulations, the morphology
> of ideas, are properly a secondary matter, and as properly,
> also, the subject of influence. Carlyle is in ['Signs of the
> Times'] stating a direct response to the England of his times:
> to Industrialism, which he was the first to name; to the feel,
> the quality, of men's general reactions – that structure of
> contemporary feeling which is only ever apprehended
> directly; as well as to the character and conflict of formal
> systems and points of view.[2]

It is undoubtedly the immediacy and urgency of Carlyle's 'direct
response to the England of his times' that makes necessary for
him the prophetic stance, though it is difficult to see how the
ideas are 'properly a secondary matter': they are indistinguishably a part of that stance and crucial to the power it
seeks. Carlyle's views were not accepted unthinkingly; they
were frequently pushed angrily to one side by other Victorian
commentators; the prophetic tone was derided as often as
admired and later evoked unconcealed disgust. Yet the areas of
concern defined by Carlyle, the 'signs' which he indicates as

[1] Matthew Arnold, 'Emerson', *Discourses in America* (1885), *Collected
Prose Works of Matthew Arnold*, R. H. Super (ed.) (11 volumes,
Michigan 1960–77), X, 166; Steven Marcus, *Engels, Manchester and the
Working Class* (1974), pp. 102–12; Norman and Jeanne Mackenzie, *The
Time Traveller: The Life of H. G. Wells* (1974), p. 60.
[2] *Culture and Society 1780–1950* (Penguin Books 1961), pp. 85–6.

characteristic of his age, lie at the heart of a complex nineteenth-
and twentieth-century debate on the organization and control of
industrial society. It is a debate conducted largely through
periodicals, books and pamphlets by intellectuals and artists,
and the influence it exerts on dominant attitudes and values
down to the present day is enormous, though of the writers
represented here only Mill, late in his life, held any formal
position of political power. Ruskin, Marx, Engels, Morris, and
Wells, all involve themselves, in very different ways, in political
agitation, but the guidance or leadership they offer are all in
extra-parliamentary forms. And, although the quality of life in
the industrial working class provides a central theme in the
debate, none of these writers comes from that class: Carlyle and
Wells are closest in their family backgrounds to the actual
experience of working-class life.

The debate they participate in is often treated as though it
existed in isolation – sometimes as English literature, sometimes
as political theory – but it was really only one particularly
articulate strand of a much wider struggle with the same issues.
From the late-eighteenth century there was a rapidly developing
working-class movement conscious of its own aims and
aspirations, and from the late 1820s, and largely in response to
working-class pressure, there was the constant activity of
reformist parliaments, marked in stages by the gradual extension
of the franchise, each of which, in 1832 and 1867 particularly,
was bitterly contested and then granted more in a mood of
capitulation than from any coherent social policy. Neither of
these forces was dependent upon the prophets for its understanding of social conditions or for the attitudes it should take to
reforms, though it was only through coming to terms with one
or other of those forces that the prophets could hope to
influence events. Not the least significant aspect of the prophetic
tradition is that its own existence is symptomatic of the social
changes it is ambitious to analyse and direct.

No truly comparable figure to the Carlylean prophet exists
before the nineteenth century. In earlier periods the prophet was
a man divinely inspired, a spokesman for, or a messenger of, the

gods, someone set apart from other men by that particular role of mediator or interpreter which gave him special insight into man's ultimate fate. His power rested on forces beyond himself which were capable of being called upon for terrible retribution if his warnings about man's declining moral or spiritual condition were not heeded. Much of this meaning is carried over into the nineteenth century, descending from Carlyle through, most centrally, Ruskin and Arnold. All three writers claim special insight into the human condition, use religious terminology to dramatize their message, and consciously encourage public images of themselves as lonely, isolated, embattled bearers of the truth. Their special status is marked by a refusal to involve themselves in what are seen as partisan, class or institutional reforms, out of fear that such involvement will dilute the purity of their message, though of course this does not prevent them from occasionally supporting or criticizing particular reforms or reformers. They claim to stand above petty intrigue and pragmatic compromise in order to speak in terms of absolute truths and on behalf of the whole of society. Although they characterize their age as one of radically disturbing change, they rarely concentrate on positive responses in society to that change: they dictate the terms of the debate and argue them out with a rhetorical ruthlessness and linguistic invention calculated to crush opposition while at the same time persuading others of the indisputable truth of their assertions.

Where they break most significantly from the age-old function of the prophet is in the secularism of their concerns, and this is the case regardless of whether they themselves hold religious beliefs. They continue to place man's spiritual nature at the centre of their ideas – his Soul-politic rather than his Body-politic in Carlyle's formulation – but their prophetic warnings can no longer be backed by threats of divine anger or retribution. The role of the Avenging Angel is now taken by democracy, and the threat posed is that if civilized society does not reform itself from within, by slowing down and controlling the pace of inevitable change, then it will be destroyed, either by physical force or by a flood of democratic ignorance. The lesson offered by the French Revolution is influential here, though not in any simplistic way. Arnold's belief that the French Revolution was 'the greatest, the most animating event' of modern times would have been shared generally by all of the writers in this anthology, as also would Carlyle's qualification in 'Signs of the Times' that the causes of Victorian discontent lay not in the Revolution itself but further back in eighteenth-century rationalism: 'The French Revolution, as is now visible enough, was not the parent of this mighty movement, but its offspring.' It was important to the prophets to demonstrate that a society deeply-rooted in tradition and custom could be overthrown with apparent ease if it allowed poverty and injustice to exist as part of its system, and the French Revolution offered, in this respect, a far more disturbing lesson than the mid-eighteenth century American 'revolution', though as the Victorian age developed the American experience began to present its own kind of disturbing challenge. The French Revolution also seemed to reveal the unreliability of egalitarian philosophies, with its original ideals swiftly perverted into periods of terror, dictatorship, war and semi-permanent political instability, while at the same time offering itself as an example to the rest of Europe. If the revolution never took hold in Britain, the fear that it could well do so is naggingly present throughout the first half of the nineteenth century, injecting a sense of urgency into both reformist parliamentarians and prophetic utterances. But the most important lesson taught to the prophets by the French Revolution cannot be explained solely in terms of class fear. It taught them that a demand for social and political change was the dominant mood of the age, that absolute statements about the inviolability of traditional rights and relationships had become virtually meaningless, and that present conditions can only be understood by studying the historical past.

It has often been said of the Victorian prophets that they were regressive in their thinking, hostile to their own time, and constantly gazing back nostalgically on idealized, usually pre-industrial, ages. Such a view is at best only half-true. The actual changes taking place may not have been welcome to the prophets, but change itself they acknowledged as a fact of modern life. Carlyle makes the point very clearly in 'Signs of the Times':

> Knowledge, education are opening the eyes of the humblest; are increasing the number of thinking minds without limit. This is as it should be; for not in turning back, not in resisting, but only in resolutely struggling forward, does our life consist.

Arnold accepted completely the necessity for political change. His consistent attitude is expressed in an early essay: 'the circumstances and conditions of government having changed, the guiding maxims of government ought to change also.' And he insisted repeatedly that the kind of 'culture' he spoke for was dynamic: 'Not a having and a resting, but a growing and a becoming.'[1] Ruskin, the Victorian prophet most open to the charge of regressive thinking, is none the less as convinced as Arnold that what is most needed in society is a dynamic not a static guide to life: 'The vital principle is not the love of *Knowledge*, but the love of *Change*. It is that strange *disquietude* of the Gothic spirit that is its greatness.' Mill would normally be excluded from the charge of being backward-looking, and necessarily so. If he lacks the rhetorical skill of Carlyle, Ruskin and Arnold, he is also more dedicated than any of them to a rational analysis of the forces transforming society. One of the main aims of 'Civilization' is to mock the stupidity of those politicians who are unwilling to see what is happening:

> The change which is thus in progress, and to a great extent consummated, is the greatest ever recorded in social affairs; the most complete, the most fruitful in consequences, and the most irrevocable. Whoever can meditate on it, and not see that so great a revolution vitiates all existing rules of government and policy, and renders all practice and all predictions grounded only on prior experience worthless, is

[1] 'Democracy' (1861), *Collected Prose Works,* II, p. 3; *Culture and Anarchy* (1869), *Collected Prose Works,* V, p. 94.

wanting in the very first and most elementary principle of statesmanship in these times.

Morris, following in this respect the pattern set by Marx and Engels, stresses in 'How We Live and How We Might Live' that 'reform' is a totally inadequate word to describe the change he desires and that only 'revolution' will do: 'So we will stick to our word, which means a change of the basis of society; it may frighten people, but it will at least warn them that there is something to be frightened about.' Ironically, it is perhaps Morris, through his utopian romance *News from Nowhere*, who seems for many modern readers to be the writer here who is most seriously limited by his admiration for the past.

In all of these cases the past is invoked as a result of the writers' consciousness of the need to prepare for the future: they all seek understanding or clarification of the present by means of historical precedents and contrasts. For Carlyle, who earned his living as a historian and ceaselessly urged others to study history, the past was indissolubly linked with the present and the future in a semi-mystical continuum. 'History,' he says cryptically, 'is a looking both before and after; as, indeed, the coming Time already waits, unseen, yet definitely shaped, predetermined and inevitable, in the Time come.'[1] Just as the French Revolution could be shown to provide a terrible warning for the present, so the Middle Ages as portrayed in Carlyle's *Past and Present* could be used as a standard of comparison for the failings of one's own age. For Carlyle it was as fateful for modern man to ignore the teaching of history as it had once been for man to ignore the words of the soothsayer. Arnold did not share this kind of mystical view of the historical process, and he loathed the Victorian obsession with medievalism, but his theory of culture is still firmly based on historical interpretation, with Ancient Greece and the Renaissance taking the place of the Middle Ages: in his more directly political writing he is committed, like Mill, to a belief in historical relativism. The most spectacular demonstration by the Victorian prophets that

---

[1] 'On History', *Critical and Miscellaneous Essays* (5 vols, 1899), II, p. 83.

involvement in the past is a way of confronting the present rather than escaping from it, is to be found in Ruskin's 'The Nature of Gothic'. As Ruskin devotes himself to reading the 'stones of Venice', finding in them the moral qualities of medieval architects and craftsmen, puzzling over the possible connections they reveal between art and the society in which it is produced, he moves by a brilliantly imaginative leap into Victorian industrialism. Through a study of the past he discovers the present and he was to be haunted by it for the rest of his life. If that moment has any rival in nineteenth-century prophetic literature then it has to be the breathtaking comprehensiveness of Marx and Engels's claim in *The Communist Manifesto* that, 'The history of all hitherto existing society is the history of class struggles.' It represents the apotheosis of historiography.

This preoccupation with the inter-connectedness of past, present and future, is one of the main distinguishing marks of modern prophetic literature. It is a process of attempted understanding and a bid for political influence, that springs from a concern with what Carlyle describes in 'Signs of the Times' as a 'deep-lying struggle in the whole fabric of society; a boundless grinding collision of the New with the Old', which then moves forward, proleptically, to pronounce on the probable results of that collision, while at the same time justifying conjectures and predictions by reference to the past. One classic illustration of this pattern – not contained in the text of this anthology – can be seen in Macaulay's review of Robert Southey's *Sir Thomas More: or, Colloquies on the Progress and Prospects of Society* (1829).[1] By the time Southey published this book his public reputation was one of a political renegade, someone whose early radicalism had been replaced by a strident conservatism: Macaulay was, archetypally, the progressive parliamentarian Whig. The *Colloquies* take the form of a dialogue between Montesinos who is a semi-portrait of Southey himself, and the ghost of Sir

[1] Quotations from the *Colloquies* are from the Cassell's National Library edition (1887); Macaulay's review is contained in his *Critical and Historical Essays* (Everyman's Library, 2 vols, 1961), and quotations here are taken from this edition.

Thomas More, the author of *Utopia* (1515). The choice of More
as a spokesman for the past is carefully calculated. As he tells
Montesinos, 'We have both speculated in the joys and freedom
of our youth upon the possible improvement of society; and
both in like manner have lived to dread with reason the effects of
that restless spirit which . . . insults heaven and disturbs the
earth.' Both men were drawn to prophecy by the restlessness of
their times, the one the age of the reformation, the other the age
of revolutions. Montesinos argues for what he calls 'progressive
melioration', a belief that in spite of the poverty and conflict of
early-nineteenth-century England, the condition of mankind
will continue gradually to improve, until, 'the progress of
knowledge and the diffusion of Christianity will bring about at
last, when men become Christians in reality as well as in name,
something like that Utopian state of which philosophers have
loved to dream.' More puts Montesinos gently in his place. Far
from gradually improving, or from having temporarily fallen
back under the impact of the new industrialism, the condition of
the 'great mass' of the population has been steadily declining
since the Middle Ages:

> They remain liable to the same indigenous diseases as their
> forefathers, and are exposed moreover to all which have been
> imported. Nor will the estimate of their condition be
> improved upon farther enquiry. They are worse fed than
> when they were hunters, fishers, and herdsmen; their
> clothing and habitations are little better, and, in comparison
> with those of the higher classes immeasurably worse. Except
> in the immediate vicinity of the collieries, they suffer more
> from cold than when the woods and turbaries were open.
> They are less religious than in the days of the Romish faith;
> and if we consider them in relation to their immediate
> superiors, we shall find reason to confess that the indepen-
> dence which has been gained since the total decay of the
> feudal system, has been dearly purchased by the loss of kindly
> feelings and ennobling attachments.

Macaulay's review of the *Colloquies* is savagely satirical. He mocks Southey's pretensions as a historian, taunts him with his change of political and religious opinions, and quotes statistics and historical evidence to disprove Southey's 'gloomy' view of the prospects of society. 'We comfort ourselves', he writes, 'with the consideration that Mr Southey is no prophet', and offers his own alternative view:

If we were to prophesy that in the year 1930 a population of fifty millions, better fed, clad, and lodged than the English of our time, will cover these islands, that Sussex and Huntingdonshire will be wealthier than the wealthiest parts of the West Riding of Yorkshire now are, that cultivation, rich as that of a flower-garden, will be carried up to the very tops of Ben Nevis and Helvellyn, that machines constructed on principles yet undiscovered will be in every house, that there will be no highways but railroads, no travelling but by steam, that our debt, vast as it seems to us, will appear to our great-grandchildren a trifling encumbrance, which might easily be paid off in a year or two, many people would think us insane. We prophesy nothing; but this we say: If any person had told the Parliament which met in perplexity and terror after the crash in 1720 that in 1830 the wealth of England would surpass all their wildest dreams, that the annual revenue would equal the principal of that debt which they considered as an intolerable burden, that for one man of ten thousand pounds then living there would be five men of fifty thousand pounds, that London would be twice as large and twice as populous, and that nevertheless the rate of mortality would have diminished to one-half of what it then was, that the post-office would bring more into the exchequer than the excise and customs had brought in together under Charles the Second, that stage coaches would run from London to York in twenty-four hours, that men would be in the habit of sailing without wind, and would be beginning to ride without horses, our ancestors would have given as much credit to the prediction as they gave to *Gulliver's Travels*. Yet the prediction would have been true.

If the conflicting views of Southey and Macaulay lack the subtlety of later prophets, the very starkness of the contrast between them also serves to highlight issues which were to become more oblique or concealed. Macaulay's vision of an England growing wealthier and wealthier as scientific knowledge expands, industrialism increases, and material benefits are diffused throughout society, was to be widely shared in the mid-Victorian period, and it remains, in essence, a familiar vision of modern capitalist societies. For Macaulay, material 'progress' would bring with it corresponding moral and educational improvement for the majority of people and an end to class conflict. The main lesson he draws from history is that individual genius will triumph over natural disasters and, more importantly, the corruption and greed of politicians. Macaulay closes his review with an appeal to the country's 'rulers' to leave 'capital to find its most lucrative course' and concentrate on their legitimate duties, 'by maintaining peace, by defending property, by diminishing the price of law, and by observing strict economy in every department of the State. Let the Government do this: the People will assuredly do the rest.'

However much the writers in this anthology would have disagreed with each other, none of them would have been willing to follow Macaulay; indeed, the questions they pose all challenge assumptions that Macaulay regards as natural. What is meant by 'the People'? Does the state not carry any moral responsibility for the well-being of society? Why should one assume that improved material conditions – in themselves desirable – should bring with them greater happiness, contentment or wisdom? Isn't it possible that 'capital' left to its own 'lucrative course' will not spread its benefits throughout society but further heighten the divisions between rich and poor? Can any of these things happen without being controlled or directed? And if not, who is to do the directing, who is to decide?

Not that Southey's views would have been generally any more welcome to the prophets than Macaulay's: Montesinos's conclusion that, 'Our sins are manifold, our danger is great, but

His mercy is infinite' was even less promising as a basis for the possible development of society than faith in material progress. But Southey's argument for the superiority of pre-industrial society, for a time when religious belief provided a stable hierarchical structure for the whole of society, was to echo throughout the wider debate – especially in Carlyle, Ruskin and Morris – and to reappear in a variety of strange guises in the twentieth century as well.[1] Macaulay's distrust of strong centralized governments leads to some of his sharpest satire against Southey's belief in paternalism: 'We cannot suppose that he would recommend popular election; for that is merely an appeal to public opinion. And to say that society ought to be governed by the opinion of the wisest and best, though true, is useless. Whose opinion is to decide who are the wisest and best?' It could as easily be Carlyle or Arnold who is being criticized there, while, turning the roles around, Sir Thomas More's understanding of the complexity of this problem is every bit as perceptive as theirs were to be:

> It is a question of degree. The just medium between too much superintendence and too little: the mystery whereby the free will of the subject is preserved, while it is directed by the fore purpose of the State (which is the secret of true polity) is yet to be found out. But this is certain, that whatever be the origin of government, its duties are patriarchal, that is to say, parental.

Referring to just this period of time, Raymond Williams has observed that, 'The growth of the new society was so confusing, even to the best minds, that positions were drawn up in terms of inherited categories, which then revealed unsuspected and even opposing implications.'[2] It is an important point and one that has as much relevance for later phases of industrial society as for the early. The continuing interest of the Victorian prophets for

[1] Alice Chandler discusses this aspect of the work of Southey, Carlyle, Ruskin and Morris in *A Dream of Order: The Medieval Ideal in Nineteenth-Century English Literature* (1971).
[2] *Culture and Society*, p. 38.

modern readers lies not in one or other of them having their predictions shown to be true or false, but in the intelligence and honesty of their concern with issues which appear as little open to an ultimate solution today as they have ever been. It is simple enough to dismiss Southey's trust in 'patriarchal' or 'parental' government, but only a fool would deny that 'the secret of true polity' is yet to be discovered.

Macaulay, of course, believed that Southey was a fool and that his foolishness was most tellingly apparent in his eagerness to talk on subjects he knew nothing about: 'He confesses that he is not versed in political economy, and that he has neither liking nor aptitude for it; and he then proceeds to read the public a lecture concerning it which fully bears out his confession.' Ignorance exposed, a statement or point of view convincingly refuted, are only ostensibly what is at stake here: interest in Macaulay's sarcastic dismissal, based on personal claims of specialized knowledge, lies in the way it becomes a standard kind of response to the prophets. Some of Arnold's best satirical writing is in answer to the charge that he was not 'practical'; Ruskin, like Southey, was attacked for meddling in questions of political economy which were clearly not his business. The crudity of the formulation is part of its deliberately reductive purpose. What right has a literary or art critic to talk about politics? What can a German intellectual know about the English working class? Isn't it just too easy for someone as wealthy as Morris to argue for a communist revolution? Responses such as these — familiar then as now — were encouraged by the prophetic method which aimed to explain not the detailed day-to-day work experience, but the wider sweep of social or political forces that could give overall sense to those experiences. The argument over the rival claims of dis-interestedness and commitment was not just part of the criticism constantly flung at the prophets: it was something that they themselves were deeply divided over. Carlyle, Mill, Arnold and Ruskin, in their different ways and however strongly they may be advocating policies which cannot sensibly be described as anything but political, all often speak as though their kind of reasoning places them above everyday involvement. Arnold, in

'The Function of Criticism at the Present Time', is quite explicit about this:

> I say, the critic must keep out of the region of immediate practice in the political, social, humanitarian sphere, if he wants to make a beginning for that more free speculative treatment of things, which may perhaps one day make its benefits felt even in this sphere, but in a natural and thence irresistible manner.

This is very close to the advice given by Bruno Bauer to the young Karl Marx:

> It would be stupid if you were to devote yourself to a practical career. Theory is now the strongest practice, and we are absolutely incapable of predicting to how large an extent it will become practical.[1]

Unlike Arnold, Marx was to speak for commitment rather than disinterestedness, but he understood, just as clearly as Arnold or Bruno Bauer, that theory was becoming the 'strongest practice' and that any contribution he could make in changing the direction of society depended on an alliance between his special kind of insight and a more practical power: 'As philosophy finds its material weapons in the proletariat, so the proletariat finds its intellectual weapons in philosophy, and as soon as the lightning of thought has struck deep into the virgin soil of the people, the emancipation of the Germans into men will be completed.'[2] If that was precisely the kind of alliance that the Victorian prophets hoped to avoid, the image of their thoughts as 'lightning' striking deep into the 'virgin soil' of other, more socially influential or politically powerful people than themselves, expresses with equal precision their shared ambitions.

This new role of the intellectual as social prophet was as much a sign of the times as his perception that modern society was characterized by class conflict. Just as his political awareness was

[1] Quoted in David McLellan, *Karl Marx: His Life and Thought* (1973), p. 34.
[2] *Karl Marx: His Life and Thought*, p. 98.

nurtured by events developing out of the French Revolution, so his belief in the power of the individual to rise above partisan involvement, comprehend the deeper patterns of social change and communicate his vision for the good of all, took its inspiration directly from late-eighteenth-century romanticism. In the early- and mid-Victorian periods the prophets seem little aware of Blake, but the example of Wordsworth – the isolated poet presenting, through the analysis of his own emotions and experiences, a message to humanity – was a powerful one. The example of Coleridge was in some respects even more powerful, though also more ambiguous. To his high poetic imagination there was added an intellectual stature that made it impossible to charge him, as Arnold was to charge Wordsworth, with not having read enough books. But at the same time he seemed to lack the strength of will required to bring his feelings and intellect together to serve a more positive social purpose. His prophetic status was badly flawed by the excesses of romanticism that the Victorians feared so much, and Carlyle's portrait of Coleridge in *The Life of John Sterling* (1851) emphasizes promise unachieved. It is admitted that Coleridge 'had, especially among young inquiring men, a higher than literary, a kind of prophetic or magician character', but he is also described as 'like a sage escaped from the inanity of life's battle'. Understandable as the desire for such an escape is, actually to submit to the temptation is to disqualify oneself as a sage: prophetic aloofness does not mean escape from social responsibility. If Coleridge was felt to have failed a crucial test, he could not be denied a place as a principal conceptualizer of the prophetic role. The word he coined for the new breed of men that he felt England so badly needed was the 'clerisy' and it did not catch on. But the idea it expressed – 'a permanent, nationalized, learned order, a national clerisy or Church' as 'an essential element of a rightly constituted nation' – was to lie behind much of the reasoning of the Victorian prophets and emerge gradually as, in several important respects, their most influential legacy to the twentieth century.[1]

---

[1] *On the Constitution of the Church and State* (1830), edited by John

The most immediately personal impact of romanticism on the Victorian prophets was, however, imaginative rather than intellectual. Carlyle, Arnold, Ruskin and Morris, all began their careers as artists conscious that their work was within the romantic tradition, and all of them gradually moved towards social criticism. This process is apparent at every stage of their work. It is in the rhetorical techniques they develop and in the way they are attracted to forms of writing which blend exposition and narrative; it is present in the emphasis they place on cultural and educational aspects of social change; and their own changes of direction become in themselves part of the debate, conversions which are employed dramatically to exemplify the unavoidable pressures of the age and the seriousness with which they must be regarded. The case of Mill is particularly interesting in this context because it takes a completely opposite direction to those of Arnold, Ruskin and Morris. Trained from the age of four to be a social philosopher, Mill's moment of conversion came with the realization that for him happiness was impossible unless the intellect was humanized by the imagination and emotions. Marx, of course, belongs to a very different cultural and philosophical tradition – there is no equivalent among the Victorian prophets to his kind of Hegelian background – but he too immersed himself in romantic literature as a young man, and while a student at Bonn University had attended lectures given by A. W. Schlegel, one of the leading interpreters of German romanticism.[1] Like the Victorian prophets Marx moved away from imaginative literature, and like them he carried his youthful romanticism into other kinds of writing.

The world Carlyle portrays in 'Signs of the Times' is one of great energy and inventiveness, of change and reform, but it is also characterized by lack of direction, by moral and social fragmentation. He recognizes the class basis of the change

Colmer, *Coleridge: Collected Works* (1976), X, p. 69; for a full discussion of the 'clerisy', see Ben Knights, *The Idea of the Clerisy in the Nineteenth Century* (1978).

[1] S. S. Prawer, *Karl Marx and World Literature* (1976), p. 9.

taking place, its origins in the startling paradox that the enormous wealth created by industrialism has brought with it enormous poverty, and the transformation of traditional kinds of relationships. By an ingenious extension of industrial imagery, the age is labelled 'Mechanical, in every outward and inward sense of that word', indicating Carlyle's awareness of modern alienation as well as its connection with the older religious sense of man as being separated from God. 'Mechanical' is further used to describe the multifarious responses to the confused situation Carlyle is analysing ('external combinations and arrangements, for institutions, constitutions'), and to stress that underlying those responses is a modern philosophy that has become overwhelmingly materialistic:

> It is no longer the moral, religious, spiritual condition of the people that is our concern, but their physical, practical, economical condition as regulated by public laws. Thus is the Body-politic more than ever worshipped and tendered; but the Soul-politic less than ever.

Although Carlyle is pessimistic about these trends, there was still within him enough of his youthful radicalism and genuine sympathy for the condition of the poor, for his final attitude not to be one of despair. But for all the perceptiveness of his analysis, Carlyle reveals no willingness to work with the trends he discerns. Instead he stands against 'mechanical' and materialistic solutions in order to argue for a 'freedom' that is 'higher' than 'political freedom': he speaks on behalf of the resurgence of forces which have been temporarily eclipsed – 'direct vision', 'wonder' and 'belief in the Invisible'. The stress in this essay and increasingly in his later work on history as demonstrating that all great human achievements have rested on the greatness of individuals, can already be seen as hero-worship: '*One* man that has a higher Wisdom, a hitherto unknown spiritual Truth in him, is stronger, not than ten men that have it not, or than ten thousand, but than *all* men that have it not.' Even without the ominous tone that the twentieth-century experience of totalitarianism has given to such a view, Carlyle lays himself completely open to Macaulay's common-sense challenge to Southey: 'To say that society ought to be governed by the opinion of the wisest and best, though true, is useless. Whose opinion is to decide who are the wisest and best?' It is not a question that would have made much sense to Carlyle: the '*one* man' who has a 'higher Wisdom' chooses himself.

Mill, on the other hand, regarded such a question as being crucially important, and 'Civilization' is largely an attempt to examine some of the problems involved in it. His basic analysis of what is happening to British society is very close to Carlyle's, though he has no 'belief in the Invisible', and, although he fears a decline of the 'heroic' in modern life, his greater dread of dictatorships prevents him from following Carlyle. Mill actually welcomes the tendency towards 'co-operation', even if at this early stage he stops short of including the trade unions in that welcome, and he accepts the spread of democracy because it is realistic to do so, the present social danger being that 'constitutional power' and 'real power' have become separated from each other. His contempt is directed at the conservative and reactionary elements in society who can not see that they have no other choice than to help make democracy work. Mill's argument is governed by the conviction that the spread of democracy will bring with it a general improvement in the material standard of life together with an overall deadening uniformity that will crush individual aspirations and attainments. Strongly influenced by Alexis de Tocqueville's *Democracy in America* (1835), Mill carefully distinguishes between the British and American situations but finds, in spite of the differences, that already the wealthy or 'refined classes' of Britain are typified by 'torpidity and cowardice', and the signs are everywhere apparent that individualism is disappearing. One example specified by Mill is the decline of literature, a prophecy which, coming at the very start of one of the greatest periods of English literature, seems curiously misguided. But behind Mill's fear is distrust of the press busily manipulating public opinion, as Carlyle had also argued, in order to destroy all sense of personal judgement, and therefore to pervert true 'literature'. Mill's dominant image of modern democratic man is of the 'individual lost in the crowd', comfortable in material terms but lacking the guiding inspiration of art and philosophy, his unformed judgements flattered and encouraged by self-seeking journalists and politicians. This early in the debate there is already an awareness of pressure groups and factions seeking to control emergent democracy by a calculated lowering of standards, and Mill's way out of this dilemma is to speak for a counterbalancing force through the organization of educational institutions. The backwardness of Oxford and Cambridge makes Mill less than optimistic but he remains convinced that ultimately hope for 'civilization' lies in the 'regeneration of individual character among our lettered and opulent classes'. In that judgement Mill reveals himself as a true disciple not only of de Tocqueville but of Coleridge as well.

Arnold clearly follows on in that line. If his interests in 'The Function of Criticism at the Present Time' seem more narrowly specialized than those of Mill, this can be explained only partly in terms of his very different personality: the main reason is the period of nearly thirty years that separates the two essays. No longer is there any need to argue the case for democracy; it is the next step that matters.

> Everything was long seen, by the young and ardent amongst us, in inseparable connection with politics and practical life. We have pretty well exhausted the benefits of seeing things in this connection, we have got all that can be got by so seeing them. Let us try a more disinterested mode of seeing them; let us betake ourselves to the serener life of the mind and spirit.

Although 'The Function of Criticism at the Present Time' is usually, and understandably, accepted as a classic of literary criticism, it is not primarily literature that Arnold has in mind. What he argues for is a frame of mind capable of apprehending 'the best that is known and thought in the world, and by in its turn making this known, to create a current of true and fresh ideas.' The extreme subtlety of Arnold's argument, as it winds through historical and cultural illustrations, and builds rhetorically into specific examples of how criticism can expose

the emptiness of political pomposity and middle-class philistinism, is directed almost entirely to the advocacy of a particular
way of examining life's problems. The question of the uses to
which the 'true and fresh ideas' are to be put is avoided, or rather
dismissed as indicative of a British obsession with practicality.
But there can be no doubt that although Arnold often seems to
be claiming that the 'free play of the mind' is something good in
itself and therefore needs no further justification, he is also
advocating an eminently practical policy. It is because an 'epoch
of concentration' is coming to a close and an 'epoch of
expansion' about to commence that criticism 'at the present
time' is so much needed:

> The mass of mankind will never have any ardent zeal for
> seeing things as they are; very inadequate ideas will always
> satisfy them. On these inadequate ideas reposes, and must
> repose, the general practice of the world. That is as much as
> saying that whoever sets himself to see things as they are will
> find himself one of a very small circle; but it is only by this
> small circle resolutely doing its own work that adequate ideas
> will ever get current at all.

In that separation of the 'general practice of the world'
conducted according to 'very inadequate ideas' and the 'small
circle' of right-thinking people, Arnold places his hope for the
future. The task of Arnold's 'small circle', like that of Mill's
regenerated members of the 'lettered classes', is to hold at bay
the vulgar materialism of a mass society and sustain cultural
values until educational reforms can, possibly, enlarge the circle.

It is noticeable that although Carlyle, Mill and Arnold all
acknowledge repeatedly the excitement and challenge of the
new ideas that have been created by industrialism and
democratic change, they are not themselves enthusiastic
supporters of those ideas. Carlyle places an ever-increasing trust
in 'eternal verities'; Mill, though infinitely more flexible and
willing to modify his opinions as the century progressed, spoke
ultimately, with Arnold, for preservation and continuity. This
element of defensiveness was built into their fears that

everything they had been taught to value could be swept away by the magnitude of the changes taking place, and is most apparent in the way they keep working-class life at a distance. Carlyle offers some vividly direct insights into working-class life, especially in *Past and Present*, though it usually exists for him as a problem. In 'Civilization', despite his admiring references to the co-operative spirit, Mill thinks in terms of 'the masses', and his surprisingly easy contrast between 'civilized' and 'savage' societies suggests that he shares Arnold's conviction that the working class is primarily interesting for what it might become rather than what it actually is.

In 'The Nature of Gothic' Ruskin abruptly shifts this emphasis, moving the industrial work-experience from the periphery to the centre of the debate. This he appears to achieve almost by accident, and the theoretical justification he advances is christian rather than socialist. For Ruskin, Gothic architecture is essentially 'moral' because it allowed constantly for the imperfect nature of man. Like the christianity of which it is the expression, Gothic encouraged man to strive towards perfection while recognizing that true perfection is attainable only in God: however flawed or imperfect the individual, he lived within a framework of belief that allowed him the full expression of his capabilities, something that modern industrialism has destroyed. It was this aspect of Ruskin's message that was to be considered so 'revolutionary' in the 1860s, even though the social structures he admires are rigidly paternalistic:

> Now, in the make and nature of every man, however rude or simple, whom we employ in manual labour, there are some powers for better things; some tardy imagination, torpid capacity of emotion, tottering steps of thought, there are, even at the worst; and in most cases it is all our own fault that they *are* tardy or torpid.

Where Ruskin is innovatory here is in his full acceptance of ruling-class blame. Carlyle, Mill and Arnold are all scathingly critical of ruling-class lethargy or obstructionism, but they exclude themselves from such criticism, or, their special role places them beyond direct responsibility. Ruskin includes himself – imperfect as all men are – in the blame, committing himself in a way that is quite new: it was for this that in 'The Function of Criticism at the Present Time' Arnold dismissed Ruskin's views as fatally compromised by his 'pugnacious political economy'. Arnold's specific reference is to *Unto this Last*, but the main step had already been taken in 'The Nature of Gothic' where the challenge is put directly to the reader: 'And observe, you are put to a stern choice in this matter. You must either make a tool of the creature, or a man of him. You cannot make both.' It is an appeal to conscience, class guilt and social responsibility of a kind to be found more often in the early-Victorian novel than in non-fictional prose, and it carries a similar emotional power. It is 'you' the reader who is told to 'look round this English room of yours' and recognize in it the evidence of a society that maintains itself by slave-labour.

Ruskin has no wish to dispense with labour – his conviction that in work lay salvation for man was as firm as Carlyle's. What he argues is that man is degraded by modern industrial labour into a machine, and he pursues his case by an imaginative use of mechanical imagery that is reminiscent of Carlyle in 'Signs of the Times'. In our manufacturing cities, he proclaims, we 'manufacture everything except men'; division of labour is a false term because it is not 'the labour that is divided; but the men: – Divided into mere segments of men – broken into small fragments and crumbs of life.' Ruskin's insistence that 'the demand for perfection is always a sign of a misunderstanding of the ends of art', something that the christian Middle Ages understood and the heathen nineteenth century did not, was to have a strong, though ambiguous, effect on late-Victorian thought. However much Ruskin protested that he was not demanding a revival of Gothic ornamentation, it was inevitable that his passionate defence of the dignity of manual labour as a way out of a society 'made up of morbid thinkers, and miserable workers' should often be reduced to a mere fashionable gesture. His ideal worker remained too exclusively the stone mason, his ideal workplace more appropriate to a medieval guild than a modern factory, his opposition to the machine no sensible way of facing the problems of a manufacturing industry. Yet the power and importance of 'The Nature of Gothic' are undeniable. In total contrast to Mill and Arnold, Ruskin denies the need for society to separate itself into the few and the many, asserting instead that it should itself be transformed so that all men can discover the creativity that lies within them.

Four years before the publication of 'The Nature of Gothic' Marx and Engels had included in *The Manifesto of the Communist Party* (1848) a caricature of 'feudal socialism' that could be taken to embrace Ruskin's kind of vision:

> Half lamentation, half lampoon; half echo of the past, half menace of the future; at times, by its bitter, witty and incisive criticism, striking the bourgeoisie to the very heart's core; but always ludicrous in its effect, through total incapacity to comprehend the march of modern history.

Like the Victorian prophets, Marx and Engels justify their predictions in terms of their understanding of the past, and there are other similarities – of rhetoric, tone, and central concerns – but at every stage of their argument the emphasis given is totally different. Modern class conflict and the industrial working class are not seen simply as the products of eighteenth-century rationalism, scientific invention and the French Revolution, but as developments in an historical process that reaches back as far as recorded history. All past epochs are characterized by a struggle between oppressors and oppressed, with every aspect of life dominated by whoever controls the means of production and exchange. This permanent state of conflict takes the form of 'an uninterrupted, now hidden, now open fight'. Just as feudalism brought the bourgeoisie into existence only to be destroyed by them so bourgeois expansion has brought into existence the industrial proletariat who will, in turn, destroy their creators: 'Modern bourgeois society . . . is like the sorcerer, who is no longer able to control the powers of the nether world whom he has called up by his spells.' Modern bourgeois society came to power by constantly revolutionizing the means of production and exchange: the modern proletariat will take over by physical force. No real indication is given as to what kind of society will emerge from the revolution, though it is assumed that the communist future will not, unlike 'all hitherto existing society', suffer from class antagonism because for the first time in history the 'immense majority' will be the controlling force. The final vision is one of total individualism:

> In place of the old bourgeois society, with its classes and class antagonisms, we shall have an association, in which the free development of each is the condition for the free development of all.

The comprehensiveness and visionary force of the *Manifesto* comes partly from the conviction that the secret of history has been revealed, and partly from the urgent need to convince the proletariat of its destined role. As Engels points out in his preface to the English edition of 1888, by the time he and Marx came to draft the *Manifesto* for the Communist League, they had moved beyond describing themselves as socialists in order to unite with those who were seeking not 'mere political revolutions' but 'total social change'. As the *Manifesto* makes clear the communists do not constitute a party separate from the proletariat, but they definitely are the guides, interpreters and prophets of the movement:

> The Communists, therefore, are on the one hand, practically the most advanced and resolute section of the working-class parties of every country, that section which pushes forward all others; on the other hand, theoretically, they have over the great mass of the proletariat the advantage of clearly understanding the line of march, the conditions, and the ultimate general results of the proletarian movement.

The only way this programme can be achieved is by the proletariat being raised 'to the position of ruling class' and 'to wrest, by degrees, all capital from the bourgeoisie, to centralize all instruments of production in the hands of the State.' In spite of their enthusiastic confidence that the revolution is near at hand, Marx and Engels never pretend that it will be an easy task; indeed it is very apparent from the *Manifesto* that the bourgeoisie are regarded with feelings of almost Macaulayesque awe at times because of the long-term revolutionary role they have played and because of the astonishing nature of their achievements: 'Subjection of Nature's forces to man, machinery, application of chemistry to industry and agriculture, steam navigation, railways, electric telegraphs, clearing of whole continents for cultivation, canalization of rivers, whole populations conjured out of the ground – what earlier century had even a presentiment that such productive forces slumbered in the lap of social labour?' This is the force that the communists are now to harness, and in the transformation the arguments, policies and theories of the Victorian prophets will be cast aside because they merely reflect the ruling ideas of the ruling class. Mill's fears for individual freedom in democratic society are groundless because they apply only to 'bourgeois individuality'. Arnold's cultural concerns when seen from the point of view of the proletariat are 'for the enormous majority, a mere training to act as a machine'. All culture in bourgeois society is 'class culture'. In their relentless focus on the majority, on the mass, Marx and Engels bring to the foreground of the prophetic debate what is always placed to one side by the Victorian prophets though still rarely absent from their minds.

The influence of Marx and Engels on Victorian thought was very small until late in the century.[1] When it did begin to make itself felt it was in a way that they themselves had foreseen. 'In times when the class-struggle nears the decisive hour . . . a small section of the ruling class cuts itself adrift, and joins the revolutionary class, the class that holds the future in its hands.' William Morris was just such a ruling-class representative. As he explains in 'How I Became a Socialist' the writings of Marx and discussions with friends about Marx clarified rather than inspired his conversion. In one sense Morris is a direct descendant of the Victorian prophets, but he also brings about a

[1] E. J. Hobsbawm, 'Dr Marx and the Victorian Critics', *Labouring Men* (1964), and S. Foner (ed.), *When Karl Marx Died: Comments in 1883* (New York 1973).

characteristically late-Victorian change in the prophetic tradition. The areas of concern stressed by Morris are now familiar enough, but gone entirely is any claim to disinterestedness and any belief in appeals in the name of the whole of society. In Morris, Ruskin and Marx are combined in almost equal measure. From Marx he brings the conviction that only by a working-class revolution can society be transformed, while from Ruskin he takes the inspiration for the kind of world he wants to see created after the revolution. By the 1880s, the extension of the franchise, a rapidly-expanding trade union movement, and the spread of socialist ideas which were already serving to create a Parliamentary Labour Party, provided a framework for reform and working-class action. Morris is involved in a variety of ways with these developments, but as firmly as Carlyle in the 1830s or Ruskin in the 1860s, his main role is to offer visionary inspiration. His artistic ability, and a good deal of his money, is dedicated to the cause of persuading others of 'how they might live' if they support socialism. Violence, he tells his audiences in lectures like 'How We Live and How We Might Live', is the necessary first step if a world of individual freedom and creativity is to be brought into being. To the combined influences of Marx and Ruskin he adds his idiosyncratic, 'decent' kind of naivety:

> Now, again, this leisure would enable me to please myself and expand my mind by travelling if I had a mind to it; because, say, for instance, that I were a shoemaker; if due social order were established, it by no means follows that I should always be obliged to make shoes in one place; a due amount of easily conceivable arrangement would enable me to make shoes in Rome, say, for three months, and to come back with new ideas of building, gathered from the sight of the works of past ages, amongst other things which would perhaps be of service in London.

As in *News from Nowhere* – which presents a more complete vision of the communist future – it is the impulse behind Morris's work that prevents such moments of naivety from being merely silly. Like many late-Victorian socialists, Morris saw a new era of individualism emerging from the revolution as man was freed from the machine, boring work and middle-class morality. Once class antagonisms disappeared, Morris could see no reason why man's natural longing for all that is rational and beautiful should not be released and satisfied.

By this time there were, however, other visions, other kinds of prophecy, which were unwilling to regard the Morrisian interpretation of utopian socialism as either probable or desirable. If Morris had accepted the 'scientific' theory of historical development, he had done so while grafting on to it a distrust of industrialism so extreme that the future began to look more than ever like the distant past. Ruskin, of course, was the dominant influence in this, but a wider distrust of science lies behind the theories of Mill and Arnold as well: the clerisy were to be learned in philosophy, literature and history, but scientific training was relegated to a minor position, though in Mill's case the 'scientific' study of humanity was to figure prominently. This discrimination was to prove one of the weakest, and most culturally divisive, features of Victorian prophecy. Engels claimed in his preface to the *Communist Manifesto* that Marx's theory was 'destined to do for history what Darwin's theory has done for biology', but the analogy was convincing only in the generalized sense that both theories claimed to explain great sweeps of human development, and for the same reason they were both to be applied in ways that their originators could not have foreseen. It was certainly possible to regard Darwinism as directly opposed to the kind of utopian future to which Marx and Engels pointed. Why was it not just as likely that science in the hands of the energetic, revolutionary bourgeoisie should raise the standard of living for the majority more successfully than a proletarian revolution? Or, as T. H. Huxley, one of the most important of late-Victorian prophets was to ask, isn't it possible that man as a species is heading not for utopia but for self-annihilation?[1]

H. G. Wells, the only major English author of his time who

---

[1] T. H. Huxley, *Evolution and Ethics* (1893).

was trained as a scientist, and who studied at Kensington under Huxley, was fascinated by both of these issues – the apparently boundless possibilities of scientific invention and the fear that science would end by destroying man long before his evolutionary span was completed.[1] In his brilliantly original science-fiction tales of the 1890s Wells gave an entirely new dimension to Victorian prophecy: the basic method remained extrapolation from a reading of the signs of the times, and the nature and quality of future life remain central points of interest, but the vast periods of time that science now envisaged and the power of science and technology to affect men's lives, to control, direct, or change them in ways inconceivable to earlier generations enter the prophetic debate decisively for the first time. In the series of articles collected together as *Anticipations* (1901) Wells began to apply his prophecies more directly to contemporary society, influenced in this respect by the growth of empirical sociology, another important attempt by late-Victorian society to identify and solve some of the problems of industrialism. 'The Life-History of Democracy' is a good example of Wells's method and his beliefs. He follows the Victorian prophets in placing the spread of democratic ideas in the political and industrial revolutions of the late-eighteenth century, though no longer is there any belief that the establishment of democracy is the inevitable end of those changes:

> Everywhere there were new elements, not as yet clearly analyzed or defined, arising as mechanism arose; everywhere the old traditional government and social system, defined and analyzed all too well, appeared increasingly obstructive, irrational and feeble in its attempts to include and direct these new powers. But now comes a point to which I am inclined to attach very great importance. The new powers were as yet shapeless. It was not the conflict of a new organization with the old. It was the preliminary dwarfing and deliquescence of

[1] For the influence of Wells's scientific training on his works, see Roslynn D. Haynes, *H. G. Wells: Discoverer of the Future* (1980).

the mature old beside the embryonic mass of the new. It was impossible then – it is, I believe, only beginning to be possible now – to estimate the proportions, possibilities, and inter-relations of the new social orders out of which a social organization has still to be built in the coming years. No formula of definite re-construction has been evolved, or has even been evolved yet, after a hundred years.

There are two points of emphasis in Wells's work which are never really brought together. First, his awareness of the emergence of a pluralistic society not structured on the lines of opposing classes but rather made up of a large variety of different kinds of actual relationships and possible relationships. It is a tendency that excites him and provokes some of his most striking prophecies of future moral and social attitudes. Secondly, there is his belief in a society that will be controlled – as inevitably as Marx believed in the proletarian revolution – by the only people who are capable of understanding it, the trained scientists. Wells's interpretation of this new class can be seen as an extension of the idea of the clerisy, except that humanistic education is replaced by science. Wells's view of modern representative democracy as nothing more than a temporary phase in the long-term development of man – a grey mass controlled and manipulated by politicians whose sole concern is to 'get office and keep office, not to do anything in office', and who, anyway, are not actually in control – has too much continuing relevance to be dismissed as harsh cynicism. Once democracy is achieved, then what? It is a question asked by every writer in this anthology. For Wells, reading the signs of the times at the turn of the century, the answer is devastating war brought about by nationalism, and followed either by the rise of dictatorships, or, the alternative he sees as the more likely, the efficient organization of society by a scientific elite, leading eventually to a world state.

'There is no future for men, however brimming with crude vitality,' George Bernard Shaw wrote in his preface to *Man and Superman* (1903), 'who are neither intelligent nor politically educated enough to be Socialists.' It sounds a dangerously bland statement, but at the turn of the century 'socialism' was open to a wide range of definitions and interpretations. There was certainly no sign that Britain was about to undergo the revolutionary transformation from a capitalist to a communist society prophesied by Marx, or even that the crucial transition period 'in which the state can be nothing but the revolutionary dictatorship of the proletariat' was near at hand.[1] Interest in Marx's thought was increasing, but even within the Labour Party it represented only one point of view among many. Yet Shaw's attitude to socialism, if not his enthusiastic endorsement of it, is to be found everywhere at this time. In 1907 John Morley, the biographer of Gladstone and a member of an ardently reformist Liberal ministry, noted ruefully that 'socialism' had become the 'key to our politics' and 'the catchword of the hour'.[2] What Morley and Shaw meant was not so much that socialism had triumphed but that the Macaulayite vision of free trade, unhindered by government interference, spreading material advantages and moral development throughout society, was gone for ever. It had been replaced, in however tentative a form, by the belief that only a strong centralized government could deal with modern social problems.

None of the prophets in this anthology would have been surprised by such a change. If they agreed on any one topic it was that modern industrial society was in danger of becoming so chaotic and inhuman that centralized institutions must be created to bring order and provide a sense of direction: they would also have been in fairly close agreement that leadership was not going to be given by the traditional rulers of British society. It is always the newness and uncertainty of the situation they find themselves in that the prophets are responding to. Their opinions on the nature and degree of central control varied considerably, and it is understandable that this should be so. It is sometimes argued against the Victorian prophets that

[1] 'Critique of the Gotha Programme' (1875) in *Marx and Engels: Selected Works* (Moscow, 2 vols, 1962), II, p. 33.
[2] Quoted in Ian Bradley, *The Optimists: Themes and Personalities in Victorian Liberalism* (1980), p. 259.

because they worked in the main outside of parliament and were often distrustful or scornful of parliamentary processes, they were out of touch with their age and ineffectual. But this is surely not the case. When, for example, Arnold spoke on behalf of a 'State' authority that would act for the country as a whole, especially in matters of educational policy, he was not being distant but involved, not out of touch with his age but ahead of it. As Lionel Trilling has pointed out, Arnold 'might as well have told the English middle class that only Popery or Mohammedanism could save the national life from meanness as that in the State lay spiritual salvation.'[1] The prophetic debate was not about the strengths and weaknesses of various tried and tested political systems: it was about shaping the kinds of institutions which were emerging haphazardly in the nineteenth century. This is why France, the United States, and comparisons drawn from distant periods of history, feature so prominently. Nearly all of the arguments for stronger central government advanced by the prophets were made in the name of greater freedom and individuality, not less. Arnold's State and Ruskin's paternalism are intended to release new kinds of creativity; Marx and Morris agree that a communist revolution will have much the same kind of effect. If the outstanding exception to these generalizations, Carlyle, can be seen as anticipating fascism – and a reading of *Shooting Niagara: And After?* (1867) doesn't provide a good deal of evidence in his defence – then this too is hardly surprising: the arguments for a working-class dictatorship, for representative democracy, for government by scientific specialists, and for the free play of economic forces, are also being tested here.

The prophetic tradition is as complex and many-sided as the new kind of society that provided its principal subject of debate, and its continuing interest lies, as has already been said, less in the rightness or wrongness of particular prophecies than in the centrality of the issues it raises. There are some dead ends and false turnings. The very assumption of the prophetic role has built into it a possibility of the kind of disillusion expressed by

[1] *Matthew Arnold* (1939, rev. ed. 1949), p. 179.

A. H. Clough's bitter comment: 'Carlyle has led us all out into the desert, and he has left us there.'[1] Marx and Engels's easy reference in the *Communist Manifesto* to the 'idiocy of rural life' or their promise that a communist society will confiscate 'all the property of all emigrants and rebels', is no less chilling, in the light of twentieth-century experience, than Carlyle's rant about 'rabid Nigger-Philanthropists'; and Morris the shoemaker deciding to make shoes for a while in Rome and learn something about architecture while doing so, is a wonderful vision of individual freedom in a communist future, but grotesque if considered in relation to the lack of individual freedom in modern communist societies. The contradictions and contrasts, the paradoxes and blind-spots, are unavoidable parts of the debate, and need to be recognized as such.

[1] H. F. Lowry (ed.), *The Letters of Matthew Arnold to A. H. Clough* (1932), p. 47.

Thomas Carlyle

Thomas Carlyle (1795–1881) was born in the village of Ecclefechan, Dumfriesshire, where his father was a stone mason, and educated at the village school, Annan Academy and Edinburgh University. Expected by his parents to enter the church, he decided instead on a career in literature and while earning his living as a school-teacher in Annan and Kirkcaldy he wrote biographical articles for an encyclopaedia and made translations from German, notably Goethe's *Wilhelm Meister's Apprenticeship* (1824). In 1826 he married Jane Baillie Welsh: at first they lived in Edinburgh but then settled at Craigenputtock farm in Dumfriesshire. Here Carlyle wrote *Sartor Resartus* (first published in *Fraser's Magazine*, 1833–4), and many essays on literature and society, including 'Signs of the Times' (*Edinburgh Review*, 1829) and a companion piece 'Characteristics' which was also published in the *Edinburgh Review* (1831). These essays were collected and published in various editions from 1838 as *Critical and Miscellaneous Essays*. In 1834 the Carlyles moved to London and Carlyle consolidated an already growing reputation with *The French Revolution* (3 vols, 1837), *Chartism* (1839), *On Heroes and Hero-Worship* (1841), and *Past and Present* (1843). This was the period of Carlyle's strongest influence: his gospel of work and fierce demands that the new industrial society should be studied and understood were important features of the early-Victorian mood. But as that mood of social urgency began to relax, Carlyle's tone became wilder. There was still respect for the historical studies of *Cromwell* (1845) and *Frederick the Great* (1858–65), but the hysteria of *Latter-Day Pamphlets* (1850), *The Nigger Question* (1853), and *Shooting Niagara: – And After?* (1867), Carlyle's defence of Governor Eyre in 1866, and his increasing admiration for Prussian militarism alienated many of his early supporters who now regarded him as dangerously illiberal. In the twentieth century he was often to be regarded as a racist and as one of the intellectual founding fathers of fascism. His *Reminiscences*, published posthumously in 1881, contain some superb sketches of his early life, and the biography by J. A. Froude (4 vols, 1882–4), though largely uncritical of Carlyle's political attitudes, is one of the outstanding Victorian biographies.

SIGNS OF THE TIMES

It is no very good symptom either of nations or individuals, that they deal much in vaticination. Happy men are full of the present, for its bounty suffices them; and wise men also, for its duties engage them. Our grand business undoubtedly is, not to *see* what lies dimly at a distance, but to *do* what lies clearly at hand.

> Know'st thou *Yesterday*, its aim and reason;
> Work'st thou well *Today*, for worthy things?
> Calmly wait the *Morrow's* hidden season,
> Need'st not fear what hap soe'er it brings.

But man's 'large discourse of reason' *will* look 'before and after'; and, impatient of the 'ignorant present time', will indulge in anticipation far more than profits him. Seldom can the unhappy be persuaded that the evil of the day is sufficient for it; and the ambitious will not be content with present splendour, but paints yet more glorious triumphs, on the cloud-curtain of the future.

The case, however, is still worse with nations. For here the prophets are not one, but many; and each incites and confirms the other; so that the fatidical fury spreads wider and wider, till at last even Saul must join in it. For there is still a real magic in the action and reaction of minds on one another. The casual deliration of a few becomes, by this mysterious reverberation, the frenzy of many; men lose the use, not only of their understandings, but of their bodily senses; while the most obdurate unbelieving hearts melt, like the rest, in the furnace where all are cast as victims and as fuel. It is grievous to think, that this noble omnipotence of Sympathy has been so rarely the Aaron's-rod of Truth and Virtue, and so often the Enchanter's-rod of Wickedness and Folly! No solitary miscreant, scarcely any solitary maniac, would venture on such actions and imaginations, as large communities of sane men have, in such circumstances, entertained as sound wisdom. Witness long scenes of the French Revolution, in these late times! Levity is no protection against such visitations, nor the utmost earnestness of character. The New-England Puritan burns witches, wrestles for months with the horrors of Satan's invisible world, and all ghastly phantasms, the daily and hourly precursors of the Last Day; then suddenly bethinks him that he is frantic, weeps bitterly, prays contritely, and the history of that gloomy season lies behind him like a frightful dream.

Old England too has had her share of such frenzies and panics; though happily, like other old maladies, they have grown milder of late: and since the days of Titus Oates have mostly passed without loss of men's lives; or indeed without much other loss than that of reason, for the time, in the sufferers. In this mitigated form, however, the distemper is of pretty regular recurrence; and may be reckoned on at intervals, like other natural visitations; so that reasonable men deal with it, as the Londoners do with their fogs, – go cautiously out into the groping crowd, and patiently carry lanterns at noon; knowing, by a well-grounded faith, that the sun is still in existence, and will one day reappear. How often have we heard, for the last fifty years, that the country was wrecked, and fast sinking; whereas, up to this date, the country is entire and afloat! The 'State in Danger' is a condition of things, which we have witnessed a hundred times; and as for the Church, it has seldom been out of 'danger' since we can remember it.

All men are aware that the present is a crisis of this sort; and why it has become so. The repeal of the Test Acts, and then of the Catholic disabilities, has struck many of their admirers with an indescribable astonishment. Those things seemed fixed and immovable; deep as the foundations of the world; and lo, in a moment they have vanished, and their place knows them no more! Our worthy friends mistook the slumbering Leviathan for an island; often as they had been assured, that Intolerance was, and could be nothing but a Monster; and so, mooring under the lee, they had anchored comfortably in his scaly rind, thinking to take good cheer; as for some space they did. But now their Leviathan has suddenly dived under; and they can no longer be fastened in the stream of time; but must drift forward on it, even like the rest of the world: no very appalling fate, we think, could they but understand it; which, however, they will not yet, for a season. Their little island is gone; sunk deep amid confused eddies; and what is left worth caring for in the universe? What is it to them that the great continents of the earth are still standing; and the polestar and all our loadstars, in the heavens, still shining and eternal? Their cherished little haven is gone, and they will not be comforted! And therefore, day after day, in all manner of periodical or perennial publications, the most lugubrious predictions are sent forth. The King has virtually abdicated; the Church is a widow, without jointure; public principle is gone; private honesty is going; society, in short, is fast falling in pieces; and a time of unmixed evil is come on us.

At such a period, it was to be expected that the rage of prophecy should be more than usually excited. Accordingly, the Millennarians have come forth on the right hand, and the Millites on the left. The Fifth-monarchy men prophesy from the Bible, and the Utilitarians from Bentham. The one announces that the last of the seals is to be opened, positively, in the year 1860; and the other assures us that 'the greatest-happiness principle' is to make a heaven of earth, in a still shorter time. We know these symptoms too well, to think it necessary or safe to interfere with them. Time and the hours will bring relief to all parties. The grand encourager of Delphic or other noises is – the Echo. Left to themselves, they will the sooner dissipate, and die away in space.

Meanwhile, we too admit that the present is an important time; as all present time necessarily is. The poorest Day that passes over us is the conflux of two Eternities; it is made up of currents that issue from the remotest Past, and flow onwards into the remotest Future. We were wise indeed, could we discern truly the signs of our own time; and by knowledge of its wants and advantages, wisely adjust our own position in it. Let us, instead of gazing idly into the obscure distance, look calmly around us, for a little, on the perplexed scene where we stand. Perhaps, on a more serious inspection, something of its perplexity will disappear, some of its distinctive characters and deeper tendencies more clearly reveal themselves; whereby our own relations to it, our own true aims and endeavours in it, may also become clearer.

Were we required to characterize this age of ours by any single epithet, we should be tempted to call it, not an Heroical, Devotional, Philosophical, or Moral Age, but, above all others, the Mechanical Age. It is the Age of Machinery, in every outward and inward sense of that word; the age which, with its whole undivided might, forwards, teaches and practises the great art of adapting means to ends. Nothing is now done directly, or by hand; all is by rule and calculated contrivance. For the simplest operation, some helps and accompaniments, some cunning abbreviating process is in readiness. Our old modes of exertion are all discredited, and thrown aside. On every hand, the living artisan is driven from his workshop, to make room for a speedier, inanimate one. The shuttle drops from the fingers of the weaver, and falls into iron fingers that ply it faster. The sailor furls his sail, and lays down his oar; and bids a strong, unwearied servant, on vaporous wings, bear him through the waters. Men have crossed oceans by steam; the Birmingham Fire-king has visited the fabulous East; and the genius of the Cape, were there any Camoens now to sing it, has again been alarmed, and with far stranger thunders than Gama's. There is no end to machinery. Even the horse is stripped of his harness, and finds a fleet fire-horse yoked in his stead. Nay, we have an artist that hatches chickens by steam; the very brood-hen is to be superseded! For all earthly, and for some unearthly purposes, we have machines and mechanic furtherances; for mincing our cabbages; for casting us into magnetic sleep. We remove mountains, and make seas our smooth highway; nothing can resist us. We war with rude Nature; and, by our resistless engines, come off always victorious, and loaded with spoils.

What wonderful accessions have thus been made, and are still making, to the physical power of mankind; how much better fed, clothed, lodged and, in all outwards respects, accommodated men now are, or might be, by a given quantity of labour, is a grateful reflection which forces itself on every one. What changes, too, this addition of power is introducing into the Social System; how wealth has more and more increased, and at the same time gathered itself more and more into masses, strangely altering the old relations, and increasing the distance between the rich and the poor, will be a question for Political Economists, and a much more complex and important one than any they have yet engaged with.

But leaving these matters for the present, let us observe how the mechanical genius of our time has diffused itself into quite other provinces. Not the external and physical alone is now managed by machinery, but the internal and spiritual also. Here too nothing follows its spontaneous course, nothing is left to be accomplished by old natural methods. Everything has its cunningly devised implements, its pre-established apparatus; it is not done by hand, but by machinery. Thus we have machines for Education: Lancastrian machines; Hamiltonian machines; monitors, maps and emblems. Instruction, that mysterious communing of Wisdom with Ignorance, is no longer an indefinable tentative process, requiring a study of individual aptitudes, and a perpetual variation of means and methods, to attain the same end; but a secure, universal, straightforward business, to be conducted in the gross, by proper mechanism, with such intellect as comes to hand. Then, we have Religious machines, of all imaginable varieties; the Bible-Society, professing a far higher and heavenly structure, is found, on inquiry, to be altogether an earthly contrivance: supported by collection of moneys, by fomenting of vanities, by puffing, intrigue and chicane; a machine for converting the Heathen. It is the same in all other departments. Has any man, or any society of men, a truth to speak, a piece of spiritual work to do; they can nowise proceed at once and with the mere natural organs, but must first call a public meeting, appoint committees, issue prospectuses, eat a public dinner; in a word, construct or borrow machinery, wherewith to speak it and do it. Without machinery they were hopeless, helpless; a colony of Hindoo weavers squatting in the heart of Lancashire. Mark, too, how every machine must have its moving power, in some of the great currents of society; every little sect among us, Unitarians, Utilitarians, Anabaptists, Phrenologists, must have its Periodical, its monthly or quarterly Magazine; – hanging out, like its windmill, into the *popularis aura*, to grind meal for the society.

With individuals, in like manner, natural strength avails little. No individual now hopes to accomplish the poorest enterprise single-handed and without mechanical aids; he must make interest with some existing corporation, and till his field with their oxen. In these days, more emphatically than ever, 'to live, signifies to unite with a party, or to make one.' Philosophy, Science, Art, Literature, all depend on machinery. No Newton, by silent meditation, now discovers the system of the world from the falling of an apple; but some quite other than Newton stands in his Museum, his Scientific Institution, and behind whole batteries of retorts, digesters, and galvanic piles imperatively 'interrogates Nature', – who, however, shows no haste to answer. In defect of Raphaels, and Angelos, and Mozarts, we have Royal Academies of Painting, Sculpture, Music; whereby the languishing spirit of Art may be strengthened, as by the more generous diet of a Public Kitchen. Literature, too, has its Paternoster-row mechanism, its Trade-dinners, its Editorial conclaves, and huge subterranean, puffing bellows; so that books are not only printed, but, in a great measure, written and sold, by machinery.

National culture, spiritual benefit of all sorts, is under the same management. No Queen Christina, in these times, needs to send for her Descartes; no King Frederick for his Voltaire, and painfully nourish him with pensions and flattery: any sovereign of taste, who wishes to enlighten his people, has only to impose a new tax, and with the proceeds establish Philosophic Institutes. Hence the Royal and Imperial Societies, the Bibliothèques, Glypothèques, Technothèques, which front us in all capital cities; like so many well-finished hives, to which it is expected the stray agencies of Wisdom will swarm of their own accord, and hive and make honey. In like manner, among ourselves, when it is thought that religion is declining, we have only to vote half-a-million's worth of bricks and mortar, and build new churches. In Ireland it seems they have gone still farther, having actually established a 'Penny-a-Week Purgatory-Society'! Thus does the Genius of Mechanism stand by to help us in all difficulties and emergencies, and with his iron back bears all our burdens.

These things, which we state lightly enough here, are yet of deep import, and indicate a mighty change in our whole manner of existence. For the same habit regulates not our modes of action alone, but our modes of thought and feeling. Men are grown mechanical in head and in heart, as well as in hand. They have lost faith in individual endeavour, and in natural force, of any kind. Not for internal perfection, but for external combinations and arrangements, for institutions, constitutions, – for Mechanism of one sort or other, do they hope and struggle. Their whole efforts, attachments, opinions, turn on mechanism, and are of a mechanical character.

We may trace this tendency in all the great manifestations of our time; in its intellectual aspect, the studies it most favours and its manner of conducting them; in its practical aspects, its politics, arts, religion, morals; in the whole sources, and throughout the whole currents, of its spiritual, no less than its material activity.

Consider, for example, the state of Science generally, in Europe, at this period. It is admitted, on all sides, that the Metaphysical and Moral Sciences are falling into decay, while the Physical are engrossing, every day, more respect and attention. In most of the European nations there is now no such thing as a Science of Mind; only more or less advancement in the general science, or the special sciences, of matter. The French were the first to desert Metaphysics; and though they have lately affected to revive their school, it has yet no signs of vitality. The land of Malebranche, Pascal, Descartes and Fénelon, has now only its Cousins and Villemains; while, in the department of Physics, it reckons far other names. Among ourselves, the Philosophy of Mind, after a rickety infancy, which never reached the vigour of manhood, fell suddenly into decay, languished and finally died out, with its last amiable cultivator, Professor Stewart. In no nation but Germany has any decisive effort been made in psychological science; not to speak of any decisive result. The science of the age, in short, is physical, chemical, physiological; in all shapes mechanical. Our favourite Mathematics, the highly-prized exponent of all these other sciences, has also become more and more mechanical. Excellence in what is called its higher departments depends less on natural genius than on acquired expertness in wielding its machinery. Without undervaluing the wonderful results which a Lagrange or Laplace educes by means of it, we may remark, that their calculus, differential and integral, is little else than a more cunningly-constructed arithmetical mill; where the factors being put in, are, as it were, ground into the true product, under cover, and without other effort on our part than steady turning of the handle. We have more Mathematics than ever; but less Mathesis. Archimedes and Plato could not have read the *Mécanique Céleste*; but neither would the whole French Institute see aught in that saying, 'God geometrises!' but a sentimental rodomontade.

Nay, our whole Metaphysics itself, from Lock's time downwards, has been physical; not a spiritual philosophy, but a material one. The singular estimation in which his Essay was so long held as a scientific work (an estimation grounded, indeed, on the estimable character of the man) will one day be thought a curious indication of the spirit of these times. His whole doctrine is mechanical, in its aim and origin, in its method and its results. It is not a philosophy of the mind: it is a mere discussion concerning the origin of our consciousness, or ideas, or whatever else they are called; a genetic history of what we see *in* the mind. The grand secrets of Necessity and Freewill, of the Mind's vital or non-vital dependence on Matter, of our mysterious relations to Time and Space, to God, to the Universe, are not, in the faintest degree touched on in these inquiries; and seem not to have the smallest connexion with them.

The last class of our Scotch Metaphysicians had a dim notion that much of this was wrong; but they knew not how to right it. The school of Reid had also from the first taken a mechanical course, not seeing any other. The singular conclusions at which Hume, setting out from their admitted premises, was arriving, brought this school into being; they let loose Instinct, as an undiscriminating ban-dog, to guard them against these conclusions; – they tugged lustily at the logical chain by which Hume was so coldly towing them and the world into bottomless abysses of Atheism and Fatalism. But the chain somehow snapped between them; and the issue has been that nobody now cares about either, – any more than about Hartley's, Darwin's, or Priestley's contemporaneous doings in England. Hartley's vibrations and vibratiuncles, one would think, were material and mechanical enough; but our Continental neighbours have gone still farther. One of their philosophers has lately discovered, that 'as the liver secretes bile, so does the brain secrete thought'; which astonishing discovery Dr Cabanis, more lately still, in his *Rapports du Physique et du Morale de l'Homme,* has pushed into its minutest developments.

The metaphysical philosophy of this last inquirer is certainly no shadowy or unsubstantial one. He fairly lays open our moral structure with his dissecting-knives and real metal probes; and exhibits it to the inspection of mankind, by Leuwenhoek microscopes, and inflation with the anatomical blowpipe. Thought, he is inclined to hold, is still secreted by the brain; but then Poetry and Religion (and it is really worth knowing) are 'a product of the smaller intestines'! We have the greatest admiration for this learned doctor: with what scientific stoicism he walks through the land of wonders, unwondering; like a wise man through some huge, gaudy, imposing Vauxhall, whose fire-works, cascades and symphonies, the vulgar may enjoy and believe in, – but where he finds nothing real but the saltpetre, pasteboard and catgut. His book may be regarded as the ultimatum of mechanical metaphysics in our time; a remarkable realization of what in Martinus Scriblerus was still only an idea, that 'as the jack had a meat-roasting quality, so had the body a thinking quality', – upon the strength of which the Nurembergers were to build a wood-and-leather man, 'who should reason as well as most country parsons.' Vaucanson did indeed make a wooden duck, that seemed to eat and digest; but that bold scheme of the Nurembergers remained for a more modern virtuoso.

This condition of the two great departments of knowledge, – the outward, cultivated exclusively on mechanical principles; the inward, finally abandoned, because, cultivated on such principles, it is found to yield no result, – sufficiently indicates the intellectual bias of our time, its all-pervading disposition towards that line of inquiry. In fact, an inward persuasion has long been diffusing itself, and now and then even comes to utterance. That, except the external, there are no true sciences; that to the inward world (if there be any) our only conceivable road is through the outward; that, in short, what cannot be investigated and understood mechanically, cannot be investigated and understood at all. We advert the more particularly to these intellectual propensities, as to prominent symptoms of our age, because Opinion is at all times doubly related to Action, first as cause, then as effect; and the speculative tendency of any age will therefore give us, on the whole, the best indications of its practical tendency.

Nowhere, for example, is the deep, almost exclusive faith we have in Mechanism more visible than in the Politics of this time. Civil government does by its nature include much that is mechanical, and must be treated accordingly. We term it indeed, in ordinary language, the Machine of Society, and talk of it as the grand working wheel from which all private machines must derive, or to which they must adapt, their movements. Considered merely as a metaphor, all this is well enough; but here, as in so many other cases, the 'foam hardens itself into a shell,' and the shadow we have wantonly evoked stands terrible before us and will not depart at our bidding. Government includes much also that is not mechanical, and cannot be treated

mechanically; of which latter truth, as appears to us, the political
speculations and exertions of our time are taking less and less
cognisance.

Nay, in the very outset, we might note the mighty interest
taken in *mere political arrangements*, as itself the sign of a
mechanical age. The whole discontent of Europe takes this
direction. The deep, strong cry of all civilized nations – a cry
which, every one now sees, must and will be answered, is: Give
us a reform of Government! A good structure of legislation, a
proper check upon the executive, a wise arrangement of the
judiciary, is *all* that is wanting for human happiness. The
Philosopher of this age is not a Socrates, a Plato, a Hooker, or
Taylor, who inculcates on men the necessity and infinite worth
of moral goodness, the great truth that our happiness depends
on the mind which is within us, and not on the circumstances
which are without us; but a Smith, a De Lolme, a Bentham, who
chiefly inculcates the reverse of this, – that our happiness
depends entirely on external circumstances; nay, that the
strength and dignity of the mind within us is itself the creature
and consequence of these. Were the laws, the government, in
good order, all were well with us; the rest would care for itself!
Dissentients from this opinion, expressed or implied, are now
rarely to be met with; widely and angrily as men differ in its
application, the principle is admitted by all.

Equally mechanical, and of equal simplicity, are the methods
proposed by both parties for completing or securing this all-
sufficient perfection of arrangement. It is no longer the moral,
religious, spiritual condition of the people that is our concern,
but their physical, practical, economical condition, as regulated
by public laws. Thus is the Body-politic more than ever
worshipped and tendered; but the Soul-politic less than ever.
Love of country, in any high or generous sense, in any other
than an almost animal sense, or mere habit, has little importance
attached to it in such reforms, or in the opposition shown them.
Men are to be guided only by their self-interests. Good
government is a good balancing of these; and, except a keen eye
and appetite for self-interest, requires no virtue in any quarter.
To both parties it is emphatically a machine: to the discontented,

a 'taxing-machine'; to the contented, a 'machine for securing property'. Its duties and its faults are not those of a father, but of an active parish-constable.

Thus it is by the mere condition of the machine, by preserving it untouched, or else by reconstructing it, and oiling it anew, that man's salvation as a social being is to be ensured and indefinitely promoted. Contrive the fabric of law aright, and without farther effort on your part, that divine spirit of Freedom, which all hearts venerate and long for, will of herself come to inhabit it; and under her healing wings every noxious influence will wither, every good and salutary one more and more expand. Nay, so devoted are we to this principle, and at the same time so curiously mechanical, that a new trade, specially grounded on it, has arisen among us, under the name of 'Codification', or codemaking in the abstract; whereby any people, for a reasonable consideration, may be accommodated with a patent code; – more easily than curious individuals with patent breeches, for the people does *not* need to be measured first.

To us who live in the midst of all this, and see continually the faith, hope and practice of every one founded on Mechanism of one kind or other, it is apt to seem quite natural, and as if it could never have been otherwise. Nevertheless, if we recollect or reflect a little, we shall find both that it has been, and might again be otherwise. The domain of Mechanism, – meaning thereby political, ecclesiastical or other outward establishments, – was once considered as embracing, and we are persuaded can at any time embrace, but a limited portion of man's interests, and by no means the highest portion.

To speak a little pedantically, there is a science of *Dynamics* in man's fortunes and nature, as well as of *Mechanics*. There is a science which treats of, and practically addresses, the primary, unmodified forces and energies of man, the mysterious springs of Love, and Fear, and Wonder, of Enthusiasm, Poetry, Religion, all which have a truly vital and *infinite* character; as well as a science which practically addresses the finite, modified developments of these, when they take the shape of immediate 'motives', as hope of reward, or as fear of punishment.

Now it is certain, that in former times the wise men, the enlightened lovers of their kind, who appeared generally as Moralists, Poets or Priests, did, without neglecting the Mechanical province, deal chiefly with the Dynamical; applying themselves chiefly to regulate, increase and purify the inward primary powers of man; and fancying that herein lay the main difficulty, and the best service they could undertake. But a wide difference is manifest in our age. For the wise men, who now appear as Political Philosophers, deal exclusively with the Mechanical province; and occupying themselves in counting-up and estimating men's motives, strive by curious checking and balancing, and other adjustments of Profit and Loss, to guide them to their true advantage: while, unfortunately, those same 'motives' are so innumerable, and so variable in every individual, that no really useful conclusion can ever be drawn from their enumeration. But though Mechanism, wisely contrived, has done much for man in a social and moral point of view, we cannot be persuaded that it has ever been the chief source of his worth or happiness. Consider the great elements of human enjoyment, the attainments and possessions that exalt man's life to its present height, and see what part of these he owes to institutions, to Mechanism of any kind; and what to the instinctive, unbounded force, which Nature herself lent him, and still continues to him. Shall we say, for example, that Science and Art are indebted principally to the founders of Schools and Universities? Did not Science originate rather, and gain advancement, in the obscure closets of the Roger Bacons, Keplers, Newtons; in the workshops of the Fausts and the Watts; wherever, and in what guise soever Nature, from the first times downwards, had sent a gifted spirit upon the earth? Again, were Homer and Shakespeare members of any beneficed guild, or made Poets by means of it? Were Painting and Sculpture created by forethought, brought into the world by institutions for that end? No; Science and Art have, from first to last, been the free gift of Nature; an unsolicited, unexpected gift; often even a fatal one. These things rose up, as it were, by spontaneous growth, in the free soil and sunshine of Nature. They were not planted or grafted, nor even greatly multiplied or improved by the culture or manuring of institutions. Generally speaking, they have derived only partial help from these; often enough have suffered damage. They made constitutions for themselves. They originated in the Dynamical nature of man, not in his Mechanical nature.

Or, to take an infinitely higher instance, that of the Christian Religion, which, under every theory of it, in the believing or unbelieving mind, must ever be regarded as the crowning glory, or rather the life and soul, of our whole modern culture: How did Christianity arise and spread abroad among men? Was it by institutions, and establishments and well-arranged systems of mechanism? Not so; on the contrary, in all past and existing institutions for those ends, its divine spirit has invariably been found to languish and decay. It arose in the mystic deeps of man's soul; and was spread abroad by the 'preaching of the word', by simple, altogether natural and individual efforts; and flew, like hallowed fire, from heart to heart, till all were purified and illuminated by it; and its heavenly light shone, as it still shines, and (as sun or star) will ever shine, through the whole dark destinies of man. Here again was no Mechanism; man's highest attainment was accomplished Dynamically, not Mechanically.

Nay, we will venture to say, that no high attainment, not even any far-extending movement among men, was ever accomplished otherwise. Strange as it may seem, if we read History with any degree of thoughtfulness, we shall find that the checks and balances of Profit and Loss have never been the grand agents with men; that they have never been roused into deep, thorough, all-pervading efforts by any computable prospect of Profit and Loss, for any visible, finite object; but always for some invisible and infinite one. The Crusades took their rise in religion; their visible object was, commercially speaking, worth nothing. It was the boundless Invisible world that was laid bare in the imaginations of those men; and in its burning light, the visible shrunk as a scroll. Not mechanical, nor produced by mechanical means, was this vast movement. No dining at Freemasons' Tavern, with the other long train of modern machinery; no cunning reconciliation of 'vested interests', was required here: only the passionate voice of one man, the rapt soul looking through the eyes of one man; and rugged, steel-clad Europe trembled beneath his words, and followed him whither he listed. In later ages it was still the same. The Reformation had an invisible, mystic and ideal aim; the result was indeed to be embodied in external things; but its spirit, its worth, was internal, invisible, infinite. Our English Revolution too originated in Religion. Men did battle, in those old days, not for Purse-sake, but for Conscience-sake. Nay, in our own days, it is no way different. The French Revolution itself had something higher in it than cheap bread and a Habeas-corpus act. Here too was an Idea; a Dynamic, not a Mechanic force. It was a struggle, though a blind and at last an insane one, for the infinite, divine nature of Right, of Freedom, of Country.

Thus does man, in every age, vindicate, consciously or unconsciously, his celestial birthright. Thus does Nature hold on her wondrous, unquestionable course; and all our systems and theories are but so many froth-eddies or sandbanks, which from time to time she casts up, and washes away. When we can drain the Ocean into mill-ponds, and bottle-up the Force of Gravity, to be sold by retail, in gas jars; then may we hope to comprehend the infinitudes of man's soul under formulas of Profit and Loss; and rule over this too, as over a patent engine, by checks, and valves, and balances.

Nay, even with regard to Government itself, can it be necessary to remind any one that Freedom, without which indeed all spiritual life is impossible, depends on infinitely more complex influences than either the extension or the curtailment of the 'democratic interest'? Who is there that, 'taking the high *priori* road,' shall point out what these influences are; what deep, subtle, inextricably entangled influences they have been and may be? For man is not the creature and product of Mechanism; but, in a far truer sense, its creator and producer: it is the noble People that makes the noble Government; rather than conversely. On the whole, Institutions are much; but they are not all. The freest and highest spirits of the world have often been found under strange outward circumstances: Saint Paul and his brother Apostles were politically slaves; Epictetus was personally one. Again, forget the influences of Chivalry and Religion, and ask: What countries produced Columbus and Las Casas? Or, descending from virtue and heroism to mere energy and spiritual talent: Cortes, Pizarro, Alba, Ximenes? The Spaniards of the sixteenth century were indisputably the noblest nation of Europe: yet they had the Inquisition and Philip II. They have the same government at this day; and are the lowest nation. The Dutch too have retained their old constitution; but no Siege of Leyden, no William the Silent, not even an Egmont or De Witt any longer appears among them. With ourselves also, where much has changed, effect has nowise followed cause as it should have done: two centuries ago, the Commons Speaker addressed Queen Elizabeth on bended knees, happy that the virago's foot did not even smite him; yet the people were then governed, not by a Castlereagh, but by a Burghley; they had their Shakespeare and Philip Sidney, where we have our Sheridan Knowles and Beau Brummel.

These and the like facts are so familiar, the truths which they preach so obvious, and have in all past times been so universally believed and acted on, that we should almost feel ashamed for repeating them; were it not that, on every hand, the memory of them seems to have passed away, or at best died into a faint tradition, of no value as a practical principle. To judge by the loud clamour of our Constitution-builders, Statists, Economists, directors, creators, reformers of Public Societies; in a word, all manner of Mechanists, from the Cartwright up to the Code-maker; and by the nearly total silence of all Preachers and Teachers who should give a voice to Poetry, Religion and Morality, we might fancy either that man's Dynamical nature was, to all spiritual intents, extinct, or else so perfected that nothing more was to be made of it by the old means; and henceforth only in his Mechanical contrivances did any hope exist for him.

To define the limits of these two departments of man's activity, which work into one another, and by means of one another, so intricately and inseparably, were by its nature an impossible attempt. Their relative importance, even to the wisest mind, will vary in different times, according to the special wants and dispositions of those times. Meanwhile, it seems clear enough that only in the right co-ordination of the two, and the vigorous forwarding of *both*, does our true line of action lie. Undue cultivation of the inward or Dynamical province leads to idle, visionary, impracticable courses, and, especially in rude eras, to Superstition and Fanaticism, with their long train of baleful and well-known evils. Undue cultivation of the outward, again, though less immediately prejudicial, and even for the time productive of many palpable benefits, must, in the long-run, by destroying Moral Force, which is the parent of all other Force, prove not less certainly, and perhaps still more hopelessly, pernicious. This, we take it, is the grand characteristic of our age. By our skill in Mechanism, it has come to pass, that in the management of external things we excel all other ages; while in whatever respects the pure moral nature, in true dignity of soul and character, we are perhaps inferior to most civilized ages.

In fact, if we look deeper, we shall find that this faith in Mechanism has now struck its roots down into man's most intimate, primary sources of conviction; and is thence sending up, over his whole life and activity, innumerable stems, – fruit-bearing and poison-bearing. The truth is, men have lost their belief in the Invisible, and believe, and hope, and work only in the Visible; or, to speak it in other words: This is not a Religious age. Only the material, the immediately practical, not the divine and spiritual, is important to us. The infinite, absolute character of Virtue has passed into a finite, conditional one; it is no longer a worship of the Beautiful and Good; but a calculation of the Profitable. Worship, indeed, in any sense, is not recognized among us, or is mechanically explained into Fear of pain, or Hope of pleasure. Our true Deity is Mechanism. It has subdued external Nature for us, and we think it will do all other things. We are Giants in physical power: in a deeper than metaphorical sense, we are Titans, that strive, by heaping mountain on mountain, to conquer Heaven also.

The strong Mechanical character, so visible in the spiritual pursuits and methods of this age, may be traced much farther into the condition and prevailing disposition of our spiritual nature itself. Consider, for example, the general fashion of Intellect in this era. Intellect, the power man has of knowing and believing, is now nearly synonymous with Logic, or the mere power of arranging and communicating. Its implement is not Meditation, but Argument. 'Cause and effect' is almost the only category under which we look at, and work with, all Nature. Our first question with regard to any object is not, What is it? but, How is it? We are no longer instinctively driven to apprehend, and lay to heart, what is Good and Lovely, but rather to inquire, as onlookers, how it is produced, whence it comes, whither it goes. Our favourite Philosophers have no love and no hatred; they stand among us not to do, nor to create anything, but as a sort of Logic-mills, to grind out the true causes and effects of all that is done and created. To the eye of a Smith, a Hume or a Constant, all is well that works quietly. An Order of Ignatius Loyola, a Presbyterianism of John Knox, a Wickliffe or a Henry the Eighth, are simply so many mechanical phenomena, caused or causing.

The *Euphuist* of our day differs much from his pleasant predecessors. An intellectual dapperling of these times boasts chiefly of his irresistible perspicacity, his 'dwelling in the daylight of truth', and so forth; which, on examination, turns out to be a dwelling in the *rush*-light of 'closet-logic', and a deep unconsciousness that there is any other light to dwell in or any other objects to survey with it. Wonder, indeed, is, on all hands, dying out: it is the sign of uncultivation to wonder. Speak to any small man of a high, majestic Reformation, of a high majestic Luther; and forthwith he sets about 'accounting' for it; how the 'circumstances of the time' called for such a character, and found him, we suppose, standing girt and road-ready, to do its errand; how the 'circumstances of the time' created, fashioned, floated him quietly along into the result; how, in short, this small man, had he been there, could have performed the like himself! For it is the 'force of circumstances' that does everything; the force of one man can do nothing. Now all this is grounded on little more than a metaphor. We figure Society as a 'Machine', and that mind is opposed to mind, as body is to body; whereby two, or at most ten, little minds must be stronger than one great mind. Notable absurdity! For the plain truth, very plain, we think is, that minds are opposed to minds in quite a different way; and *one* man that has a higher Wisdom, a hitherto unknown spiritual Truth in him, is stronger, not than ten men that have it not, or than ten thousand, but than *all* men that have it not; and stands among them with a quite ethereal, angelic power, as with a sword out of Heaven's own armory, sky-tempered, which no buckler, and no tower of brass, will finally withstand.

But to us, in these times, such considerations rarely occur. We enjoy, we see nothing by direct vision; but only by reflection, and in anatomical dismemberment. Like Sir Hudibras, for every Why we must have a Wherefore. We have our little *theory* on all human and divine things. Poetry, the workings of genius itself, which in all times, with one or another meaning, has been called Inspiration, and held to be mysterious and inscrutable, is no longer without its scientific exposition. The building of the lofty rhyme is like any other masonry or bricklaying; we have theories of its rise, height, decline and fall, – which latter, it would seem, is now near, among all people. Of our 'Theories of Taste', as they are called, wherein the deep, infinite, unspeakable Love of Wisdom and Beauty, which dwells in all men, is 'explained', made mechanically visible, from 'Association' and the like, why should we say anything? Hume has written us a 'Natural History of Religion'; in which one Natural History all the rest are included. Strangely too does the general feeling coincide with Hume's in this wonderful problem; for whether his 'Natural History' be the right one or not, that Religion must have a Natural History, all of us, cleric and laic, seem to be agreed. He indeed regards it as a Disease, we again as Health; so far there is a difference; but in our first principle we are at one.

To what extent theological Unbelief, we mean intellectual dissent from the Church, in its view of Holy Writ, prevails at this day, would be a highly important, were it not, under any circumstances, an almost impossible inquiry. But the Unbelief, which is of a still more fundamental character, every man may see prevailing, with scarcely any but the faintest contradiction, all around him; even in the Pulpit itself. Religion in most countries, more or less in every country, is no longer what it was, and should be, – a thousand-voiced psalm from the heart of Man to his invisible Father, the fountain of all Goodness, Beauty, Truth, and revealed in every revelation of these; but for the most part, a wise prudential feeling grounded on mere calculation; a matter, as all others now are, of Expediency and Utility; whereby some smaller quantum of earthly enjoyment may be exchanged for a far larger quantum of celestial enjoyment. Thus Religion too is Profit, a working for wages; not Reverence, but vulgar Hope or Fear. Many, we know, very many we hope, are still religious in a far different sense; were it not so, our case were too desperate: but to witness that such is the temper of the times, we take any calm observant man, who agrees or disagrees in our feeling on the matter, and ask him whether our *view* of it is not in general well-founded.

Literature too, if we consider it, gives similar testimony. At no former era has Literature, the printed communication of Thought, been of such importance as it is now. We often hear that the Church is in danger; and truly so it is, – in a danger it seems not to know of: for, with its tithes in the most perfect safety, its functions are becoming more and more superseded. The true Church of England, at this moment, lies in the Editors of its Newspapers. These preach to the people daily, weekly; admonishing kings themselves; advising peace or war, with an authority which only the first Reformers, and a long-past class of Popes, were possessed of; inflicting moral censure; imparting moral encouragement, consolation, edification; in all ways diligently 'administering the Discipline of the Church'. It may be said too, that in private disposition the new Preachers some-what resemble the Mendicant Friars of old times: outwardly full of holy zeal; inwardly not without stratagem, and hunger for terrestrial things. But omitting this class, and the boundless host of watery personages who pipe, as they are able, on so many scrannel straws, let us look at the higher regions of Literature, where, if anywhere, the pure melodies of Poesy and Wisdom should be heard. Of natural talent there is no deficiency: one or two richly-endowed individuals even give us a superiority in

this respect. But what is the song they sing? Is it a tone of the
Memnon Statue, breathing music as the *light* first touches it? A
'liquid wisdom', disclosing to our sense the deep, infinite
harmonies of Nature and man's soul? Alas, no! It is not a matin
or vesper hymn to the Spirit of Beauty, but a fierce clashing of
cymbals, and shouting of multitudes, as children pass through
the fire to Moloch! Poetry itself has no eye for the Invisible.
Beauty is no longer the god it worships, but some brute image of
Strength; which we may call an idol, for true Strength is one and
the same with Beauty, and its worship also is a hymn. The meek,
silent Light can mould, create and purify all Nature; but the loud
Whirlwind, the sign and product of Disunion, of Weakness,
passes on, and is forgotten. How widely this veneration for the
physically Strongest has spread itself through Literature, any
one may judge who reads either criticism or poem. We praise a
work, not as 'true', but as 'strong'; our highest praise is that it
has 'affe cted' us, has 'terrified' us. All this, it has been well
observed, is the 'maximum of the Barbarous', the symptom, not
of vigorous refinement, but of luxurious corruption. It speaks
much, too, for men's indestructible love of truth, that nothing of
this kind will abide with them; that even the talent of a Byron
cannot permanently seduce us into idol-worship; that he too,
with all his wild siren charming, already begins to be
disregarded and forgotten.

Again, with respect to our Moral condition: here also he who
runs may read that the same physical, mechanical influences are
everywhere busy. For the 'superior morality', of which we hear
so much, we too would desire to be thankful: at the same time, it
were but blindness to deny that this 'superior morality' is
properly rather an 'inferior criminality', produced not by greater
love of Virtue, but by greater perfection of Police; and of that far
subtler and stronger Police, called Public Opinion. This last
watches over us with its Argus eyes more keenly than ever; but
the 'inward eye' seems heavy with sleep. Of any belief in
invisible, divine things, we find as few traces in our Morality as
elsewhere. It is by tangible, material considerations that we are
guided, not by inward and spiritual. Self-denial, the parent of all
virtue, in any true sense of that word, has perhaps seldom been

rarer: so rare is it, that the most, even in their abstract speculations, regard its existence as a chimera. Virtue is Pleasure, is Profit; no celestial, but an earthly thing. Virtuous men, Philanthropists, Martyrs are happy accidents; their 'taste' lies the right way! In all senses, we worship and follow after Power; which may be called a physical pursuit. No man now loves Truth, as Truth must be loved, with an infinite love; but only with a finite love, and as it were *par amours*. Nay, properly speaking, he does not *believe* and know it, but only '*thinks*' it, and that 'there is every probability!' He preaches it aloud, and rushes courageously forth with it, – if there is a multitude huzzaing at his back; yet ever keeps looking over his shoulder, and the instant the huzzaing languishes, he too stops short.

In fact, what morality we have takes the shape of Ambition, of 'Honour': beyond money and money's worth, our only rational blessedness is Popularity. It were but a fool's trick to die for conscience. Only for 'character', by duel, or in case of extremity, by suicide, is the wise man bound to die. By arguing on the 'force of circumstances', we have argued away all force from ourselves; and stand leashed together, uniform in dress and movement, like the rowers of some boundless galley. This and that may be right and true; *but* we must not do it. Wonderful 'Force of Public Opinion'! We must act and walk in all points as it prescribes; follow the traffic it bids us, realize the sum of money, the degree of 'influence' it expects of us, *or* we shall be lightly esteemed; certain mouthfuls of articulate wind will be blown at us, and this what mortal courage can front? Thus, while civil liberty is more and more secured to us, our moral liberty is all but lost. Practically considered, our creed is Fatalism; and, free in hand and foot, we are shackled in heart and soul with far straiter than feudal chains. Truly may we say, with the Philosopher, 'the deep meaning of the Laws of Mechanism lies heavy on us'; and in the closet, in the market-place, in the temple, by the social hearth, encumbers the whole movements of our mind, and over our noblest faculties is spreading a nightmare sleep.

These dark features, we are aware, belong more or less to other ages, as well as to ours. This faith in Mechanism, in the all-importance of physical things, is in every age the common refuge of Weakness and blind Discontent; of all who believe, as many will ever do, that man's true good lies without him, not within. We are aware also, that, as applied to ourselves in all their aggravation, they form but half a picture; that in the whole picture there are bright lights as well as gloomy shadows. If we here dwell chiefly on the latter, let us not be blamed: it is in general more profitable to reckon up our defects than to boast of our attainments.

Neither, with all these evils more or less clearly before us, have we at any time despaired of the fortunes of society. Despair, or even despondency, in that respect, appears to us, in all cases, a groundless feeling. We have a faith in the imperishable dignity of man; in the high vocation to which, throughout this his earthly history, he has been appointed. However it may be with individual nations, whatever melancholic speculators may assert, it seems a well-ascertained fact, that in all times, reckoning even from those of the Heraclides and Pelasgi, the happiness and greatness of mankind at large have been continually progressive. Doubtless this age also is advancing. Its very unrest, its ceaseless activity, its discontent contains matter of promise. Knowledge, education are opening the eyes of the humblest; are increasing the number of thinking minds without limit. This is as it should be; for not in turning back, not in resisting, but only in resolutely struggling forward, does our life consist.

Nay, after all, our spiritual maladies are but of Opinion; we are but fettered by chains of our own forging, and which ourselves also can rend asunder. This deep, paralyzed subjection to physical objects comes not from Nature, but from our own unwise mode of *viewing* Nature. Neither can we understand that man wants, at this hour, any faculty of heart, soul or body, that ever belonged to him. 'He, who has been born, has been a First Man'; has had lying before his young eyes, and as yet unhardened into scientific shapes, a world as plastic, infinite, divine, as lay before the eyes of Adam himself. If Mechanism, like some glass bell, encircles and imprisons us; if the soul looks forth on a fair heavenly country which it cannot reach, and pines, and in its scanty atmosphere is ready to perish, – yet the bell is but of glass; 'one bold stroke to break the bell in pieces, and thou art delivered!' Not the invisible world is wanting, for it dwells in man's soul, and this last is still here. Are the solemn temples, in which the Divinity was once visibly revealed among us, crumbling away? We can repair them, we can rebuild them. The wisdom, the heroic worth of our forefathers, which we have lost, we can recover. That admiration of old nobleness, which now so often shows itself as a faint *dilettantism*, will one day become a generous emulation, and man may again be all that he has been, and more than he has been. Nor are these the mere daydreams of fancy; they are clear possibilities; nay, in this time they are even assuming the character of hopes. Indications we do see in other countries and in our own, signs infinitely cheering to us, that Mechanism is not always to be our hard taskmaster, but one day to be our pliant, all-ministering servant; that a new and brighter spiritual era is slowly evolving itself for all men. But on these things our present course forbids us to enter.

Meanwhile, that great outward changes are in progress can be doubtful to no one. The time is sick and out of joint. Many things have reached their height; and it is a wise adage that tells us, 'the darkest hour is nearest the dawn.' Wherever we can gather indication of the public thought, whether from printed books, as in France or Germany, or from Carbonari rebellions and other political tumults, as in Spain, Portugal, Italy and Greece, the voice it utters is the same. The thinking minds of all nations call for change. There is a deep-lying struggle in the whole fabric of society; a boundless grinding collision of the New with the Old. The French Revolution, as is now visible enough, was not the parent of this mighty movement, but its offspring. Those two hostile influences, which always exist in human things, and on the constant intercommunion of which depends their health and safety, had lain in separate masses, accumulating through generations, and France was the scene of their fiercest explosion; but the final issue was not unfolded in that country: nay, it is not yet anywhere unfolded. Political freedom is hitherto the object of these efforts; but they will not and cannot stop there. It is towards a higher freedom than mere freedom from oppression by his fellow-mortal, that man dimly aims. Of this higher, heavenly freedom, which is 'man's reasonable service', all his noble institutions, his faithful endeavours and loftiest attainments, are but the body, and more and more approximated emblem.

On the whole, as this wondrous planet, Earth, is journeying with its fellows through infinite Space, so are the wondrous destinies embarked on it journeying through infinite Time, under a higher guidance than ours. For the present, as our astronomy informs us, its path lies towards *Hercules*, the constellation of *Physical Power*: but that is not our most pressing concern. Go where it will, the deep HEAVEN will be around it. Therein let us have hope and sure faith. To reform a world, to reform a nation, no wise man will undertake; and all but foolish men know, that the only solid, though a far slower reformation, is what each begins and perfects on *himself*.

John Stuart Mill

John Stuart Mill (1806–73) was born in Pentonville, London and educated at home by his father James Mill, an historian and ardent disciple of the utilitarian philosopher Jeremy Bentham. The rigorous educational training given to the young John Stuart Mill was intended to make him the great exponent of utilitarianism and is described vividly in his *Autobiography* (1873). The policy was successful in that Mill became one of the most noted intellectuals of his age, but it also bred in him a reaction against narrow utilitarianism together with a humanist concern that was to inspire much of his best work. In 1823, following the example of his father, Mill entered the East India Company and remained there until 1858. In the late 1820s and the 1830s he was an active member of the Philosophical Radicals who were to exert a formative influence on mid-Victorian Liberalism, and editor of the *London and Westminster Review*. Among the many essays and reviews he wrote at this time are, 'The Spirit of the Age', 'Coleridge', 'Bentham', 'De Tocqueville on Democracy in America' and 'Civilization', which was first published in the *London and Westminster Review*, April 1836, and later reprinted in *Dissertations and Discussions* (2 vols, 1859). Mill's early full-length works *A System of Logic* (1843) and *Principles of Political Economy* (2 vols, 1848) reveal him as both the advocate of a new scientific study of society, based on inductive and empirical methods, and a theorist of the economics and politics of society. Throughout his work there is an impressive willingness to learn from different approaches and methods and a strongly pragmatic interest in the ways in which social institutions work. In 1851 he married Harriet Taylor with whom he had had a long and intimate friendship. After her death in 1858 and, as he always insisted, largely through her inspiration, he published his most lasting works, *On Liberty*

(1859), *Considerations on Representative Government* (1861), *Utilitarianism* (1863) and *The Subjection of Women* (1869), exploring in these books the questions of individual freedom and liberty in modern democratic societies that had been a major preoccupation throughout his life. He was MP for Westminster from 1865 to 1868.

CIVILIZATION

The word Civilization, like many other terms of the philosophy of human nature, is a word of double meaning. It sometimes stands for *human improvement* in general, and sometimes for *certain kinds* of improvement in particular.

We are accustomed to call a country more civilized if we think it more improved; more eminent in the best characteristics of Man and Society; farther advanced in the road to perfection; happier, nobler, wiser. This is one sense of the word civilization. But in another sense it stands for that kind of improvement only, which distinguishes a wealthy and powerful nation from savages or barbarians. It is in this sense that we may speak of the vices or the miseries of civilization; and that the question has been seriously propounded, whether civilization is on the whole a good or an evil? Assuredly, we entertain no doubt on this point; we hold that civilization is a good, that it is the cause of much good, and not incompatible with any; but we think there is other good, much even of the highest good, which civilization in this sense does not provide for, and some which it has a tendency (though that tendency may be counteracted) to impede.

The inquiry into which these considerations would lead, is calculated to throw light upon many of the characteristic features of our time. The present era is pre-eminently the era of civilization in the narrow sense; whether we consider what has already been achieved, or the rapid advances making towards still greater achievements. We do not regard the age as either equally advanced or equally progressive in many of the other kinds of improvement. In some it appears to us stationary, in some even retrograde. Moreover, the irresistible consequences of a state of advancing civilization; the new position in which that advance has placed, and is every day more and more placing, mankind; the entire inapplicability of old rules to this new position, and the necessity, if we would either realize the benefits of the new state or preserve those of the old, that we should adopt many new rules, and new courses of action; are topics which seem to require a more comprehensive examination than they have usually received.

We shall on the present occasion use the word civilization only in the restricted sense: not that in which it is synonymous with improvement, but that in which it is the direct converse or contrary of rudeness or barbarism. Whatever be the characteristics of what we call savage life, the contrary of these, or the qualities which society puts on as it throws off these, constitute civilization. Thus, a savage tribe consists of a handful of individuals, wandering or thinly scattered over a vast tract of country: a dense population, therefore, dwelling in fixed habitations, and largely collected together in towns and villages, we term civilized. In savage life there is no commerce, no manufactures, no agriculture, or next to none: a country rich in the fruits of agriculture: commerce, and manufactures, we call civilized. In savage communities each person shifts for himself; except in war (and even then very imperfectly), we seldom see any joint operations carried on by the union of many; nor do savages, in general, find much pleasure in each other's society. Wherever, therefore, we find human beings acting together for common purposes in large bodies, and enjoying the pleasures of social intercourse, we term them civilized. In savage life there is little or no law, or administration of justice; no systematic employment of the collective strength of society, to protect individuals against injury from one another; every one trusts to his own strength or cunning, and where that fails, he is generally without resource. We accordingly call a people civilized, where the arrangements of society, for protecting the persons and property of its members, are sufficiently perfect to maintain peace among them; *i.e.* to induce the bulk of the community to rely for their security mainly upon social arrangements, and renounce for the most part, and in ordinary circumstances, the vindication of their interests (whether in the way of aggression or of defence) by their individual strength or courage.

These ingredients of civilization are various, but consideration will satisfy us that they are not improperly classed together. History, and their own nature, alike show that they begin together, always co-exist, and accompany each other in their growth. Wherever there has arisen sufficient knowledge of the arts of life, and sufficient security of property and person, to render the progressive increase of wealth and population possible, the community becomes and continues progressive in all the elements which we have just enumerated. These elements exist in modern Europe, and especially in Great Britain, in a more eminent degree, and in a state of more rapid progression, than at any other place or time. We propose to consider some of the consequences which that high and progressive state of civilization has already produced, and of the further ones which it is hastening to produce.

The most remarkable of those consequences of advancing civilization, which the state of the world is now forcing upon the attention of thinking minds, is this: that power passes more and more from individuals, and small knots of individuals, to masses: that the importance of the masses becomes constantly greater, that of individuals less.

The causes, evidences, and consequences of this law of human affairs, well deserve attention.

There are two elements of importance and influence among mankind: the one is, property; the other, powers and acquirements of mind. Both of these, in an early stage of civilization, are confined to a few persons. In the beginnings of society, the power of the masses does not exist; because property and intelligence have no existence beyond a very small portion of the community, and even if they had, those who possessed the smaller portions would be, from their incapacity of co-operation, unable to cope with those who possessed the larger.

In the more backward countries of the present time, and in all Europe at no distant date, we see property entirely concentrated in a small number of hands; the remainder of the people being, with few exceptions, either the military retainers and dependents of the possessors of property, or serfs, stripped and tortured at pleasure by one master, and pillaged by a hundred. At no period could it be said that there was literally no middle class – but that class was extremely feeble, both in numbers and in power: while the labouring people, absorbed in manual toil, with difficulty earned, by the utmost excess of exertion, a more or less scanty and always precarious subsistence. The character of this state of society was the utmost excess of poverty and impotence in the masses; the most enormous importance and uncontrollable power of a small number of individuals, each of whom, within his own sphere, knew neither law nor superior.

We must leave to history to unfold the gradual rise of the trading and manufacturing classes, the gradual emancipation of the agricultural, the tumults and *bouleversements* which accompanied these changes in their course, and the extraordinary alterations in institutions, opinions, habits, and the whole of social life, which they brought in their train. We need only ask the reader to form a conception of all that is implied in the words, growth of a middle class; and then to reflect on the immense increase of the numbers and property of that class throughout Great Britain, France, Germany, and other countries, in every successive generation, and the novelty of a labouring class receiving such wages as are now commonly earned by nearly the whole of the manufacturing, that is, of the most numerous portion of the operative classes of this country – and ask himself whether, from causes so unheard-of, unheard-of effects ought not to be expected to flow. It must at least be evident, that if, as civilization advances, property and intelligence become thus widely diffused among the millions, it must also be an effect of civilization, that the portion of either of these which can belong to an individual must have a tendency to become less and less influential, and all results must more and more be decided by the movements of masses; provided that the power of combination among the masses keeps pace with the progress of their resources. And that it does so, who can doubt?

There is not a more accurate test of the progress of civilization than the progress of the power of co-operation.

Consider the savage: he has bodily strength, he has courage, enterprise, and is often not without intelligence; what makes all savage communities poor and feeble? The same cause which prevented the lions and tigers from long ago extirpating the race of men – incapacity of co-operation. It is only civilized beings who can combine. All combination is compromise: it is the sacrifice of some portion of individual will, for a common purpose. The savage cannot bear to sacrifice, for any purpose, the satisfaction of his individual will. His social cannot even temporarily prevail over his selfish feelings, nor his impulses bend to his calculations. Look again at the slave: he is used indeed to make his will give way; but to the commands of a master, not to a superior purpose of his own. He is wanting in intelligence to form such a purpose; above all, he cannot frame to himself the conception of a fixed rule: nor if he could, has he the capacity to adhere to it; he is habituated to control, but not to self-control; when a driver is not standing over him with a whip, he is found more incapable of withstanding any temptation, or restraining any inclination, than the savage himself.

We have taken extreme cases, that the fact we seek to illustrate might stand out more conspicuously. But the remark itself applies universally. As any people approach to the condition of savages or of slaves, so are they incapable of acting in concert. Consider even war, the most serious business of a barbarous people; see what a figure rude nations, or semi-civilized and enslaved nations, have made against civilized ones, from Marathon downwards. Why? Because discipline is more powerful than numbers, and discipline, that is, perfect co-operation, is an attribute of civilization. To come to our own times, the whole history of the Peninsular War bears witness to the incapacity of an imperfectly civilized people for co-operation. Amidst all the enthusiasm of the Spanish nation struggling against Napoleon, no one leader, military or political, could act in concert with another; no one would sacrifice one iota of his consequence, his authority, or his opinion, to the most obvious demands of the common cause; neither generals nor soldiers could observe the simplest rules of the military art. If there be an interest which one might expect to act forcibly upon the minds even of savages, it is the desire of simultaneously crushing a formidable neighbour whom none of them are strong enough to resist single-handed; yet none but civilized nations have ever been capable of forming an alliance. The native states of India have been conquered by the English one by one; Turkey made peace with Russia in the very moment of her invasion by France; the nations of the world never could form a confederacy against the Romans, but were swallowed up in succession, some of them being always ready to aid in the subjugation of the rest. Enterprises requiring the voluntary co-operation of many persons independent of one another, in the hands of all but highly civilized nations, have always failed.

It is not difficult to see why this incapacity of organized combination characterizes savages, and disappears with the growth of civilization. Co-operation, like other difficult things, can be learnt only by practice: and to be capable of it in great things, a people must be gradually trained to it in small. Now, the whole course of advancing civilization is a series of such training. The labourer in a rude state of society works singly, or if several are brought to work together by the will of a master, they work side by side, but not in concert; one man digs his piece of ground, another digs a similar piece of ground close by him. In the situation of an ignorant labourer, tilling even his own field with his own hands, and associating with no one except his wife and his children, what is there that can teach him to co-operate? The division of employments – the accomplishment by the combined labour of several, of tasks which could not be achieved by any number of persons singly – is the great school of co-operation. What a lesson, for instance, is navigation, as soon as it passes out of its first simple stage; the safety of all, constantly depending upon the vigilant performance by each, of the part peculiarly allotted to him in the common task. Military operations, when not wholly undisciplined, are a similar school; so are all the operations of commerce and manufactures which require the employment of many hands upon the same thing at the same time. By these operations, mankind learn the value of combination; they see how much and with what ease it accomplishes, which never could be accomplished without it; they learn a practical lesson of submitting themselves to guidance, and subduing themselves to act as interdependent parts of a complex whole. A people thus progressively trained to combination by the business of their lives, become capable of carrying the same habits into new things. For it holds universally, that the one only mode of learning to do anything, is actually doing something of the same kind under easier circumstances. Habits of discipline once acquired, qualify human beings to accomplish all other things for which discipline is needed. No longer either spurning control, or incapable of seeing its advantages; whenever any object presents itself which can be attained by co-operation, and which they see or believe to be beneficial, they are ripe for attaining it.

The characters, then, of a state of high civilization being the diffusion of property and intelligence, and the power of co-operation; the next thing to observe is the unexampled development which all these elements have assumed of late years.

The rapidity with which property has accumulated and is accumulating in the principal countries of Europe, but especially in this island, is obvious to every one. The capital of the industrious classes overflows into foreign countries, and into all kinds of wild speculations. The amount of capital annually exported from Great Britain alone, surpasses probably the whole wealth of the most flourishing commercial republics of antiquity. But this capital, collectively so vast, is mainly composed of small portions; very generally so small that the owners cannot, without other means of livelihood, subsist on the profits of them. While such is the growth of property in the hands of the mass, the circumstances of the higher classes have undergone nothing like a corresponding improvement. Many large fortunes have, it is true, been accumulated, but many others have been wholly or partially dissipated; for the inheritors of immense fortunes, as a class, always live at least up to their incomes when at the highest, and the unavoidable vicissitudes of those incomes are always sinking them deeper and deeper into debt. A large proportion of the English landlords, as they themselves are constantly telling us, are so overwhelmed with mortgages, that they have ceased to be the real owners of the bulk of their estates. In other countries the large properties have very generally been broken down; in France, by revolution, and the revolutionary law of inheritance; in Prussia, by successive edicts of that substantially democratic, though formally absolute government.

With respect to knowledge and intelligence, it is the truism of the age, that the masses, both of the middle and even of the working classes, are treading upon the heels of their superiors.

If we now consider the progress made by those same masses in the capacity and habit of co-operation, we find it equally surprising. At what period were the operations of productive industry carried on upon anything like their present scale? Were so many hands ever before employed at the same time upon the same work, as now in all the principal departments of manufactures and commerce? To how enormous an extent is business now carried on by joint-stock companies – in other words, by many small capitals thrown together to form one great one. The country is covered with associations. There are societies for political, societies for religious, societies for philanthropic purposes. But the greatest novelty of all is the spirit of combination which has grown up among the working classes. The present age has seen the commencement of benefit societies; and they now, as well as the more questionable Trades Unions, overspread the whole country. A more powerful, though not so ostensible, instrument of combination than any of these, has but lately become universally accessible – the newspaper. The newspaper carries home the voice of the many to every individual among them; by the newspaper, each learns that others are feeling as he feels, and that if he is ready, he will find them also prepared to act upon what they feel. The newspaper is the telegraph which carries the signal throughout the country, and the flag round which it rallies. Hundreds of newspapers speaking in the same voice at once, and the rapidity of communication afforded by improved means of locomotion, were what enabled the whole country to combine in that simultaneous energetic demonstration of determined will which carried the Reform Act. Both these facilities are on the increase, every one may see how rapidly; and they will enable the people on all decisive occasions to form a collective will, and render that collective will irresistible.

To meet this wonderful development of physical and mental power on the part of the masses, can it be said that there has been any corresponding quantity of intellectual power or moral energy unfolded among those individuals or classes who have enjoyed superior advantages? No one, we think, will affirm it. There is a great increase of humanity, a decline of bigotry, as well as of arrogance and the conceit of caste, among our conspicuous classes; but there is, to say the least, no increase of shining ability, and a very marked decrease of vigour and energy. With all the advantages of this age, its facilities for mental cultivation, the incitements and the rewards which it holds out to exalted talents, there can scarcely be pointed out in the European annals any stirring times which have brought so little that is distinguished, either morally or intellectually, to the surface.

That this, too, is no more than was to be expected from the tendencies of civilization, when no attempt is made to correct them, we shall have occasion to show presently. But even if civilization did nothing to lower the eminences, it would produce an exactly similar effect by raising the plains. When the masses become powerful, an individual, or a small band of individuals, can accomplish nothing considerable except by influencing the masses; and to do this becomes daily more difficult, from the constantly increasing number of those who are vying with one another to attract the public attention. Our position, therefore, is established, that by the natural growth of civilization, power passes from individuals to masses, and the weight and importance of an individual, as compared with the mass, sink into greater and greater insignificance.

The change which is thus in progress, and to a great extent consummated, is the greatest ever recorded in social affairs; the most complete, the most fruitful in consequences, and the most irrevocable. Whoever can meditate on it, and not see that so great a revolution vitiates all existing rules of government and policy, and renders all practice and all predictions grounded only on prior experience worthless, is wanting in the very first and most elementary principle of statesmanship in these times.

'Il faut,' as M. de Tocqueville has said, 'une science politique nouvelle à un monde tout nouveau.' The whole face of society is reversed — all the natural elements of power have definitively changed places, and there are people who talk of standing up for ancient institutions, and the duty of sticking to the British Constitution settled in 1688! What is still more extraordinary, these are the people who accuse others of disregarding variety of circumstances, and imposing their abstract theories upon all states of society without discrimination.

We put it to those who call themselves Conservatives, whether, when the chief power in society is passing into the hands of the masses, they really think it possible to prevent the masses from making that power predominant as well in the government as elsewhere? The triumph of democracy, or, in other words, of the government of public opinion, does not depend upon the opinion of any individual or set of individuals that it ought to triumph, but upon the natural laws of the progress of wealth, upon the diffusion of reading, and the increase of the facilities of human intercourse. If Lord Kenyon or the Duke of Newcastle could stop these, they might accomplish something. There is no danger of the prevalence of democracy in Syria or Timbuctoo. But he must be a poor politician who does not know, that whatever is the growing power in society will force its way into the government, by fair means or foul. The distribution of constitutional power cannot long continue very different from that of real power, without a convulsion. Nor, if the institutions which impede the progress of democracy could be by any miracle preserved, could even they do more than render that progress a little slower. Were the Constitution of Great Britain to remain henceforth unaltered, we are not the less under the dominion, becoming every day more irresistible, of public opinion.

With regard to the advance of democracy, there are two

different positions which it is possible for a rational person to take up, according as he thinks the masses prepared, or unprepared, to exercise the control which they are acquiring over their destiny, in a manner which would be an improvement upon what now exists. If he thinks them prepared, he will aid the democratic movement; or if he deem it to be proceeding fast enough without him, he will at all events refrain from resisting it. If, on the contrary, he thinks the masses unprepared for complete control over their government – seeing at the same time that, prepared or not, they cannot long be prevented from acquiring it – he will exert his utmost efforts in contributing to preparing them; using all means, on the one hand, for making the masses themselves wiser and better; on the other, for so rousing the slumbering energy of the opulent and lettered classes, so storing the youth of those classes with the profoundest and most valuable knowledge, so calling forth whatever of individual greatness exists or can be raised up in the country, as to create a power which might partially rival the mere power of the masses, and might exercise the most salutary influence over them for their own good. When engaged earnestly in works like these, one can understand how a rational person might think that in order to give more time for the performance of them, it were well if the current of democracy, which can in no sort be stayed, could be prevailed upon for a time to flow less impetuously. With Conservatives of this sort, all democrats of corresponding enlargement of aims could fraternize as frankly and cordially as with most of their own friends: and we speak from an extensive knowledge of the wisest and most high-minded of that body, when we take upon ourselves to answer for them, that they would never push forward their own political projects in a spirit or with a violence which could tend to frustrate any rational endeavours towards the object nearest their hearts, the instruction of the understandings and the elevation of the characters of all classes of their countrymen.

But who is there among the political party calling themselves Conservatives, that professes to have any such object in view? Do they seek to employ the interval of respite which they might hope to gain by withstanding democracy, in qualifying the people to wield the democracy more wisely when it comes? Would they not far rather resist any such endeavour, on the principle that knowledge is power, and that its further diffusion would make the dreaded evil come sooner? Do the leading Conservatives in either house of parliament feel that the character of the higher classes needs renovating, to qualify them for a more arduous task and a keener strife than has yet fallen to their lot? Is not the character of a Tory lord or country gentleman, or a Church of England parson, perfectly satisfactory to them? Is not the existing constitution of the two Universities — those bodies whose especial duty it was to counteract the debilitating influence of the circumstances of the age upon individual character, and to send forth into society a succession of minds, not the creatures of their age, but capable of being its improvers and regenerators — the Universities, by whom this their especial duty has been basely neglected, until, as is usual with all neglected duties, the very consciousness of it as a duty has faded from their remembrance — is not, we say, the existing constitution and the whole existing system of these Universities, down to the smallest of their abuses, the exclusion of Dissenters, a thing for which every Tory, though he may not, as he pretends, die in the last ditch, will at least vote in the last division? The Church, professedly the other great instrument of national culture, long since perverted (we speak of rules, not exceptions) into a grand instrument for discouraging all culture inconsistent with blind obedience to established maxims and constituted authorities — what Tory has a scheme in view for any changes in this body, but such as may pacify assailants, and make the institution wear a less disgusting appearance to the eye? What political Tory will not resist to the very last moment any alteration in that Church, which would prevent its livings from being the provision for a family, its dignities the reward of political or of private services? The Tories, those at least connected with parliament or office, do not aim at having good institutions, or even at preserving the present ones; their object is to profit by them while they exist.

We scruple not to express our belief that a truer spirit of

conservation, as to everything good in the principles and professed objects of our old institutions, lives in many who are determined enemies of those institutions in their present state, than in most of those who call themselves Conservatives. But there are many well-meaning people who always confound attachment to an end, with pertinacious adherence to any set of means by which it either is, or is pretended to be, already pursued; and have yet to learn, that bodies of men who live in honour and importance upon the pretence of fulfilling ends which they never honestly seek, are the great hindrance to the attainment of those ends; and that whoever has the attainment really at heart, must expect a war of extermination with all such confederacies.

Thus far as to the political effects of Civilization. Its moral effects, which as yet we have only glanced at, demand further elucidation. They may be considered under two heads: the direct influence of Civilization itself upon individual character, and the moral effects produced by the insignificance into which the individual falls in comparison with the masses.

One of the effects of a high state of civilization upon character, is a relaxation of individual energy: or rather the concentration of it within the narrow sphere of the individual's money-getting pursuits. As civilization advances, every person becomes dependent, for more and more of what most nearly concerns him, not upon his own exertions, but upon the general arrangements of society. In a rude state, each man's personal security, the protection of his family, his property, his liberty itself, depend greatly upon his bodily strength and his mental energy or cunning: in a civilized state, all this is secured to him by causes extrinsic to himself. The growing mildness of manners is a protection to him against much that he was before exposed to, while for the remainder he may rely with constantly increasing assurance upon the soldier, the policeman, and the judge; and (where the efficiency of purity of those instruments, as is usually the case, lags behind the general march of civilization) upon the advancing strength of public opinion. There remain, as inducements to call forth energy of character, the desire of wealth or of personal aggrandizement, the passion of philanthropy, and the love of active virtue. But the objects to which these various feelings point are matters of choice, not of necessity, nor do the feelings act with anything like equal force upon all minds. The only one of them which can be considered as anything like universal, is the desire of wealth; and wealth being, in the case of the majority, the most accessible means of gratifying all their other desires, nearly the whole of the energy of character which exists in highly civilized societies concentrates itself on the pursuit of that object. In the case, however, of the most influential classes – those whose energies, if they had them, might be exercised on the greatest scale and with the most considerable result – the desire of wealth is already sufficiently satisfied, to render them averse to suffer pain or incur much voluntary labour for the sake of any further increase. The same classes also enjoy, from their station alone, a high degree of personal consideration. Except the high offices of the State, there is hardly anything to tempt the ambition of men in their circumstances. Those offices, when a great nobleman could have them for asking for, and keep them with less trouble than he could manage his private estates, were, no doubt, desirable enough possessions for such persons; but when they become posts of labour, vexation, and anxiety, and besides cannot be had without paying the price of some previous toil, experience shows that among men unaccustomed to sacrifice their amusements and their ease, the number upon whom these high offices operate as incentives to activity, or in whom they call forth any vigour of character, is extremely limited. Thus it happens that in highly civilized countries, and particularly among ourselves, the energies of the middle classes are almost confined to money-getting, and those of the higher classes are nearly extinct.

There is another circumstance to which we may trace much both of the good and of the bad qualities which distinguish our civilization from the rudeness of former times. One of the effects of civilization (not to say one of the ingredients in it) is, that the spectacle, and even the very idea, of pain, is kept more and more out of the sight of those classes who enjoy in their fulness the benefits of civilization. The state of perpetual personal conflict, rendered necessary by the circumstances of former times, and from which it was hardly possible for any person, in whatever rank of society, to be exempt, necessarily habituated every one to the spectacle of harshness, rudeness, and violence, to the struggle of one indomitable will against another, and to the alternate suffering and infliction of pain. These things, consequently, were not as revolting even to the best and most actively benevolent men of former days, as they are to our own; and we find the recorded conduct of those men frequently such as would be universally considered very unfeeling in a person of our own day. They, however, thought less of the infliction of pain, because they thought less of pain altogether. When we read of actions of the Greeks and Romans, or of our own ancestors, denoting callousness to human suffering, we must not think that those who committed these actions were as cruel as we must become before we could do the like. The pain which they inflicted, they were in the habit of voluntarily undergoing from slight causes; it did not appear to them as great an evil, as it appears, and as it really is, to us, nor did it in any way degrade their minds. In our own time the necessity of personal collision between one person and another is, comparatively speaking, almost at an end. All those necessary portions of the business of society which oblige any person to be the immediate agent or ocular witness of the infliction of pain, are delegated by common consent to peculiar and narrow classes: to the judge, the soldier, the surgeon, the butcher, and the executioner. To most people in easy circumstances, any pain, except that inflicted upon the body by accident or disease, and upon the mind by the inevitable sorrows of life, is rather a thing known of than actually experienced. This is much more emphatically true in the more refined classes, and as refinement advances: for it is in avoiding the presence not only of actual pain, but of whatever suggests offensive or disagreeable ideas, that a great part of refinement consists. We may remark too, that this is possible only by a perfection of mechanical arrangements impracticable in any but a high state of civilization. Now, most kinds of pain and annoyance appear much more unendurable to those who have little experience of them, than to those who have much. The consequence is that, compared with former times, there is in the more opulent classes of modern civilized communities much more of the amiable and humane, and much less of the heroic. The heroic essentially consists in being ready, for a worthy object, to do and to suffer, but especially to do, what is painful or disagreeable: and whoever does not early learn to be capable of this, will never be a great character. There has crept over the refined classes, over the whole class of gentlemen in England, a moral effeminacy, an inaptitude for every kind of struggle. They shrink from all effort, from everything which is troublesome and disagreeable. The same causes which render them sluggish and unenterprising, make them, it is true, for the most part, stoical under inevitable evils. But heroism is an active, not a passive quality; and when it is necessary not to bear pain but to seek it, little needs be expected from the men of the present day. They cannot undergo labour, they cannot brook ridicule, they cannot brave evil tongues: they have not hardihood to say an unpleasant thing to any one whom they are in the habit of seeing, or to face, even with a nation at their back, the coldness of some little coterie which surrounds them. This torpidity and cowardice, as a general characteristic, is new in the world: but (modified by the different temperaments of different nations) it is a natural consequence of the progress of civilization, and will continue until met by a system of cultivation adapted to counteract it.

If the source of great virtues thus dries up, great vices are placed, no doubt, under considerable restraint. The *régime* of public opinion is adverse to at least the indecorous vices: and as that restraining power gains strength, and certain classes or individuals cease to possess a virtual exemption from it, the change is highly favourable to the outward decencies of life. Nor can it be denied that the diffusion of even such knowledge as civilization naturally brings, has no slight tendency to rectify, though it be but partially, the standard of public opinion; to undermine many of those prejudices and superstitions which made mankind hate each other for things not really odious; to make them take a juster measure of the tendencies of actions, and weigh more correctly the evidence on which they condemn or applaud their fellow-creatures; to make, in short, their approbation direct itself more correctly to good actions, and their disapprobation to bad. What are the limits to this natural improvement in public opinion, when there is no other sort of cultivation going on than that which is the accompaniment of civilization, we need not at present inquire. It is enough that within those limits there is an extensive range; that as much improvement in the general understanding, softening of the feelings, and decay of pernicious errors, as naturally attends the progress of wealth and the spread of reading, suffices to render the judgement of the public upon actions and persons, so far as evidence is before them, much more discriminating and correct.

But here presents itself another ramification of the effects of civilization, which it has often surprised us to find so little attended to. The individual becomes so lost in the crowd, that though he depends more and more upon opinion, he is apt to depend less and less upon well-grounded opinion; upon the opinion of those who know him. An established character becomes at once more difficult to gain, and more easily to be dispensed with.

It is in a small society, where everybody knows everybody, that public opinion, so far as well directed, exercises its most salutary influence. Take the case of a tradesman in a small country town: to every one of his customers he is long and accurately known; their opinion of him has been formed after repeated trials; if he could deceive them once, he cannot hope to go on deceiving them in the quality of his goods; he has no other customers to look for if he loses these, while, if his goods are really what they profess to be, he may hope, among so few competitors, that this also will be known and recognized, and that he will acquire the character, individually and professionally, which his conduct entitles him to. Far different is the case of a man setting up in business in the crowded streets of a great city. If he trust solely to the quality of his goods, to the honesty and faithfulness with which he performs what he undertakes, he may remain ten years without a customer: be he ever so honest, he is driven to cry out on the housetops that his wares are the best of wares, past, present, and to come; while if he proclaim this, however false, with sufficient loudness to excite the curiosity of passers by, and can give his commodities 'a gloss, a saleable look', not easily to be seen through at a superficial glance, he may drive a thriving trade though no customer ever enter his shop twice. There has been much complaint of late years, of the growth, both in the world of trade and in that of intellect, of quackery, and especially of puffing: but nobody seems to have remarked, that these are the inevitable fruits of immense competition; of a state of society where any voice, not pitched in an exaggerated key, is lost in the hubbub. Success, in so crowded a field, depends not upon what a person is, but upon what he seems: mere marketable qualities become the object instead of substantial ones, and a man's labour and capital are expended less in doing anything, than in persuading other people that he has done it. Our own age has seen this evil brought to its consummation. Quackery there always was, but it once was a test of the absence of sterling qualities: there was a proverb that good wine needed no bush. It is our own age which has seen the honest dealer driven to quackery, by hard necessity, and the certainty of being undersold by the dishonest. For the first time, arts for attracting public attention form a necessary part of the qualifications even of the deserving: and skill in these goes farther than any other quality towards ensuring success. The same intensity of competition drives the trading public more and more to play high for success, to throw for all or nothing; and this, together with the difficulty of sure calculations in a field of commerce so widely extended, renders bankruptcy no longer disgraceful, because no longer an almost certain presumption either of dishonesty or imprudence: the discredit which it still incurs belongs to it, alas! mainly as an indication of poverty. Thus public opinion loses another of those simple criteria of desert, which, and which alone, it is capable of correctly applying; and the very cause which has rendered it omnipotent in the gross, weakens the precision and force with which its judgement is brought home to individuals.

It is not solely on the private virtues, that this growing insignificance of the individual in the mass, is productive of mischief. It corrupts the very fountain of the improvement of public opinion itself; it corrupts public teaching; it weakens the influence of the more cultivated few over the many. Literature has suffered more than any other human production by the common disease. When there were few books, and when few read at all save those who had been accustomed to read the best authors, books were written with the well-grounded expectation that they would be read carefully, and if they deserved it, would be read often. A book of sterling merit, when it came out, was sure to be heard of, and might hope to be read, by the whole reading class; it might succeed by its real excellencies, though not got up to strike at once; and even if so got up, unless it had the support of genuine merit, it fell into oblivion. The rewards were then for him who wrote *well*, not *much*; for the laborious and learned, not the crude and ill-informed writer. But now the case is reversed. 'This is a reading age; and precisely because it is so reading an age, any book which is the result of profound meditation is, perhaps, less likely to be duly and profitably read than at a former period. The world reads too much and too quickly to read well. When books were few, to get through one was a work of time and labour: what was written with thought was read with thought, and with a desire to extract from it as much of the materials of knowledge as possible. But when almost every person who can spell, can and will write, what is to be done? It is difficult to know what to read, except by reading everything; and so much of the world's business is now transacted through the press, that it is necessary to know what is printed, if we desire to know what is going on. Opinion weighs with so vast a weight in the balance of events, that ideas of no value in themselves are of importance from the mere circumstance that they *are* ideas, and have a *bonâ fide* existence as such anywhere out of Bedlam. The world, in consequence, gorges itself with intellectual food, and in order to swallow the more, *bolts* it. Nothing is now read slowly, or twice over. Books are run through with no less rapidity, and scarcely leave a more durable impression, than a newspaper article. It is for this, among other causes, that so few books are produced of any value. The lioness in the fable boasted that though she produced only one at a birth, that one was a lion. But if each lion only counted for one, and each leveret for one, the advantage would all be on the side of the hare. When every unit is individually weak, it is only multitude that tells. What wonder that the newspapers should carry all before them? A book produces hardly a greater effect than an article, and there can be 365 of these in one year. He, therefore, who should and would write a book, and write it in the proper manner of writing a book, now dashes down his first hasty thoughts, or what he mistakes for thoughts, in a periodical. And the public is in the predicament of an indolent man, who cannot bring himself to apply his mind vigorously to his own affairs, and over whom, therefore, not he who speaks most wisely, but he who speaks most frequently, obtains the influence.'

Hence we see that literature is becoming more and more ephemeral: books, of any solidity, are almost gone by; even reviews are not now considered sufficiently light; the attention cannot sustain itself on any serious subject, even for the space of a review-article. In the more attractive kinds of literature, novels and magazines, though the demand has so greatly increased, the supply has so outstripped it, that even a novel is seldom a lucrative speculation. It is only under circumstances of rare attraction that a bookseller will now give anything to an author for copyright. As the difficulties of success thus progressively increase, all other ends are more and more sacrificed for the attainment of it; literature becomes more and more a mere reflection of the current sentiments, and has almost entirely abandoned its mission as an enlightener and improver of them.

There are now in this country, we may say, but two modes left in which an individual mind can hope to produce much direct effect upon the minds and destinies of his countrymen generally; as a member of parliament, or an editor of a London newspaper. In both these capacities much may still be done by an individual, because, while the power of the collective body is very great, the number of participants in it does not admit of much increase. One of these monopolies will be opened to competition when the newspaper stamp is taken off; whereby the importance of the newspaper press in the aggregate, considered as the voice of public opinion, will be increased, and the influence of any one writer in helping to form that opinion necessarily diminished. This we might regret, did we not remember to what ends that influence is now used, and is sure to be so while newspapers are a mere investment of capital for the sake of mercantile profit.

Is there, then, no remedy? Are the decay of individual energy, the weakening of the influence of superior minds over the multitude, the growth of charlatanerie, and the diminished efficacy of public opinion as a restraining power, – are these the price we necessarily pay for the benefits of civilization; and can they only be avoided by checking the diffusion of knowledge, discouraging the spirit of combination, prohibiting improvements in the arts of life, and repressing the further increase of wealth and of production? Assuredly not. Those advantages which civilization cannot give – which in its uncorrected influence it has even a tendency to destroy – may yet co-exist with civilization; and it is only when joined to civilization that they can produce their fairest fruits. All that we are in danger of losing we may preserve, all that we have lost we may regain, and bring to a perfection hitherto unknown; but not by slumbering, and leaving things to themselves, no more than by ridiculously trying our strength against their irresistible tendencies: only by establishing counter-tendencies, which may combine with those tendencies, and modify them.

The evils are, that the individual is lost and becomes impotent in the crowd, and that individual character itself becomes relaxed and enervated. For the first evil, the remedy is, greater and more perfect combination among individuals; for the second, national institutions of education, and forms of polity calculated to invigorate the individual character.

The former of these desiderata, as its attainment depends upon a change in the habits of society itself, can only be realized by degrees, as the necessity becomes felt; but circumstances are even now to a certain extent forcing it on. In Great Britain especially (which so far surpasses the rest of the old world in the extent and rapidity of the accumulation of wealth) the fall of profits, consequent upon the vast increase of population and capital, is rapidly extinguishing the class of small dealers and small producers, from the impossibility of living on their diminished profits, and is throwing business of all kinds more and more into the hands of large capitalists, – whether these be rich individuals, or joint-stock companies formed by the aggregation of many small capitals. We are not among those who believe that this progress is tending to the complete extinction of competition, or that the entire productive resources of the country will within any assignable number of ages, if ever, be administered by, and for the benefit of, a general association of the whole community. But we believe that the multiplication of competitors in all branches of business and in all professions – which renders it more and more difficult to obtain success by merit alone, more and more easy to obtain it by plausible pretence – will find a limiting principle in the progress of the spirit of co-operation; that in every overcrowded department there will arise a tendency among individuals so to unite their labour or their capital, that the purchaser or employer will have to choose, not among innumerable individuals, but among a few groups. Competition will be as active as ever, but the number of competitors will be brought within manageable bounds.

Such a spirit of co-operation is most of all wanted among the intellectual classes and professions. The amount of human labour, and labour of the most precious kind, now wasted, and wasted too in the cruelest manner, for want of combination, is incalculable. What a spectacle, for instance, does the medical profession present! One successful practitioner burthened with more work than mortal man can perform, and which he performs so summarily that it were often better let alone; – in the surrounding streets twenty unhappy men, each of whom has been as laboriously and expensively trained as he has to do the very same thing, and is possibly as well qualified, wasting their capabilities and starving for want of work. Under better arrangements these twenty would form a corps of subalterns marshalled under their more successful leader; who (granting him to be really the ablest physician of the set, and not merely the most successful impostor) is wasting time in physicking people for headaches and heartburns, which he might with better economy of mankind's resources turn over to his subordinates, while he employed his maturer powers and greater experience in studying and treating those more obscure and difficult cases upon which science has not yet thrown sufficient light, and to which ordinary knowledge and abilities would not be adequate. By such means every person's capacities would be turned to account, and the highest minds being kept for the highest things, these would make progress, while ordinary occasions would be no losers.

But it is in literature, above all, that a change of this sort is of most pressing urgency. There the system of individual competition has fairly worked itself out, and things can hardly continue much longer as they are. Literature is a province of exertion upon which more, of the first value to human nature, depends, than upon any other; a province in which the highest and most valuable order of works, those which most contribute to form the opinions and shape the characters of subsequent ages, are, more than in any other class of productions, placed beyond the possibility of appreciation by those who form the bulk of the purchasers in the book-market; insomuch that, even in ages when these were a far less numerous and more select class than now, it was an admitted point that the only success which writers of the first order could look to was the verdict of posterity. That verdict could, in those times, be confidently expected by whoever was worthy of it; for the good judges, though few in number, were sure to read every work of merit which appeared; and as the recollection of one book was not in those days immediately obliterated by a hundred others, they remembered it, and kept alive the knowledge of it to subsequent ages. But in our day, from the immense multitude of writers (which is now not less remarkable than the multitude of readers), and from the manner in which the people of this age are obliged to read, it is difficult for what does not strike during its novelty, to strike at all: a book either misses fire altogether, or is so read as to make no permanent impression; and the good equally with the worthless are forgotten by the next day.

For this there is no remedy, while the public have no guidance beyond booksellers' advertisements, and the ill-considered and hasty criticisms of newspapers and small periodicals, to direct them in distinguishing what is not worth reading from what is. The resource must in time be, some organized co-operation among the leading intellects of the age, whereby works of first-rate merit, of whatever class, and of whatever tendency in point of opinion, might come forth with the stamp on them, from the first, of the approval of those whose names would carry authority. There are many causes why we must wait long for such a combination; but (with enormous defects, both in plan and in execution) the Society for the Diffusion of Useful Knowledge was as considerable a step towards it, as could be expected in the present state of men's minds, and in a first attempt. Literature has had in this country two ages; it must now have a third. The age of patronage, as Johnson a century ago proclaimed, is gone. The age of booksellers, it has been proclaimed by Mr Carlyle, has well nigh died out. In the first there was nothing intrinsically base, nor in the second anything inherently independent and liberal. Each has done great things; both have had their day. The time is perhaps coming when authors, as a collective guild, will be their own patrons and their own booksellers.

These things must bide their time. But the other of the two great desiderata, the regeneration of individual character among our lettered and opulent classes, by the adaptation to that purpose of our institutions, and, above all, of our educational institutions, is an object of more urgency, and for which more might be immediately accomplished, if the will and the understanding were not alike wanting.

This, unfortunately, is a subject on which, for the inculcation of rational views, everything is yet to be done; for, all that we would inculcate, all that we deem of vital importance, all upon which we conceive the salvation of the next and all future ages to rest, has the misfortune to be almost equally opposed to the most popular doctrines of our own time, and to the prejudices of those who cherish the empty husk of what has descended from ancient times. We are at issue equally with the admirers of

Oxford and Cambridge, Eton and Westminster, and with the generality of their professed reformers. We regard the system of those institutions, as administered for two centuries past, with sentiments little short of utter abhorrence. But we do not conceive that their vices would be cured by bringing their studies into a closer connexion with what it is the fashion to term 'the business of the world'; by dismissing the logic and classics which are still professedly taught, to substitute modern languages and experimental physics. We would have classics and logic taught far more really and deeply than at present, and we would add to them other studies more alien than any which yet exist to the 'business of the world', but more germane to the great business of every rational being – the strengthening and enlarging of his own intellect and character. The empirical knowledge which the world demands, which is the stock in trade of money-getting life, we would leave the world to provide for itself; content with infusing into the youth of our country a spirit, and training them to habits, which would ensure their acquiring such knowledge easily, and using it well. These, we know, are not the sentiments of the vulgar; but we believe them to be those of the best and wisest of all parties: and we are glad to corroborate our opinion by a quotation from a work written by a friend to the Universities, and by one whose tendencies are rather Conservative than Liberal; a book which, though really, and not in form merely, one of fiction, contains much subtle and ingenious thought, and the results of much psychological experience, combined, we are compelled to say, with much caricature, and very provoking (though we are convinced unintentional) distortion and misinterpretation of the opinions of some of those with whose philosophy that of the author does not agree.

'You believe' (a clergyman *loquitur*) 'that the University is to prepare youths for a successful career in society: I believe the sole object is to give them that manly character which will enable them to resist the influences of society. I do not care to prove that I am right, and that any university which does not stand upon this basis will be rickety in its childhood, and useless or mischievous in its manhood; I care only to assert that this was the notion of those who founded Oxford and Cambridge. I fear that their successors are gradually losing sight of this principle – are gradually beginning to think that it is their business to turn out clever lawyers and serviceable Treasury clerks – are pleased when the world compliments them upon the goodness of the article with which they have furnished it – and that this low vanity is absorbing all their will and their power to create great men, whom the age will scorn, and who will save it from the scorn of the times to come.'

'One or two such men,' said the Liberal, 'in a generation, may be very useful; but the University gives us two or three thousand youths every year. I suppose you are content that a portion shall do week-day services.'

'I wish to have a far more hard-working and active race than we have at present,' said the clergyman; 'men more persevering in toil, and less impatient of reward; but all experience, a thing which the schools are not privileged to despise, though the world is – all experience is against the notion, that the means to procure a supply of good ordinary men is to attempt nothing higher. I know that nine-tenths of those whom the University sends out must be hewers of wood and drawers of water; but, if I train the ten-tenths to be so, depend upon it the wood will be badly cut, the water will be spilt. Aim at something noble; make your system such that a great man may be formed by it, and there will be a manhood in your little men of which you do not dream. But when some skilful rhetorician, or lucky rat, stands at the top of the ladder – when the University, instead of disclaiming the creature, instead of pleading, as an excuse for themselves, that the healthiest mother may, by accident, produce a shapeless abortion, stands shouting, that the world may know what great things they can do, "we taught the boy!" – when the hatred which worldly men will bear to religion always, and to learning whenever it teaches us to soar and not to grovel, is met, not with a frank defiance, but rather with a deceitful argument to show that trade is the better for them; is it wonderful that a puny beggarly feeling should pervade the mass of our young men? that they should scorn all noble achievements, should have no higher standard of action than the world's opinion, and should conceive of no higher reward than to sit down amidst loud cheering, which continues for several moments?'*

Nothing can be more just or more forcible than the description here given of the objects which University education should aim at: we are at issue with the writer, only on the proposition that these objects ever were attained, or ever could be so, consistently with the principle which has always been the foundation of the English Universities; a principle, unfortunately, by no means confined to them. The difficulty which continues to oppose either such reform of our old academical institutions, or the establishment of such new ones, as shall give us an education capable of forming great minds, is, that in order to do so it is necessary to begin by eradicating the idea which nearly all the upholders and nearly all the impugners of the Universities rootedly entertain, as to the objects not merely of academical education, but of education itself. What is this idea? That the object of education is, not to qualify the pupil for judging what is true or what is right, but to provide that he shall think true what we think true, and right what we think right – that to teach, means to inculcate our own opinions, and that our business is not to make thinkers or inquirers, but disciples. This is the deep-seated error, the inveterate prejudice, which the real reformer of English education has to struggle against. Is it astonishing that great minds are not produced, in a country where the test of a great mind is, agreeing in the opinions of the small minds? where every institution for spiritual culture which the country has – the Church, the Universities, and almost every dissenting community – are constituted on the following as their avowed principle: that the object is, *not* that the individual should go forth determined and qualified to seek truth ardently, vigorously, and disinterestedly; *not* that he be furnished at setting out with the needful aids and facilities, the needful materials and instruments for that search, and then left to the unshackled use of them; *not* that, by a free communion with the

*From the novel of 'Eustace Conway', attributed to Mr Maurice.

thoughts and deeds of the great minds which preceded him, he be inspired at once with the courage to dare all which truth and conscience require, and the modesty to weigh well the grounds of what others think, before adopting contrary opinions of his own: *not* this – no; but that the triumph of the system, the merit, the excellence in the sight of God which it possesses, or which it can impart to its pupil, is that his speculations shall terminate in the adoption, in words, of a particular set of opinions. That provided he adhere to these opinions, it matters little whether he receive them from authority or from examination; and worse, that it matters little by what temptations of interest or vanity, by what voluntary or involuntary sophistication with his intellect, and deadening of his noblest feelings, that result is arrived at; that it even matters comparatively little whether to his mind the words are mere words, or the representatives of realities – in what sense he receives the favoured set of propositions, or whether he attaches to them any sense at all. Were ever great minds thus formed? Never. The few great minds which this country has produced have been formed in spite of nearly everything which could be done to stifle their growth. And all thinkers, much above the common order, who have grown up in the Church of England, or in any other Church, have been produced in latitudinarian epochs, or while the impulse of intellectual emancipation which gave existence to the Church had not quite spent itself. The flood of burning metal which issued from the furnace, flowed on a few paces before it congealed.

That the English Universities have, throughout, proceeded on the principle, that the intellectual association of mankind must be founded upon articles, *i.e.* upon a promise of belief in certain opinions; that the scope of all they do is to prevail upon their pupils, by fair means or foul, to acquiesce in the opinions which are set down for them; that the abuse of the human faculties so forcibly denounced by Locke under the name of 'principling' their pupils, is their sole method in religion, politics, morality, or philosophy – is vicious indeed, but the vice is equally prevalent without and within their pale, and is no farther disgraceful to them than inasmuch as a better doctrine has been taught for a century past by the superior spirits, with whom in point of intelligence it was their duty to maintain themselves on a level. But, that when this object was attained they cared for no other; that if they could make churchmen, they cared not to make religious men; that if they could make Tories, whether they made patriots was indifferent to them; that if they could prevent heresy, they cared not if the price paid were stupidity – this constitutes the peculiar baseness of those bodies. Look at them. While their sectarian character, while the exclusion of all who will not sign away their freedom of thought, is contended for as if life depended upon it, there is hardly a trace in the system of the Universities that any other object whatever is seriously cared for. Nearly all the professorships have degenerated into sinecures. Few of the professors ever deliver a lecture. One of the few great scholars who have issued from either University for a century (and he was such before he went thither), the Rev. Connop Thirlwall, has published to the world that in his University at least, even theology – even Church of England theology is not taught; and his dismissal, for this piece of honesty, from the tutorship of his college, is one among the daily proofs how much safer it is for twenty men to neglect their duty, than for one man to impeach them of the neglect. The only studies really encouraged are classics and mathematics; neither of them a useless study, though the last, as an exclusive instrument for fashioning the mental powers, greatly overrated; but Mr Whewell, a high authority against his own University, has published a pamphlet, chiefly to prove that the kind of mathematical attainment by which Cambridge honours are gained, expertness in the use of the calculus, is not that kind which has any tendency to produce superiority of intellect.* The mere shell and husk of the

*The erudite and able writer in the 'Edinburgh Review' [Sir William Hamilton], who has expended an almost superfluous weight of argument and authority in combating the position incidentally maintained in Mr Whewell's pamphlet, of the great value of mathematics as an exercise of the mind, was, we think, bound to have noticed the fact that the far more direct object of the pamphlet was one which partially coincided with that of its reviewer. We do not think that

syllogistic logic at the one University, the wretchedest smattering of Locke and Paley at the other, are all of moral or psychological science that is taught at either.* As a means of educating the many, the Universities are absolutely null. The youth of England are not educated. The attainments of any kind required for taking all the degrees conferred by these bodies are, at Cambridge, utterly contemptible; at Oxford, we believe, of late years, somewhat higher, but still very low. Honours, indeed, are not gained but by a severe struggle; and if even the candidates for honours were mentally benefitted, the system would not be worthless. But what have the senior wranglers done, even in mathematics? Has Cambridge produced, since Newton, one great mathematical genius? We do not say an Euler, a Laplace, or a Lagrange, but such as France has produced a score of during the same period. How many books which have thrown light upon the history, antiquities, philosophy, art, or literature of the ancients, have the two Universities sent forth since the Reformation? Compare them, not merely with Germany, but even with Italy or France. When a man is pronounced by them to have excelled in their studies, what do the Universities do? They give him an income, not for continuing to learn, but for having learnt; not for doing anything, but for what he has already done: on condition solely of living like a monk, and putting on the livery of the Church at the end of seven years. They bribe men by high rewards to get their arms ready, but do not require them to fight.†

Mr Whewell has done well what he undertook: he is vague, and is always attempting to be a profounder metaphysician than he can be; but the main proposition of his pamphlet is true and important, and he is entitled to no little credit for having discerned that important truth, and expressed it so strongly.
*We should except, at Oxford, the Ethics, Politics, and Rhetoric of Aristotle. These are part of the course of classical instruction, and are so far an exception to the rule, otherwise pretty faithfully observed at both Universities, of cultivating only the least useful parts of ancient literature.
†Much of what is here said of the Universities, has, in a great measure, ceased to be true. The Legislature has at last asserted its right of

Are these the places of education which are to send forth minds capable of maintaining a victorious struggle with the debilitating influences of the age, and strengthening the weak side of Civilization by the support of a higher Cultivation? This, however, is what we require from these institutions; or, in their default, from others which should take their place. And the very first step towards their reform should be to unsectarianize them wholly – not by the paltry measure of allowing Dissenters to come and be taught orthodox sectarianism, but by putting an end to sectarian teaching altogether. The principle itself of dogmatic religion, dogmatic morality, dogmatic philosophy, is what requires to be rooted out; not any particular manifestation of that principle.

The very corner-stone of an education intended to form great minds, must be the recognition of the principle, that the object is to call forth the greatest possible quantity of intellectual *power*, and to inspire the intensest *love of truth*; and this without a particle of regard to the results to which the exercise of that power may lead, even though it should conduct the pupil to opinions diametrically opposite to those of his teachers. We say this, not because we think opinions unimportant, but because of the immense importance which we attach to them; for in proportion to the degree of intellectual power and love of truth which we succeed in creating, is the certainty that (whatever may happen in any one particular instance) in the aggregate of instances true opinions will be the result; and intellectual power and practical love of truth are alike impossible where the reasoner is shown his conclusions, and informed beforehand that he is expected to arrive at them.

We are not so absurd as to propose that the teacher should not set forth his own opinions as the true ones, and exert his utmost powers to exhibit their truth in the strongest light. To abstain from this would be to nourish the worst intellectual habit of all, that of not finding, and not looking for, certainty in anything. But the teacher himself should not be held to any creed; nor

interference; and even before it did so, the bodies had already entered into a course of as decided improvement as any other English institutions. But I leave these pages unaltered, as matter of historical record, and as an illustration of tendencies. [1859.]

should the question be whether his own opinions are the true ones, but whether he is well instructed in those of other people, and, in enforcing his own, states the arguments for all conflicting opinions fairly. In this spirit it is that all the great subjects are taught from the chairs of the German and French Universities. As a general rule, the most distinguished teacher is selected, whatever be his particular views, and he consequently teaches in the spirit of free inquiry, not of dogmatic imposition.

Such is the principle of all academical instruction which aims at forming great minds. The details cannot be too various and comprehensive. Ancient literature would fill a large place in such a course of instruction; because it brings before us the thoughts and actions of many great minds, minds of many various orders of greatness, and these related and exhibited in a manner tenfold more impressive, tenfold more calculated to call forth high aspirations, than in any modern literature. Imperfectly as these impressions are made by the current modes of classical teaching, it is incalculable what we owe to this, the sole ennobling feature in the slavish, mechanical thing which the moderns call education. Nor is it to be forgotten among the benefits of familiarity with the monuments of antiquity, and especially those of Greece, that we are taught by it to appreciate and to admire intrinsic greatness, amidst opinions, habits, and institutions most remote from ours; and are thus trained to that large and catholic toleration, which is founded on understanding, not on indifference – and to a habit of free, open sympathy with powers of mind and nobleness of character, howsoever exemplified. Were but the languages and literature of antiquity so taught that the glorious images they present might stand before the student's eyes as living and glowing realities – that, instead of lying a *caput mortuum* at the bottom of his mind, like some foreign substance in no way influencing the current of his thoughts or the tone of his feelings, they might circulate through it, and become assimilated, and be part and parcel of himself! – then should we see how little these studies have yet done for us, compared with what they have yet to do.

An important place in the system of education which we contemplate would be occupied by history: because it is the record of all great things which have been achieved by mankind, and because when philosophically studied it gives a certain largeness of conception to the student, and familiarizes him with the action of great causes. In no other way can he so completely realize in his own mind (howsoever he may be satisfied with the proof of them as abstract propositions) the great principles by which the progress of man and the condition of society are governed. Nowhere else will the infinite varieties of human nature be so vividly brought home to him, and anything cramped or one-sided in his own standard of it so effectually corrected; and nowhere else will he behold so strongly exemplified the astonishing pliability of our nature, and the vast effects which may under good guidance be produced upon it by honest endeavour. The literature of our own and other modern nations should be studied along with the history, or rather as part of the history.

In the department of pure intellect, the highest place will belong to logic and the philosophy of mind: the one, the instrument for the cultivation of all sciences; the other, the root from which they all grow. It scarcely needs be said that the former ought not to be taught as a mere system of technical rules, nor the latter as a set of concatenated abstract propositions. The tendency, so strong everywhere, is strongest of all here, to receive opinions into the mind without any real understanding of them, merely because they seem to follow from certain admitted premises, and to let them lie there as forms of words, lifeless and void of meaning. The pupil must be led to interrogate his own consciousness, to observe and experiment upon himself: of the mind, by any other process, little will he ever know.

With these should be joined all those sciences, in which great and certain results are arrived at by mental processes of some length or nicety: not that all persons should study all these sciences, but that some should study all, and all some. These may be divided into sciences of mere ratiocination, as mathematics; and sciences partly of ratiocination, and partly of what is far more difficult, comprehensive observation and analysis. Such are, in their *rationale*, even the sciences to which mathematical processes are applicable: and such are all those which relate to human nature. The philosophy of morals, of government, of law, of political economy, of poetry and art, should form subjects of systematic instruction, under the most eminent professors who could be found; these being chosen, not for the particular doctrines they might happen to profess, but as being those who were most likely to send forth pupils qualified in point of disposition and attainments to choose doctrines for themselves. And why should not religion be taught in the same manner? Not until then will one step be made towards the healing of religious differences: not until then will the spirit of English religion become catholic instead of sectarian, favourable instead of hostile to freedom of thought and the progress of the human mind.

With regard to the changes, in forms of polity and social arrangements, which, in addition to reforms in education, we conceive to be required for regenerating the character of the higher classes; to express them even summarily would require a long discourse. But the general idea from which they all emanate, may be stated briefly. Civilization has brought about a degree of security and fixity in the possession of all advantages once acquired, which has rendered it possible for a rich man to lead the life of a Sybarite, and nevertheless enjoy throughout life a degree of power and consideration which could formerly be earned or retained only by personal activity. We cannot undo what civilization has done, and again stimulate the energy of the higher classes by insecurity of property, or danger of life or limb. The only adventitious motive it is in the power of society to hold out, is reputation and consequence; and of this as much use as possible should be made for the encouragement of desert. The main thing which social changes can do for the improvement of the higher classes – and it is what the progress of democracy is insensibly but certainly accomplishing – is gradually to put an end to every kind of unearned distinction, and let the only road open to honour and ascendancy be that of personal qualities.

Karl Marx
and
Frederick Engels

Karl Marx (1818–83) was born in Trier, Prussia. His parents were Jewish, though his father – a lawyer by profession – was baptized a Christian shortly before Marx's birth. He was educated at the Trier High School, the University of Bonn, and the University of Berlin where he became associated with the Young Hegelians and was for a while influenced by the radical theology of Bruno Bauer. In 1841 Marx received a doctorate from the University of Jena: the same year saw the publication of Ludwig Feuerbach's *Essence of Christianity* which reinforced Marx's own determination to interpret Hegel's theory of the dialectic in materialistic terms. For a short while Marx was editor of the *Rheinische Zeitung* but pressure from the Prussian government forced him and Jenny von Westphalen, whom he had married in 1843, first to Paris, then Brussels, Cologne, and finally London which remained his home for the rest of his life. Throughout these early unsettled years Marx was meeting and arguing with leading European radicals, intellectuals, bohemians and social theorists; much of his own writing at this time, some of which was to be reworked in his later books, has only recently begun to be widely known. Marx first met Frederick Engels (1820–95) in Paris in 1844. Engels came from a family of German industrialists. He left school at the age of sixteen to enter the family business at Barmen, near Düsseldorf, though his main interests were intellectual, and throughout his life he was to be simultaneously a successful businessman and a revolutionary writer. After a spell of military service in Berlin where he came, like Marx, under the influence of the Young Hegelians and Feuerbach, he was sent to the Manchester branch of the family business. Here he became friendly with Chartists and Owenite socialists, and began gathering the material for *The Condition of the Working Class in England* (1845). The friendship between Marx and Engels was immediate and life-long.

In 1847 Marx and Engels were approached in London by a German secret society, The League of the Just – soon to be renamed the Communist League – for help in drafting a declaration of communist beliefs. Engels drew up a list of 'Principles of Communism' and working from this Marx wrote the pamphlet. Written in German *The Manifesto of the Communist Party* was published in London in 1848, 'the year of revolutions'. An English translation by Helen Macfarlane was published in the radical newspaper *The Red Republican* in 1850, and various unauthorized translations were published in Britain and America, but the familiar English version by Samuel Moore and Engels (with annotations also by Engels) was first published in 1888, and is the edition reprinted here. Many of Marx's works were not published in complete editions during his lifetime – for example *The German Ideology* which was written in 1845 by Marx and Engels and which outlines their materialistic theory of history – while of the books that were published, English translations were not made until late in the century, for example, *The Poverty of Philosophy* (1847), *The Eighteenth Brumaire of Louis Bonaparte* (1852) and *A Contribution to the Critique of Political Economy* (1859).

Although always connected with revolutionary and workers' movements, and involved most notably with the founding of the International Working Men's Association in 1864, Marx's life in London was mainly dedicated to historical research for *Capital*, the work which was intended to give a full justification of the argument that history is determined by economic factors. Only the first volume was completed and published, though Engels arranged the publication of a further two volumes after Marx's death. From 1851 to 1862 Marx was the European correspondent of the *New York Daily Tribune* and although this brought him some money, many of the articles were actually written by Engels. Even apart from this kind of help it is doubtful whether Marx and his family could have survived at all in London without Engels's financial support. After Marx's death, Engels devoted his time to spreading knowledge of the theories which he always insisted came predominantly from Marx, and books like *The Origin of the Family* (1891) and especially *Socialism: Utopian and Scientific* (1892) were to be very influential in the development of Marxism throughout the world.

Preface

The 'Manifesto' was published as the platform of the 'Communist League', a working-men's association, first exclusively German, later on international, and, under the political conditions of the Continent before 1848, unavoidably a secret society. At a Congress of the League, held in London in November, 1847, Marx and Engels were commissioned to prepare for publication a complete theoretical and practical party-programme. Drawn up in German, in January, 1848, the manuscript was sent to the printer in London a few weeks before the French revolution of February 24th. A French translation was brought out in Paris, shortly before the insurrection of June, 1848. The first English translation, by Miss Helen Macfarlane, appeared in George Julian Harney's *Red Republican*, London, 1850. A Danish and a Polish edition had also been published.

The defeat of the Parisian insurrection of June, 1848, – the first great battle between Proletariat and Bourgeoisie – drove again into the background, for a time, the social and political aspirations of the European working class. Thenceforth, the struggle for supremacy was again, as it had been before the revolution of February, solely between different sections of the propertied class; the working class was reduced to a fight for political elbow-room, and to the position of extreme wing of the middle-class Radicals. Wherever independent proletarian movements continued to show signs of life, they were ruthlessly hunted down. Thus the Prussian police hunted out the Central Board of the Communist League, then located in Cologne. The members were arrested, and, after eighteen months' imprisonment, they were tried in October, 1852. This celebrated 'Cologne Communist trial' lasted from October 4th till November 12th; seven of the prisoners were sentenced to terms of imprisonment in a fortress, varying from three to six years. Immediately after the sentence, the League was formally dissolved by the remaining members. As to the 'Manifesto', it seemed thenceforth to be doomed to oblivion.

When the European working class had recovered sufficient strength for another attack on the ruling classes, the International Working Men's Association sprang up. But this association, formed with the express aim of welding into one body the whole militant proletariat of Europe and America, could not at once proclaim the principles laid down in the 'Manifesto'. The International was bound to have a programme broad enough to be acceptable to the English Trades' Unions, to the followers of Proudhon in France, Belgium, Italy, and Spain, and to the Lasselleans * in Germany. Marx, who drew up this programme to the satisfaction of all parties, entirely trusted to the intellectual development of the working class, which was sure to result from combined action and mutual discussion. The very events and vicissitudes of the struggle against Capital, the defeats even more than the victories, could not help bringing home to men's minds the insufficiency of their various favourite nostrums, and preparing the way for a more complete insight into the true conditions of working-class emancipation. And Marx was right. The International, on its breaking up in 1874, left the workers quite different men from what it had found them in 1864. Proudhonism in France, Lassalleanism in Germany were dying out, and even the Conservative English Trades' Unions, though most of them had long since severed their connexion with the International, were gradually advancing towards that point at which, last year at Swansea, their President could say in their name 'Continental Socialism has lost its terrors for us'. In fact: the principles of the 'Manifesto' had made considerable headway among the working men of all countries.

---

*Lassalle personally, to us, always acknowledged himself to be a disciple of Marx, and, as such, stood on the ground of the 'Manifesto'. But in his public agitation, 1862–4, he did not go beyond demanding co-operative workshops supported by State credit.

The Manifesto itself thus came to the front again. The German text had been, since 1850, reprinted several times in Switzerland, England and America. In 1872, it was translated into English in New York, where the translation was published in 'Woodhull and Claflin's Weekly'. From this English version, a French one was made in 'Le Socialiste' of New York. Since then at least two more English translations, more or less mutilated, have been brought out in America, and one of them has been reprinted in England. The first Russian translation, made by Bakounine, was published at Herzen's 'Kolokol' office in Geneva, about 1863; a second one, by the heroic Vera Zasulitch, also in Geneva, 1882. A new Danish edition is to be found in 'Socialdemokratisk Bibliothek', Copenhagen, 1885; a fresh French translation in 'Le Socialiste', Paris, 1886. From this latter a Spanish version was prepared and published in Madrid, 1886. The German reprints are not to be counted, there have been twelve altogether at the least. An Armenian translation, which was to be published in Constantinople some months ago, did not see the light, I am told, because the publisher was afraid of bringing out a book with the name of Marx on it, while the translator declined to call it his own production. Of further translations into other languages I have heard, but have not seen them. Thus the history of the Manifesto reflects, to a great extent, the history of the modern working-class movement; at present it is undoubtedly the most widespread, the most international production of all Socialist Literature, the common platform acknowledged by millions of working men from Siberia to California.

Yet, when it was written, we could not have called it a *Socialist* Manifesto. By Socialists, in 1847, were understood, on the one hand, the adherents of the various Utopian systems: Owenites in England, Fourierists in France, both of them already reduced to the position of mere sects, and gradually dying out; on the other hand, the most multifarious social quacks, who, by all manners of tinkering, professed to redress, without any danger to capital and profit, all sorts of social grievances, in both cases men outside the working-class movement, and looking rather to the 'educated' classes for support. Whatever portion of the working class had become convinced of the insufficiency of mere political revolutions, and had proclaimed the necessity of a total social change, that portion, then, called itself Communist. It was a crude, rough-hewn, purely instinctive sort of Communism; still, it touched the cardinal point and was powerful enough amongst the working class to produce the Utopian Communism, in France, of Cabet, and in Germany, of Weitling. Thus, Socialism was, in 1847, a middle-class movement, Communism a working-class movement. Socialism was, on the Continent at least, 'respectable'; Communism was the very opposite. And as our notion, from the very beginning, was that 'the emancipation of the working class must be the act of the working class itself', there could be no doubt as to which of the two names we must take. Moreover, we have, ever since, been far from repudiating it.

The 'Manifesto' being our joint production, I consider myself bound to state that the fundamental proposition which forms its nucleus, belongs to Marx. That proposition is: that in every historical epoch, the prevailing mode of economic production and exchange, and the social organization necessarily following from it, form the basis upon which is built up, and from which alone can be explained, the political and intellectual history of that epoch; that consequently the whole history of mankind (since the dissolution of primitive tribal society, holding land in common ownership) has been a history of class struggles, contests between exploiting and exploited, ruling and oppressed classes; that the history of these class struggles form a series of evolution in which, nowadays, a stage has been reached where the exploited and oppressed class – the proletariat – cannot attain its emancipation from the sway of the exploiting and ruling class – the bourgeoisie – without, at the same time, and once and for all, emancipating society at large from all exploitation, oppression, class-distinctions and class-struggles.

This proposition which, in my opinion, is destined to do for history what Darwin's theory has done for biology, we, both of us, had been gradually approaching for some years before 1845. How far I had independently progressed towards it, is best

shown by my 'Condition of the Working Class in England'.*
But when I again met Marx at Brussels, in spring, 1845, he had it
ready worked out, and put it before me, in terms almost as clear
as those in which I have stated it here.

From our joint preface to the German edition of 1872, I quote
the following:—

'However much the state of things may have altered during
the last twenty-five years, the general principles laid down in this
Manifesto are, on the whole, as correct today as ever. Here and
there some detail might be improved. The practical application
of the principles will depend, as the manifesto itself states,
everywhere and at all times, on the historical conditions for the
time being existing, and, for that reason, no special stress is laid
on the revolutionary measures proposed at the end of Section II.
That passage would, in many respects, be very dif-
ferently worded today. In view of the gigantic strides of Modern
Industry since 1848, and of the accompanying improved and
extended organization of the working class, in view of the
practical experience gained, first in the February revolution, and
then, still more, in the Paris Commune, where the proletariat for
the first time held political power for two whole months, this
programme has in some details become antiquated. One thing
especially was proved by the Commune, viz., that "the working
class cannot simply lay hold of the ready-made State machinery,
and wield it for its own purposes". (See 'The Civil War in
France; Address of the General Council of the International
Working-men's Association', London, Truelove, 1871, p. 15,
where this point is further developed). Further, it is self-evident,
that the criticism of socialist literature is deficient in relation to
the present time, because it comes down only to 1847; also, that
the remarks on the relation of the Communists to the various
opposition-parties (Section IV), although in principle still
correct, yet in practice are antiquated, because the political
situation has been entirely changed, and the progress of history

*The Condition of the Working Class in England in 1844. By Frederick
Engels. Translated by Florence K. Wischnewetzky, New York, Lovell
— London, W. Reeves, 1888.

has swept from off the earth the greater portion of the political parties there enumerated.

But then, the Manifesto has become a historical document which we have no longer any right to alter.'

The present translation is by Mr Samuel Moore, the translator of the greater portion of Marx's 'Capital'. We have revised it in common, and I have added a few notes explanatory of historical allusions.

London, 30 January 1888.   FREDERICK ENGELS.

Manifesto of the Communist Party

A spectre is haunting Europe – the spectre of Communism. All the Powers of old Europe have entered into a holy alliance to exorcize this spectre; Pope and Czar, Metternich and Guizot, French Radicals and German police-spies.

Where is the party in opposition that has not been decried as communistic by its opponents in power? Where the Opposition that has not hurled back the branding reproach of Communism, against the more advanced opposition parties, as well as against its reactionary adversaries?

Two things result from this fact.

I. Communism is already acknowledged by all European Powers to be itself a Power.

II. It is high time that Communists should openly, in the face of the whole world, publish their views, their aims, their tendencies, and meet this nursery tale of the Spectre of Communism with a Manifesto of the party itself.

To this end, Communists of various nationalities have assembled in London, and sketched the following manifesto, to be published in the English, French, German, Italian, Flemish and Danish languages.

I

BOURGEOIS AND PROLETARIANS.*

The history of all hitherto existing society† is the history of class struggles.

*By bourgeoisie is meant the class of modern Capitalists, owners of the means of social production and employers of wage-labour. By proletariat, the class of modern wage-labourers who, having no means of production of their own, are reduced to selling their labour power in order to live.

†That is, all *written* history. In 1847, the pre-history of society, the social

Freeman and slave, patrician and plebeian, lord and serf, guild-master* and journeyman, in a word, oppressor and oppressed, stood in constant opposition to one another, carried on an uninterrupted, now hidden, now open fight, a fight that each time ended, either in a revolutionary re-constitution of society at large, or in the common ruin of the contending classes.

In the earlier epochs of history, we find almost everywhere a complicated arrangement of society into various orders, a manifold gradation of social rank. In ancient Rome we have patricians, knights, plebeians, slaves; in the middle ages, feudal lords, vassals, guild-masters, journeymen, apprentices, serfs; in almost all of these classes, again, subordinate gradations.

The modern bourgeois society that has sprouted from the ruins of feudal society, has not done away with class antagonisms. It has but established new classes, new conditions of oppression, new forms of struggle in place of the old ones.

Our epoch, the epoch of the bourgeoisie, possesses, however, this distinctive feature; it has simplified the class antagonisms. Society as a whole is more and more splitting up into two great hostile camps, into two great classes directly facing each other: Bourgeoisie and Proletariat.

From the serfs of the middle ages sprang the chartered

organization existing previous to recorded history, was all but unknown. Since then, Haxthausen discovered common ownership of land in Russia, Maurer proved it to be the social foundation from which all Teutonic races started in history, and by and bye village communities were found to be, or to have been the primitive form of society everywhere from India to Ireland. The inner organization of this primitive Communistic society was laid bare, in its typical form, by Morgan's crowning discovery of the true nature of the *gens* and its relation to the *tribe*. With the dissolution of these primaeval communities society begins to be differentiated into separate and finally antagonistic classes. I have attempted to retrace this process of dissolution in: 'Der Ursprung der Familie des, Privateigenthums und des Staats,' 2nd edition, Stuttgart 1886.

*Guild-master, that is a full member of a guild, a master within, not a head of a guild.

burghers of the earliest towns. From these burgesses the first elements of the bourgeoisie were developed.

The discovery of America, the rounding of the Cape, opened up fresh ground for the rising bourgeoisie. The East-Indian and Chinese markets, the colonization of America, trade with the colonies, the increase in the means of exchange and in commodities generally, gave to commerce, to navigation, to industry, an impulse never before known, and thereby, to the revolutionary element in the tottering feudal society, a rapid development.

The feudal system of industry, under which industrial production was monopolized by close guilds, now no longer sufficed for the growing wants of the new markets. The manufacturing system took its place. The guild-masters were pushed on one side by the manufacturing middle class; division of labour between the different corporate guilds vanished in the face of division of labour in each single workshop.

Meantime the markets kept ever growing, the demand ever rising. Even manufacture no longer sufficed. Thereupon, steam and machinery revolutionized industrial production. The place of manufacture was taken by the giant, Modern Industry, the place of the industrial middle class, by industrial millionaires, the leaders of whole industrial armies, the modern bourgeois.

Modern Industry has established the world-market, for which the discovery of America paved the way. This market has given an immense development to commerce, to navigation, to communication by land. This development has, in its turn, reacted on the extension of industry; and in proportion as industry, commerce, navigation, railways extended, in the same proportion the bourgeoisie developed, increased its capital, and pushed into the background every class handed down from the Middle Ages.

We see, therefore, how the modern bourgeoisie is itself the product of a long course of development, of a series of revolutions in the modes of production and of exchange.

Each step in the development of the bourgeoisie was accompanied by a corresponding political advance of that class. An oppressed class under the sway of the feudal nobility, an armed and self-governing association in the medieval commune*, here independent urban republic (as in Italy and Germany), there taxable 'third estate' of the monarchy (as in France), afterwards, in the period of manufacture proper, serving either the semi-feudal or the absolute monarchy as a counterpoise against the nobility, and, in fact, corner-stone of the great monarchies in general, the bourgeoisie has at last, since the establishment of Modern Industry and of the world-market, conquered for itself, in the modern representative State, exclusive political sway. The executive of the modern State is but a committee for managing the common affairs of the whole bourgeoisie.

The bourgeoisie, historically, has played a most revolutionary part.

The bourgeoisie, wherever it has got the upper hand, has put an end to all feudal, patriarchal, idyllic relations. It has pitilessly torn asunder the motley feudal ties that bound man to his 'natural superiors', and has left remaining no other nexus between man and man than naked self-interest, than callous 'cash payment'. It has drowned the most heavenly ecstacies of religious fervour, of chivalrous enthusiasm, of philistine sentimentalism, in the icy water of egotistical calculation. It has resolved personal worth into exchange value, and in place of the numberless indefeasible chartered freedoms, has set up that single, unconscionable freedom – Free Trade. In one word, for exploitation, veiled by religious and political illusions, it has substituted naked, shameless, direct, brutal exploitation.

The bourgeoisie has stripped of its halo every occupation hitherto honoured and looked up to with reverent awe. It has converted the physician, the lawyer, the priest, the poet, the man of science, into its paid wage-labourers.

The bourgeoisie has torn away from the family its sentimental

*'Commune' was the name taken, in France, by the nascent towns even before they had conquered from their feudal lords and masters, local self-government and political rights as 'the Third Estate'. Generally speaking, for the economical development of the bourgeoisie, England is here taken as the typical country, for its political development, France.

veil, and has reduced the family relation to a mere money relation.

The bourgeoisie has disclosed how it came to pass that the brutal display of vigour in the Middle Ages, which Reactionists so much admire, found its fitting complement in the most slothful indolence. It has been the first to shew what man's activity can bring about. It has accomplished wonders far surpassing Egyptian pyramids, Roman aqueducts, and Gothic cathedrals; it has conducted expeditions that put in the shade all former Exoduses of nations and crusades.

The bourgeoisie cannot exist without constantly revolutionizing the instruments of production, and thereby the relations of production, and with them the whole relations of society. Conservation of the old modes of production in unaltered form, was, on the contrary, the first condition of existence for all earlier industrial classes. Constant revolutionizing of production, uninterrupted disturbance of all social conditions, everlasting uncertainty and agitation distinguish the bourgeois epoch from all earlier ones. All fixed, fast-frozen relations, with their train of ancient and venerable prejudices and opinions, are swept away, all new-formed ones become antiquated before they can ossify. All that is solid melts into air, all that is holy is profaned, and man is at last compelled to face with sober senses, his real conditions of life, and his relations with his kind.

The need of a constantly expanding market for its products chases the bourgeoisie over the whole surface of the globe. It must nestle everywhere, settle everywhere, establish connexions everywhere.

The bourgeoisie has through its exploitation of the world-market given a cosmopolitan character to production and consumption in every country. To the great chagrin of Reactionists, it has drawn from under the feet of industry the national ground on which it stood. All old-established national industries have been destroyed or are daily being destroyed. They are dislodged by new industries, whose introduction becomes a life and death question for all civilized nations, by industries that no longer work up indigenous raw material, but raw material drawn from the remotest zones; industries whose products are consumed, not only at home, but in every quarter of the globe. In place of the old wants, satisfied by the productions of the country, we find new wants, requiring for their satisfaction the products of distant lands and climes. In place of the old local and national seclusion and self-sufficiency, we have intercourse in every direction, universal interdependence of nations. And as in material, so also in intellectual production. The intellectual creations of individual nations become common property. National one-sidedness and narrow-mindedness become more and more impossible, and from the numerous national and local literatures, there arises a world-literature.

The bourgeoisie, by the rapid improvement of all instruments of production, by the immensely facilitated means of communication, draws all, even the most barbarian, nations into civilization. The cheap prices of its commodities are the heavy artillery with which it batters down all Chinese walls, with which it forces the barbarians' intensely obstinate hatred of foreigners to capitulate. It compels all nations, on pain of extinction, to adopt the bourgeois mode of production; it compels them to introduce what it calls civilization into their midst, i.e., to become bourgeois themselves. In one word, it creates a world after its own image.

The bourgeoisie has subjected the country to the rule of the towns. It has created enormous cities, has greatly increased the urban population as compared with the rural, and has thus rescued a considerable part of the population from the idiocy of rural life. Just as it has made the country dependent on the towns, so it has made barbarian and semi-barbarian countries dependent on the civilized ones, nations of peasants on nations of bourgeois, the East on the West.

The bourgeoisie keeps more and more doing away with the scattered state of the population, of the means of production, and of property. It has agglomerated population, centralized means of production, and has concentrated property in a few hands. The necessary consequence of this was political centralization. Independent, or but loosely connected provinces, with separate interests, laws, governments and systems of taxation, became lumped together into one nation, with one government, one code of laws, one national class-interest, one frontier and one customs-tariff.

The bourgeoisie, during its rule of scarce one hundred years, has created more massive and more colossal productive forces than have all preceding generations together. Subjection of Nature's forces to man, machinery, application of chemistry to industry and agriculture, steam-navigation, railways, electric telegraphs, clearing of whole continents for cultivation, canalization of rivers, whole populations conjured out of the ground – what earlier century had even a presentiment that such productive forces slumbered in the lap of social labour?

We see then: the means of production and of exchange on whose foundation the bourgeoisie built itself up, were generated in feudal society. At a certain stage in the development of these means of production and of exchange, the conditions under which feudal society produced and exchanged, the feudal organization of agriculture and manufacturing industry, in one word, the feudal relations of property became no longer compatible with the already developed productive forces; they became so many fetters. They had to be burst asunder; they were burst asunder.

Into their place stepped free competition, accompanied by a social and political constitution adapted to it, and by the economical and political sway of the bourgeois class.

A similar movement is going on before our own eyes. Modern bourgeois society with its relations of production, of exchange and of property, a society that has conjured up such gigantic means of production and of exchange, is like the sorcerer, who is no longer able to control the powers of the nether world whom he has called up by his spells. For many a decade past the history of industry and commerce is but the history of the revolt of modern productive forces against modern conditions of production, against the property relations that are the conditions for the existence of the bourgeoisie and of its rule. It is enough to mention the commercial crises that by their periodical return put on its trial, each time more threateningly, the existence of the entire bourgeois society. In these crises a great part not only of the existing products, but also of the previously created productive forces, are periodically destroyed. In these crises there breaks out an epidemic that, in all earlier epochs, would have seemed an absurdity – the epidemic of over-production. Society suddenly finds itself put back into a state of momentary barbarism; it appears as if a famine, a universal war of devastation had cut off the supply of every means of subsistence; industry and commerce seem to be destroyed; and why? Because there is too much civilization, too much means of subsistence, too much industry, too much commerce. The productive forces at the disposal of society no longer tend to further the development of the conditions of bourgeois property; on the contrary, they have become too powerful for these conditions, by which they are fettered, and so soon as they overcome these fetters, they bring disorder into the whole of bourgeois society, endanger the existence of bourgeois property. The conditions of bourgeois society are too narrow to comprise the wealth created by them. And how does the bourgeoisie get over these crises? On the one hand by enforced destruction of a mass of productive forces; on the other, by the conquest of new markets, and by the more thorough exploitation of the old ones. That is to say, by paving the way for more extensive and more destructive crises, and by diminishing the means whereby crises are prevented.

The weapons with which the bourgeoisie felled feudalism to the ground are now turned against the bourgeoisie itself.

But not only has the bourgeoisie forged the weapons that bring death to itself; it has also called into existence the men who are to wield those weapons – the modern working class – the proletarians.

In proportion as the bourgeoisie, i.e., capital, is developed, in the same proportion is the proletariat, the modern working class, developed, a class of labourers, who live only so long as they find work, and who find work only so long as their labour increases capital. These labourers, who must sell themselves piecemeal, are a commodity, like every other article of commerce, and are consequently exposed to all the vicissitudes of competition, to all the fluctuations of the market.

Owing to the extensive use of machinery and to division of labour, the work of the proletarians has lost all individual character, and, consequently, all charm for the workman. He becomes an appendage of the machine, and it is only the most simple, most monotonous, and most easily acquired knack, that is required of him. Hence, the cost of production of a workman is restricted, almost entirely, to the means of subsistence that he requires for his maintenance, and for the propagation of his race. But the price of a commodity, and therefore also of labour, is equal to its cost of production. In proportion, therefore, as the repulsiveness of the work increases, the wage decreases. Nay more, in proportion as the use of machinery and division of labour increases, in the same proportion the burden of toil also increases, whether by prolongation of the working hours, by increase of the work exacted in a given time, or by increased speed of the machinery, etc.

Modern industry has converted the little workshop of the patriarchal master, into the great factory of the industrial capitalist. Masses of labourers, crowded into the factory, are organized like soldiers. As privates of the industrial army they are placed under the command of a perfect hierarchy of officers and sergeants. Not only are they slaves of the bourgeois class, and of the bourgeois State, they are daily and hourly enslaved by the machine, by the over-looker, and, above all, by the individual bourgeois manufacturer himself. The more openly this despotism proclaims gain to be its end and aim, the more petty, the more hateful and the more embittering it is.

The less the skill and exertion of strength implied in manual labour, in other words, the more modern industry becomes developed, the more is the labour of men superseded by that of women. Differences of age and sex have no longer any distinctive social validity for the working class. All are instruments of labour, more or less expensive to use, according to their age and sex.

No sooner is the exploitation of the labourer by the manufacturer, so far, at an end, that he receives his wages in cash, than he is set upon by the other portions of the bourgeoisie, the landlord, the shopkeeper, the pawnbroker, etc.

The lower strata of the middle class – the small tradespeople, shopkeepers, and retired tradesmen generally, the handicraftsmen and peasants – all these sink gradually into the proletariat, partly because their diminutive capital does not suffice for the scale on which Modern Industry is carried on, and is swamped in the competition with the large capitalists, partly because their specialized skill is rendered worthless by new methods of production. Thus the proletariat is recruited from all classes of the population.

The proletariat goes through various stages of development. With its birth begins its struggle with the bourgeoisie. At first the contest is carried on by individual labourers, then by the workpeople of a factory, then by the operatives of one trade, in one locality, against the individual bourgeois who directly exploits them. They direct their attacks not against the bourgeois conditions of production, but against the instruments of production themselves; they destroy imported wares that compete with their labour, they smash to pieces machinery, they set factories ablaze, they seek to restore by force the vanished status of the workman of the Middle Ages.

At this stage the labourers still form an incoherent mass scattered over the whole country, and broken up by their mutual competition. If anywhere they unite to form more compact bodies, this is not yet the consequence of their own active union, but of the union of the bourgeoisie, which class, in order to attain its own political ends, is compelled to set the whole proletariat in motion, and is moreover yet, for a time, able to do so. At this stage, therefore, the proletarians do not fight their enemies, but the enemies of their enemies, the remnants of absolute monarchy, the landowners, the non-industrial bourgeois, the petty bourgeoisie. Thus the whole historical movement is concentrated in the hands of the bourgeoisie; every victory so obtained is a victory for the bourgeoisie.

But with the development of industry the proletariat not only increases in number; it becomes concentrated in greater masses, its strength grows, and it feels that strength more. The various interests and conditions of life within the ranks of the proletariat are more and more equalized, in proportion as machinery obliterates all distinctions of labour, and nearly everywhere reduces wages to the same low level. The growing competition among the bourgeois, and the resulting commercial crises, make the wages of the workers ever more fluctuating. The unceasing improvement of machinery, ever more rapidly developing, makes their livelihood more and more precarious; the collisions between individual workmen and individual bourgeois take more and more the character of collisions between two classes. Thereupon the workers begin to form combinations (Trades' Unions) against the bourgeois; they club together in order to keep up the rate of wages; they found permanent associations in order to make provision beforehand for these occasional revolts. Here and there the contest breaks out into riots.

Now and then the workers are victorious, but only for a time. The real fruit of their battles lies, not in the immediate result, but in the ever-expanding union of the workers. This union is helped on by the improved means of communication that are created by modern industry, and that place the workers of different localities in contact with one another. It was just this contact that was needed to centralize the numerous local struggles, all of the same character, into one national struggle between classes. But every class struggle is a political struggle. And that union, to attain which the burghers of the Middle Ages, with their miserable highways, required centuries, the modern proletarians, thanks to railways, achieve in a few years.

This organization of the proletarians into a class, and consequently into a political party, is continually being upset again by the competition between the workers themselves. But it ever rises up again, stronger, firmer, mightier. It compels legislative recognition of particular interests of the workers, by taking advantage of the divisions among the bourgeoisie itself. Thus the ten-hours'-bill in England was carried.

Altogether collisions between the classes of the old society further, in many ways, the course of development of the proletariat. The bourgeoisie finds itself involved in a constant battle. At first with the aristocracy; later on, with those portions of the bourgeoisie itself, whose interests have become antagonistic to the progress of industry; at all times, with the bourgeoisie of foreign countries. In all these battles it sees itself compelled to appeal to the proletariat, to ask for its help, and thus, to drag it into the political arena. The bourgeoisie itself, therefore, supplies the proletariat with its own elements of political and general education, in other words, it furnishes the proletariat with weapons for fighting the bourgeoisie.

Further, as we have already seen, entire sections of the ruling classes are, by the advance of industry, precipitated into the proletariat, or are at least threatened in their conditions of existence. These also supply the proletariat with fresh elements of enlightenment and progress.

Finally, in times when the class-struggle nears the decisive hour, the process of dissolution going on within the ruling class, in fact within the whole range of old society, assumes such a violent, glaring character, that a small section of the ruling class cuts itself adrift, and joins the revolutionary class, the class that holds the future in its hands. Just as, therefore, at an earlier period, a section of the nobility went over to the bourgeoisie, so now a portion of the bourgeoisie goes over to the proletariat, and in particular, a portion of the bourgeois ideologists, who have raised themselves to the level of comprehending theoretically the historical movement as a whole.

Of all the classes that stand face to face with the bourgeoisie today, the proletariat alone is a really revolutionary class. The other classes decay and finally disappear in the face of modern industry; the proletariat is its special and essential product.

The lower middle class, the small manufacturer, the shopkeeper, the artisan, the peasant, all these fight against the bourgeoisie, to save from extinction their existence as fractions of the middle class. They are therefore not revolutionary, but conservative. Nay more, they are reactionary, for they try to roll back the wheel of history. If by chance they are revolutionary, they are so, only in view of their impending transfer into the proletariat, they thus defend not their present, but their future interests, they desert their own standpoint to place themselves at that of the proletariat.

The 'dangerous class', the social scum, that passively rotting mass thrown off by the lowest layers of old society, may, here and there, be swept into the movement by a proletarian revolution; its conditions of life, however, prepare it far more for the part of a bribed tool of reactionary intrigue.

In the conditions of the proletariat, those of old society at large are already virtually swamped. The proletarian is without property; his relation to his wife and children has no longer anything in common with the bourgeois family-relations; modern industrial labour, modern subjection to capital, the same in England as in France, in America as in Germany, has stripped him of every trace of national character. Law, morality, religion, are to him so many bourgeois prejudices, behind which lurk in ambush just as many bourgeois interests.

All the preceding classes that got the upper hand, sought to fortify their already acquired status by subjecting society at large to their conditions of appropriation. The proletarians cannot become masters of the productive forces of society, except by abolishing their own previous mode of appropriation, and thereby also every other previous mode of appropriation. They have nothing of their own to secure and to fortify; their mission is to destroy all previous securities for, and insurances of, individual property.

All previous historical movements were movements of minorities, or in the interest of minorities. The proletarian movement is the self-conscious, independent movement of the immense majority, in the interest of the immense majority. The proletariat, the lowest stratum of our present society, cannot stir, cannot raise itself up, without the whole superincumbent strata of official society being sprung into the air.

Though not in substance, yet in form, the struggle of the proletariat with the bourgeoisie is at first a national struggle. The proletariat of each country must, of course, first of all settle matters with its own bourgeoisie.

In depicting the most general phases of the development of the proletariat, we traced the more or less veiled civil war, raging within existing society, up to the point where that war breaks out into open revolution, and where the violent overthrow of the bourgeoisie, lays the foundation for the sway of the proletariat.

Hitherto, every form of society has been based, as we have already seen, on the antagonism of oppressing and oppressed classes. But in order to oppress a class, certain conditions must be assured to it under which it can, at least, continue its slavish existence. The serf, in the period of serfdom, raised himself to membership in the commune, just as the petty bourgeois, under the yoke of feudal absolutism, managed to develop into a bourgeois. The modern labourer, on the contrary, instead of rising with the progress of industry, sinks deeper and deeper below the conditions of existence of his own class. He becomes a pauper, and pauperism develops more rapidly than population and wealth. And here it becomes evident, that the bourgeoisie is unfit any longer to be the ruling class in society, and to impose its conditions of existence upon society as an over-riding law. It is unfit to rule because it is incompetent to assure an existence to its slave within his slavery, because it cannot help letting him sink into such a state, that it has to feed him, instead of being fed by him. Society can no longer live under this bourgeoisie, in other words, its existence is no longer compatible with society.

The essential condition for the existence, and for the sway of the bourgeois class, is the formation and augmentation of capital; the condition for capital is wage-labour. Wage-labour rests exclusively on competition between the labourers. The advance of industry, whose involuntary promoter is the bourgeoisie, replaces the isolation of the labourers, due to competition, by their revolutionary combination, due to association. The development of Modern Industry, therefore, cuts from under its feet the very foundation on which the bourgeoisie produces and appropriates products. What the bourgeoisie therefore produces, above all, are its own grave-diggers. Its fall and the victory of the proletariat are equally inevitable.

II

PROLETARIANS AND COMMUNISTS

In what relation do the Communists stand to the proletarians as a whole?

The Communists do not form a separate party opposed to other working-class parties.

They have no interests separate and apart from those of the proletariat as a whole.

They do not set up any sectarian principles of their own, by which to shape and mould the proletarian movement.

The Communists are distinguished from the other working-class parties by this only: 1. In the national struggles of the proletarians of the different countries, they point out and bring to the front the common interests of the entire proletariat, independently of all nationality. 2. In the various stages of development which the struggle of the working class against the bourgeoisie has to pass through, they always and everywhere represent the interests of the movement as a whole.

The Communists, therefore, are on the one hand, practically, the most advanced and resolute section of the working-class parties of every country, that section which pushes forward all others; on the other hand, theoretically, they have over the great mass of the proletariat the advantage of clearly understanding the line of march, the conditions, and the ultimate general results of the proletarian movement.

The immediate aim of the Communists is the same as that of all the other proletarian parties: formation of the proletariat into a class, overthrow of the bourgeois supremacy, conquest of political power by the proletariat.

The theoretical conclusions of the Communists are in no way based on ideas or principles that have been invented, or discovered, by this or that would-be universal reformer.

They merely express, in general terms, actual relations springing from an existing class struggle, from a historical movement going on under our very eyes. The abolition of existing property-relations is not at all a distinctive feature of Communism.

All property relations in the past have continually been subject to historical change consequent upon the change in historical conditions.

The French Revolution, for example, abolished feudal property in favour of bourgeois property.

The distinguishing feature of Communism is not the abolition of property generally, but the abolition of bourgeois property. But modern bourgeois private property is the final and most complete expression of the system of producing and appropriating products, that is based on class antagonisms, on the exploitation of the many by the few.

In this sense, the theory of the Communists may be summed up in the single sentence: Abolition of private property.

We Communists have been reproached with the desire of abolishing the right of personally acquiring property as the fruit of a man's own labour, which property is alleged to be the ground work of all personal freedom, activity and independence.

Hard-won, self-acquired, self-earned property! Do you mean the property of the petty artisan and of the small peasant, a form of property that preceded the bourgeois form? There is no need to abolish that; the development of industry has to a great extent already destroyed it, and is still destroying it daily.

Or do you mean modern bourgeois private property?

But does wage-labour create any property for the labourer? Not a bit. It creates capital, i.e., that kind of property which exploits wage-labour, and which cannot increase except upon condition of begetting a new supply of wage-labour for fresh exploitation. Property, in its present form, is based on the antagonism of capital and wage-labour. Let us examine both sides of this antagonism.

To be a capitalist, is to have not only a purely personal, but a social *status* in production. Capital is a collective product, and only by the united action of many members, nay, in the last resort, only by the united action of all members of society, can it be set in motion.

Capital is therefore not a personal, it is a social power.

When, therefore, capital is converted into common property, into the property of all members of society, personal property is not thereby transformed into social property. It is only the social character of the property that is changed. It loses its class-character.

Let us now take wage-labour.

The average price of wage-labour is the minimum wage, i.e., that quantum of the means of subsistence, which is absolutely requisite to keep the labourer in bare existence as a labourer. What, therefore, the wage-labourer appropriates by means of his labour, merely suffices to prolong and reproduce a bare existence. We by no means intend to abolish this personal appropriation of the products of labour, an appropriation that is made for the maintenance and reproduction of human life, and that leaves no surplus wherewith to command the labour of others. All that we want to do away with, is the miserable character of this appropriation, under which the labourer lives merely to increase capital, and is allowed to live only in so far as the interest of the ruling class requires it.

In bourgeois society, living labour is but a means to increase accumulated labour. In Communist society, accumulated labour is but a means to widen, to enrich, to promote the existence of the labourer.

In bourgeois society, therefore, the past dominates the present; in communist society, the present dominates the past. In bourgeois society capital is independent and has individuality, while the living person is dependent and has no individuality.

And the abolition of this state of things is called by the bourgeois, abolition of individuality and freedom! And rightly so. The abolition of bourgeois individuality, bourgeois independence, and bourgeois freedom is undoubtedly aimed at.

By freedom is meant, under the present bourgeois conditions of production, free trade, free selling and buying.

But if selling and buying disappears, free selling and buying disappears also. This talk about free selling and buying, and all the other 'brave words' of our bourgeoisie about freedom in general, have a meaning, if any, only in contrast with restricted selling and buying, with the fettered traders of the Middle Ages, but have no meaning when opposed to the Communistic abolition of buying and selling, of the bourgeois conditions of production, and of the bourgeoisie itself.

You are horrified at our intending to do away with private property. But in your existing society, private property is already done away with for nine-tenths of the population; its existence for the few is solely due to its non-existence in the hands of those nine-tenths. You reproach us, therefore, with intending to do away with a form of property, the necessary condition for whose existence is, the non-existence of any property for the immense majority of society.

In one word, you reproach us with intending to do away with your property. Precisely so: that is just what we intend.

From the moment when labour can no longer be converted into capital, money, or rent, into a social power capable of being monopolized, i.e., from the moment when individual property can no longer be transformed into bourgeois property, into capital, from that moment, you say, individuality vanishes.

You must, therefore, confess that by 'individual' you mean no other person than the bourgeois, than the middle-class owner of property. This person must, indeed, be swept out of the way, and made impossible.

Communism deprives no man of the power to appropriate the products of society: all that it does is to deprive him of the power to subjugate the labour of others by means of such appropriation.

It has been objected, that upon the abolition of private property all work will cease, and universal laziness will overtake us.

According to this, bourgeois society ought long ago to have gone to the dogs through sheer idleness; for those of its members who work, acquire nothing, and those who acquire anything, do not work. The whole of this objection is but another expression of the tautology: that there can no longer be any wage-labour when there is no longer any capital.

All objections urged against the Communistic mode of

producing and appropriating material products, have, in the same way, been urged against the Communistic modes of producing and appropriating intellectual products. Just as, to the bourgeois, the disappearance of class property is the disappearance of production itself, so the disappearance of class culture is to him identical with the disappearance of all culture.

That culture, the loss of which he laments, is, for the enormous majority, a mere training to act as a machine.

But don't wrangle with us so long as you apply, to our intended abolition of bourgeois property, the standard of your bourgeois notions of freedom, culture, law, etc. Your very ideas are but the outgrowth of the conditions of your bourgeois production and bourgeois property, just as your jurisprudence is but the will of your class made into a law for all, a will, whose essential character and direction are determined by the economical conditions of existence of your class.

The selfish misconception that induces you to transform into eternal laws of nature and of reason, the social forms springing from your present mode of production and form of property – historical relations that rise and disappear in the progress of production – this misconception you share with every ruling class that has preceded you. What you see clearly in the case of ancient property, what you admit in the case of feudal property, you are of course forbidden to admit in the case of your own bourgeois form of property.

Abolition of the family! Even the most radical flare up at this infamous proposal of the Communists.

On what foundation is the present family, the bourgeois family, based? On capital, on private gain. In its completely developed form this family exists only among the bourgeoisie. But this state of things finds its complement in the practical absence of the family among the proletarians, and in public prostitution.

The bourgeois family will vanish as a matter of course when its complement vanishes, and both will vanish with the vanishing of capital.

Do you charge us with wanting to stop the exploitation of children by their parents? To this crime we plead guilty.

But, you will say, we destroy the most hallowed of relations, when we replace home education by social.

And your education! Is not that also social, and determined by the social conditions under which you educate, by the intervention, direct or indirect, of society by means of schools, etc.? The communists have not invented the intervention of society in education; they do but seek to alter the character of that intervention, and to rescue education from the influence of the ruling class.

The bourgeois clap-trap about the family and education, about the hallowed co-relation of parent and child, become all the more disgusting, the more, by the action of Modern Industry, all family ties among the proletarians are torn asunder, and their children transformed into simple articles of commerce and instruments of labour.

But you Communists would introduce community of women, screams the whole bourgeoisie in chorus.

The bourgeois sees in his wife a mere instrument of production. He hears that the instruments of production are to be exploited in common, and, naturally, can come to no other conclusion, than that the lot of being common to all will likewise fall to the women.

He has not even a suspicion that the real point aimed at is to do away with the status of women as mere instruments of production.

For the rest, nothing is more ridiculous than the virtuous indignation of our bourgeois at the community of women which, they pretend, is to be openly and officially established by the Communists. The Communists have no need to introduce community of women; it has existed almost from time immemorial.

Our bourgeois, not content with having the wives and daughters of their proletarians at their disposal, not to speak of common prostitutes, take the greatest pleasure in seducing each other's wives.

Bourgeois marriage is in reality a system of wives in common and thus, at the most, what the Communists might possibly be reproached with, is that they desire to introduce, in substitution for a hypocritically concealed, an openly legalized community of women. For the rest, it is self-evident, that the abolition of the present system of production must bring with it the abolition of the community of women springing from that system, i.e., of prostitution both public and private.

The Communists are further reproached with desiring to abolish countries and nationality.

The working men have no country. We cannot take from them what they have not got. Since the proletariat must first of all acquire political supremacy, must rise to be the leading class of the nation, must constitute itself *the* nation, it is, so far, itself national, though not in the bourgeois sense of the word.

National differences, and antagonisms between peoples, are daily more and more vanishing, owing to the development of the bourgeoisie, to freedom of commerce, to the world-market, to uniformity in the mode of production and in the conditions of life corresponding thereto.

The supremacy of the proletariat will cause them to vanish still faster. United action, of the leading civilized countries at least, is one of the first conditions for the emancipation of the proletariat.

In proportion as the exploitation of one individual by another is put an end to, the exploitation of one nation by another will also be put an end to. In proportion as the antagonism between classes within the nation vanishes, the hostility of one nation to another will come to an end.

The charges against Communism made from a religious, a philosophical, and, generally, from an ideological standpoint, are not deserving of serious examination.

Does it require deep intuition to comprehend that man's ideas, views, and conceptions, in one word, man's consciousness, changes with every change in the conditions of his material existence, in his social relations and in his social life?

What else does the history of ideas prove, than that intellectual production changes its character in proportion as material production is changed? The ruling ideas of each age have ever been the ideas of its ruling class.

When people speak of ideas that revolutionize society, they do but express the fact, that within the old society, the elements of a new one have been created, and that the dissolution of the old ideas keeps even pace with the dissolution of the old conditions of existence.

When the ancient world was in its last throes, the ancient religions were overcome by Christianity. When Christian ideas succumbed in the eighteenth century to rationalist ideas, feudal society fought its death-battle with the then revolutionary bourgeoisie. The ideas of religious liberty and freedom of conscience, merely gave expression to the sway of free competition within the domain of knowledge.

'Undoubtedly,' it will be said, 'religious, moral, philosophical and juridical ideas have been modified in the course of historical development. But religion, morality, philosophy, political science, and law, constantly survived this change.'

'There are besides, eternal truths, such as Freedom, Justice, etc., that are common to all states of society. But Communism abolishes eternal truths, it abolishes all religion, and all morality, instead of constituting them on a new basis; it therefore acts in contradiction to all past historical experience.'

What does this accusation reduce itself to? The history of all past society has consisted in the development of class antagonisms, antagonisms that assumed different forms at different epochs.

But whatever form they may have taken, one fact is common to all past ages, viz., the exploitation of one part of society by the other. No wonder, then, that the social consciousness of past ages, despite all the multiplicity and variety it displays, moves within certain common forms, or general ideas, which cannot completely vanish except with the total disappearance of class antagonisms.

The Communist revolution is the most radical rupture with traditional property-relations; no wonder that its development involves the most radical rupture with traditional ideas.

But let us have done with the bourgeois objections to Communism.

We have seen above, that the first step in the revolution by the working class, is to raise the proletariat to the position of ruling class, to win the battle of democracy.

The proletariat will use its political supremacy, to wrest, by degrees, all capital from the bourgeoisie, to centralize all instruments of production in the hands of the State, i.e., of the proletariat organized as the ruling class; and to increase the total of productive forces as rapidly as possible.

Of course, in the beginning, this cannot be effected except by means of despotic inroads on the rights of property, and on the conditions of bourgeois production; by means of measures, therefore, which appear economically insufficient and untenable, but which, in the course of the movement, outstrip themselves, necessitate further inroads upon the old social order, and are unavoidable as a means of entirely revolutionizing the mode of production.

These measures will of course be different in different countries.

Nevertheless in the most advanced countries, the following will be pretty generally applicable.

1. Abolition of property in land and application of all rents of land to public purposes.

2. A heavy progressive or graduated income tax.

3. Abolition of all right of inheritance.

4. Confiscation of the property of all emigrants and rebels.

5. Centralization of credit in the hands of the State, by means of a national bank with State capital and an exclusive monopoly.

6. Centralization of the means of communication and transport in the hands of the State.

7. Extension of factories and instruments of production owned by the State: the bringing into cultivation of waste lands, and the improvement of the soil generally in accordance with a common plan.

8. Equal liability of all to labour. Establishment of industrial armies, especially for agriculture.

9. Combination of agriculture with manufacturing industries: gradual abolition of the distinction between town and country, by a more equable distribution of the population over the country.

10. Free education for all children in public schools. Abolition of children's factory labour in its present form. Combination of education with industrial production, etc., etc.

When, in the course of development, class distinctions have disappeared, and all production has been concentrated in the hands of a vast association of the whole nation, the public power will lose its political character. Political power, properly so called, is merely the organized power of one class for oppressing another. If the proletariat during its contest with the bourgeoisie is compelled, by the force of circumstances, to organize itself as a class, if, by means of a revolution, it makes itself the ruling class, and, as such, sweeps away by force the old conditions of production, then it will, along with these conditions, have swept away the conditions for the existence of class antagonisms, and of classes generally, and will thereby have abolished its own supremacy as a class.

In place of the old bourgeois society, with its classes and class antagonisms, we shall have an association, in which the free development of each is the condition for the free development of all.

III

SOCIALIST AND COMMUNIST LITERATURE

REACTIONARY SOCIALISM
Feudal Socialism

Owing to their historical position, it became the vocation of the aristocracies of France and England to write pamphlets against modern bourgeois society. In the French revolution of July 1830, and in the English reform agitation, these aristocracies again succumbed to the hateful upstart. Thenceforth, a serious political contest was altogether out of question. A literary battle alone remained possible. But even in the domain of literature the old cries of the restoration period* had become impossible.

In order to arouse sympathy, the aristocracy were obliged to lose sight, apparently, of their own interests, and to formulate their indictment against the bourgeoisie in the interest of the exploited working class alone. Thus the aristocracy took their revenge by singing lampoons on their new master, and whispering in his ears sinister prophecies of coming catastrophe.

In this way arose feudal socialism: half lamentation, half lampoon; half echo of the past, half menace of the future; at times, by its bitter, witty and incisive criticism, striking the bourgeoisie to the very hearts' core, but always ludicrous in its effect, through total incapacity to comprehend the march of modern history.

The aristocracy, in order to rally the people to them, waved the proletarian alms-bag in front for a banner. But the people, so often as it joined them, saw on their hindquarters the old feudal coats of arms, and deserted with loud and irreverent laughter.

One section of the French Legitimists, and 'Young England', exhibited this spectacle.

In pointing out that their mode of exploitation was different to that of the bourgeoisie, the feudalists forget that they exploited under circumstances and conditions that were quite different, and that are now antiquated. In showing that, under their rule, the modern proletariat never existed, they forget that the modern bourgeoisie is the necessary offspring of their own form of society.

For the rest, so little do they conceal the reactionary character of their criticism, that their chief accusation against the bourgeoisie amounts to this, that under the bourgeois *régime* a class is being developed, which is destined to cut up root and branch the old order of society.

What they upbraid the bourgeoisie with is not so much that it creates a proletariat, as that it creates a *revolutionary* proletariat.

In political practice, therefore, they join in all coercive

---

*Not the English Restoration 1660 to 1689, but the French Restoration 1814 to 1830.

measures against the working class; and in ordinary life, despite their high falutin phrases, they stoop to pick up the golden apples dropped from the tree of industry, and to barter truth, love, and honour for traffic in wool, beetroot-sugar, and potato spirit*.

As the parson has ever gone hand in hand with the landlord, so has Clerical Socialism with Feudal Socialism.

Nothing is easier than to give Christian asceticism a Socialist tinge. Has not Christianity declaimed against private property, against marriage, against the State? Has it not preached in the place of these, charity and poverty, celibacy and mortification of the flesh, monastic life and Mother Church? Christian Socialism is but the Holy Water with which the priest consecrates the heart-burnings of the aristocrat.

Petty Bourgeois Socialism

The feudal aristocracy was not the only class that was ruined by the bourgeoisie, not the only class whose conditions of existence pined and perished in the atmosphere of modern bourgeois society. The medieval burgesses and the small peasant proprietors were the precursors of the modern bourgeoisie. In those countries which are but little developed, industrially and commercially, these two classes still vegetate side by side with the rising bourgeoisie.

In countries where modern civilization has become fully developed, a new class of petty bourgeois has been formed, fluctuating between proletariat and bourgeoisie, and ever renewing itself as a supplementary part of bourgeois society. The individual members of this class, however, are being constantly hurled down into the proletariat by the action of

*This applies chiefly to Germany where the landed aristocracy and squirearchy have large portions of their estates cultivated for their own account by stewards, and are, moreover, extensive beetroot-sugar manufacturers and distillers of potato spirits. The wealthier British aristocracy are, as yet, rather above that; but they, too, know how to make up for declining rents by lending their names to floaters of more or less shady joint-stock companies.

competition, and, as modern industry develops, they even see the moment approaching when they will completely disappear as an independent section of modern society, to be replaced, in manufactures, agriculture and commerce, by overlookers, bailiffs and shopmen.

In countries, like France, where the peasants constitute far more than half of the population, it was natural that writers who sided with the proletariat against the bourgeoisie, should use, in their criticism of the bourgeois *régime*, the standard of the peasant and petty bourgeois, and from the standpoint of these intermediate classes should take up the cudgels for the working class. Thus arose petty bourgeois Socialism. Sismondi was the head of this school, not only in France but also in England.

This school of Socialism dissected with great acuteness the contradictions in the conditions of modern production. It laid bare the hypocritical apologies of economists. It proved, incontrovertibly, the disastrous effects of machinery and division of labour; the concentration of capital and land in a few hands; overproduction and crises; it pointed out the inevitable ruin of the petty bourgeois and peasant, the misery of the proletariat, the anarchy in production, the crying inequalities in the distribution of wealth, the industrial war of extermination between nations, the dissolution of old moral bonds, of the old family relations, of the old nationalities.

In its positive aims, however, this form of Socialism aspires either to restoring the old means of production and of exchange, and with them the old property relations, and the old society, or to cramping the modern means of production and of exchange, within the frame work of the old property relations that have been, and were bound to be, exploded by those means. In either case, it is both reactionary and Utopian.

Its last words are: corporate guilds for manufacture; patriarchal relations in agriculture.

Ultimately, when stubborn historical facts had dispersed all intoxicating effects of self-deception, this form of Socialism ended in a miserable fit of the blues.

GERMAN OR 'TRUE' SOCIALISM

The Socialist and Communist literature of France, a literature that originated under the pressure of a bourgeoisie in power, and that was the expression of the struggle against this power, was introduced into Germany at a time when the bourgeoisie, in that country, had just begun its contest with feudal absolutism.

German philosophers, would-be philosophers, and *beaux esprits*, eagerly seized on this literature, only forgetting, that when these writings immigrated from France into Germany, French social conditions had not immigrated along with them. In contact with German social conditions, this French literature lost all its immediate practical significance, and assumed a purely literary aspect. Thus, to the German philosophers of the eighteenth century, the demands of the first French Revolution were nothing more than the demands of 'Practical Reason' in general, and the utterance of the will of the revolutionary French bourgeoisie signified in their eyes the laws of pure Will, of Will as it was bound to be, of true human Will generally.

The work of the German *literati* consisted solely in bringing the new French ideas into harmony with their ancient philosophical conscience, or rather, in annexing the French ideas without deserting their own philosophic point of view.

This annexation took place in the same way in which a foreign language is appropriated, namely by translation.

It is well known how the monks wrote silly lives of Catholic Saints *over* the manuscripts on which the classical works of ancient heathendom had been written. The German *literati* reversed this process with the profane French literature. They wrote their philosophical nonsense beneath the French original. For instance, beneath the French criticism of the economic functions of money, they wrote 'Alienation of Humanity', and beneath the French criticism of the bourgeois State they wrote, 'Dethronement of the Category of the General', and so forth.

The introduction of these philosophical phrases at the back of the French historical criticisms they dubbed 'Philosophy of Action', 'True Socialism', 'German Science of Socialism', 'Philosophical Foundation of Socialism', and so on.

The French Socialist and Communist literature was thus completely emasculated. And, since it ceased in the hands of the German to express the struggle of one class with the other, he felt conscious of having overcome 'French one-sidedness' and of representing, not true requirements, but the requirements of Truth, not the interests of the proletariat, but the interests of Human Nature, of Man in general, who belongs to no class, has no reality, who exists only in the misty realm of philosophical fantasy.

This German Socialism, which took its schoolboy task so seriously and solemnly, and extolled its poor stock-in-trade in such mountebank fashion, meanwhile gradually lost its pedantic innocence.

The fight of the German, and, especially, of the Prussian bourgeoisie, against feudal aristocracy and absolute monarchy, in other words, the liberal movement, became more earnest.

By this, the long wished-for opportunity was offered to 'True Socialism' of confronting the political movement with the socialist demands, of hurling the traditional anathemas against liberalism, against representative government, against bourgeois competition, bourgeois freedom of the press, bourgeois legislation, bourgeois liberty and equality, and of preaching to the masses that they had nothing to gain, and everything to lose, by this bourgeois movement. German Socialism forgot, in the nick of time, that the French criticism, whose silly echo it was, presupposed the existence of modern bourgeois society, with its corresponding economic conditions of existence, and the political constitution adapted thereto, the very things whose attainment was the object of the pending struggle in Germany.

To the absolute governments, with their following of parsons, professors, country squires and officials, it served as a welcome scarecrow against the threatening bourgeoisie.

It was a sweet finish after the bitter pills of floggings and bullets, with which these same governments, just at that time, dosed the German working-class risings.

While this 'True' Socialism thus served the governments as a weapon for fighting the German bourgeoisie, it, at the same time, directly represented a reactionary interest, the interest of the German Philistines. In Germany the *petty bourgeois* class, a *relique* of the sixteenth century, and since then constantly cropping up again under various forms, is the real social basis of the existing state of things.

To preserve this class, is to preserve the existing state of things in Germany. The industrial and political supremacy of the bourgeoisie threatens it with certain destruction; on the one hand, from the concentration of capital; on the other, from the rise of a revolutionary proletariat. 'True' Socialism appeared to kill these two birds with one stone. It spread like an epidemic.

The robe of speculative cobwebs, embroidered with flowers of rhetoric, steeped in the dew of sickly sentiment, this transcendental robe in which the German Socialists wrapped their sorry 'eternal truths' all skin and bone, served to wonderfully increase the sale of their goods amongst such a public.

And on its part, German Socialism recognized, more and more, its own calling as the bombastic representative of the petty bourgeois Philistine.

It proclaimed the German nation to be the model nation, and the German petty Philistine to be the typical man. To every villainous meanness of this model man it gave a hidden, higher, socialistic interpretation, the exact contrary of its real character. It went to the extreme length of directly opposing the 'brutally destructive' tendency of Communism, and of proclaiming its supreme and impartial contempt of all class struggles. With very few exceptions, all the so-called Socialist and Communist publications that now (1847) circulate in Germany belong to the domain of this foul and enervating literature.

CONSERVATIVE OR BOURGEOIS SOCIALISM

A part of the bourgeoisie is desirous of redressing social grievances, in order to secure the continued existence of bourgeois society.

To this section belong economists, philanthropists, humanitarians, improvers of the condition of the working class, organizers of charity, members of societies for the prevention of cruelty to animals, temperance fanatics, hole and corner reformers of every imaginable kind. This form of Socialism has, moreover, been worked out into complete systems.

We may cite Proudhon's *Philosophie de la Misère* as an example of this form.

The socialistic bourgeois want all the advantages of modern social conditions without the struggles and dangers necessarily resulting therefrom. They desire the existing state of society minus its revolutionary and disintegrating elements. They wish for a bourgeoisie without a proletariat. The bourgeoisie naturally conceives the world in which it is supreme to be the best; and bourgeois socialism develops this comfortable conception into various more or less complete systems. In requiring the proletariat to carry out such a system, and thereby to march straightway into the social New Jerusalem, it but requires in reality, that the proletariat should remain within the bounds of existing society, but should cast away all its hateful ideas concerning the bourgeoisie.

A second and more practical, but less systematic form of this socialism sought to depreciate every revolutionary movement in the eyes of the working class, by showing that no mere political reform, but only a change in the material conditions of existence in economical relations, could be of any advantage to them. By changes in the material conditions of existence, this form of Socialism, however, by no means understands abolition of the bourgeois relations of production, an abolition that can be effected only by a revolution, but administrative reforms, based on the continued existence of these relations; reforms, therefore, that in no respect affect the relations between capital and labour, but, at the best, lessen the cost, and simplify the administrative work, of bourgeois government.

Bourgeois Socialism attains adequate expression, when, and only when, it becomes a mere figure of speech.

Free trade: for the benefit of the working class. Protective duties: for the benefit of the working class. Prison Reform: for the benefit of the working class. This is the last word and the only seriously meant word of bourgeois Socialism.

It is summed up in the phrase: the bourgeois is a bourgeois – for the benefit of the working class.

CRITICAL-UTOPIAN SOCIALISM AND COMMUNISM

We do not here refer to that literature which, in every great modern revolution, has always given voice to the demands of the proletariat: such as the writings of Babeuf and others.

The first direct attempts of the proletariat to attain its own ends, made in times of universal excitement, when feudal society was being overthrown, these attempts necessarily failed, owing to the then undeveloped state of the proletariat, as well as to the absence of the economic conditions for its emancipation, conditions that had yet to be produced, and could be produced by the impending bourgeois epoch alone. The revolutionary literature that accompanied these first movements of the proletariat had necessarily a reactionary character. It inculcated universal asceticism and social levelling in its crudest form.

The Socialist and Communist systems properly so called, those of St Simon, Fourier, Owen and others, spring into existence in the early undeveloped period, described above, of the struggle between proletariat, and bourgeoisie, (see section I. Bourgeoisie and Proletariat.)

The founders of these systems see, indeed, the class antagonisms, as well as the action of the decomposing elements in the prevailing form of society. But the proletariat, as yet in its infancy, offers to them the spectacle of a class without any historical initiative or any independent political movement.

Since the development of class antagonism keeps even pace with the development of industry, the economic situation, as they find it, does not as yet offer to them the material conditions for the emancipation of the proletariat. They therefore search after a new social science, after new social laws, that are to create these conditions.

Historical action is to yield to their personal inventive action, historically created conditions of emancipation to fantastic ones, and the gradual, spontaneous class-organization of the proletariat to an organization of society specially contrived by these inventors. Future history resolves itself, in their eyes, into the propaganda and the practical carrying out of their social plans.

In the formation of their plans they are conscious of caring chiefly for the interests of the working class, as being the most suffering class. Only from the point of view of being the most suffering class does the proletariat exist for them.

The undeveloped state of the class struggle, as well as their own surroundings, cause Socialists of this kind to consider themselves far superior to all class antagonisms. They want to improve the condition of every member of society, even that of the most favoured. Hence, they habitually appeal to society at large, without distinction of class; nay, by preference, to the ruling class. For how can people, when once they understand their system, fail to see in it the best possible plan of the best possible state of society?

Hence, they reject all political, and especially all revolutionary action: they wish to attain their ends by peaceful means, and endeavour, by small experiments, necessarily doomed to failure, and by the force of example, to pave the way for the new social Gospel.

Such fantastic pictures of future society, painted at a time when the proletariat is still in a very undeveloped state, and has but a fantastic conception of its own position, correspond with the first instinctive yearnings of that class for a general reconstruction of society.

But these Socialist and Communist publications contain also a critical element. They attack every principle of existing society. Hence they are full of the most valuable materials for the enlightenment of the working class. The practical measures proposed in them, such as the abolition of the distinction between town and country, of the family, of the carrying on of industries for the account of private individuals, and of the wage system, the proclamation of social harmony, the conversion of the functions of the State into a mere superintendence of production, all these proposals point solely to the disappearance of class-antagonisms which were, at that time, only just cropping up, and which, in these publications, are recognized under their earliest, indistinct and undefined forms only. These proposals, therefore, are of a purely Utopian character.

The significance of Critical-Utopian Socialism and Communism bears an inverse relation to historical development. In proportion as the modern class struggle develops and takes definite shape, this fantastic standing apart from the contest, these fantastic attacks on it lose all practical value and all theoretical justification. Therefore, although the originators of these systems were, in many respects, revolutionary, their disciples have, in every case, formed mere reactionary sects. They hold fast by the original views of their masters, in opposition to the progressive historical development of the proletariat. They, therefore, endeavour, and that consistently, to deaden the class struggle and to reconcile the class antagonisms. They still dream of experimental realization of their social Utopias, of founding isolated 'phalanstères', of establishing 'Home Colonies', of setting up a 'Little Icaria'* – duodecimo editions of the New Jerusalem, and to realize all these castles in the air, they are compelled to appeal to the feelings and purses of the bourgeois. By degrees they sink into the category of the reactionary conservative Socialists depicted above, differing from these only by more systematic pedantry, and by their fanatical and superstitious belief in the miraculous effects of their social science.

They, therefore, violently oppose all political action on the part of the working class; such action, according to them, can only result from blind unbelief in the new Gospel.

The Owenites in England, and the Fourierists in France, respectively oppose the Chartists and the 'Réformistes'.

IV

POSITION OF THE COMMUNISTS IN RELATION TO THE VARIOUS EXISTING OPPOSITION PARTIES

Section II has made clear the relations of the Communists to the existing working-class parties, such as the Chartists in England and the Agrarian Reformers in America.

*Phalanstères were socialist colonies on the plan of Charles Fourier; Icaria was the name given by Cabet to his Utopia and, later on, to his American Communist colony.

The Communists fight for the attainment of the immediate aims, for the enforcement of the momentary interests of the working class; but in movement of the present, they also represent and take care of the future of that movement. In France the Communists ally themselves with the Social-Democrats*, against the conservative and radical bourgeoisie, reserving, however, the right to take up a critical position in regard to phrases and illusions traditionally handed down from the great Revolution.

In Switzerland they support the Radicals, without losing sight of the fact that this party consists of antagonistic elements, partly of Democratic Socialists, in the French sense, partly of radical bourgeois.

In Poland they support the party that insists on an agrarian revolution, as the prime condition for national emancipation, that party which fomented the insurrection of Cracow in 1846.

In Germany they fight with the bourgeoisie whenever it acts in a revolutionary way, against the absolute monarchy, the feudal squirearchy, and the petty bourgeoisie.

But they never cease, for a single instant, to instil into the working class the clearest possible recognition of the hostile antagonism between bourgeoisie and proletariat, in order that the German workers may straightway use, as so many weapons against the bourgeoisie, the social and political conditions that the bourgeoisie must necessarily introduce along with its supremacy, and in order that, after the fall of the reactionary classes in Germany, the fight against the bourgeoisie itself may immediately begin.

The Communists turn their attention chiefly to Germany, because that country is on the eve of a bourgeois revolution, that is bound to be carried out under more advanced conditions of European civilization, and with a much more developed proletariat, than that of England was in the seventeenth, and of

---

* The party then represented in parliament by Ledru-Rollin, in literature by Louis Blanc, in the daily press by the *Réforme*. The name of Social Democracy signified, with these its inventors, a section of the Democratic or Republican party more or less tinged with Socialism.

France in the eighteenth century, and because the bourgeois revolution in Germany will be but the prelude to an immediately following proletarian revolution.

In short, the Communists everywhere support every revolutionary movement against the existing social and political order of things.

In all these movements they bring to the front, as the leading question in each, the property question, no matter what its degree of development at the time.

Finally, they labour everywhere for the union and agreement of the democratic parties of all countries.

The Communists disdain to conceal their views and aims. They openly declare that their ends can be attained only by the forcible overthrow of all existing social conditions. Let the ruling classes tremble at a Communistic revolution. The proletarians have nothing to lose but their chains. They have a world to win.

Working men of all countries unite!

John Ruskin

John Ruskin (1819–1900) was the only son of a wealthy London wine merchant. Both of his parents were strict evangelicals and Ruskin's austere childhood is described memorably in his autobiography *Praeterita* (1889). Until going to Oxford in 1836, Ruskin was educated at home. His rather isolated early life was varied in ways that were to be important for his intellectual development by accompanying his father on business journeys throughout Britain and Europe. Ruskin established his reputation as a writer with the first volume of *Modern Painters* (1843), a defence of modern landscape painting centring on the work of Turner; a further four volumes were published between 1846 and 1860. *The Seven Lamps of Architecture* (1849) shows Ruskin moving towards the theory that art reflects the moral qualities of the age in which it is produced, the underlying theme of 'The Nature of Gothic' which was first published in the second volume of *The Stones of Venice* (3 vols, 1853). From this point Ruskin became increasingly concerned with social issues. The serialization of *Unto This Last* in the *Cornhill Magazine* (August–November 1860) was stopped because of readers' objections to Ruskin's views, though his attack on political economy was no more severe than those of Carlyle and Dickens, and the future society he envisaged was strongly paternalistic: many of the specific reforms proposed in *Unto This Last* are now accepted as unobjectionable features of welfare state societies. Ruskin continued to write and lecture on social topics. The lectures contained in *Crown of Wild Olives* are among the best of his work, while *Fors Clavigera* (1871–4), a series of monthly letters written to 'the workmen and labourers of Great Britain', though often neglected, is one of the most revealing, and moving, studies of class-consciousness in modern English literature. In 1869 Ruskin was appointed Slade Professor of Fine

Art at Oxford, and this position he used to publicize his increasingly idiosyncratic social and artistic ideals. The large sums of money he inherited were employed for the same purpose. He set up art museums, founded the Guild of St George to put into practice his theories of co-operative living and financed numerous social schemes. During the last years of his life, which were spent at Brantwood in the Lake District, he was subject to fits of depression bordering on insanity but it was also the period of his greatest influence, with his writings on art and society attracting followers throughout the world.

THE NATURE OF GOTHIC

If the reader will look back to the division of our subject which was made in the first chapter of the first volume, he will find that we are now about to enter upon the examination of that school of Venetian architecture which forms an intermediate step between the Byzantine and Gothic forms; but which I find may be conveniently considered in its connexion with the latter style. In order that we may discern the tendency of each step of this change, it will be wise in the outset to endeavour to form some general idea of its final result. We know already what the Byzantine architecture is from which the transition was made, but we ought to know something of the Gothic architecture into which it led. I shall endeavour therefore to give the reader in this chapter an idea, at once broad and definite, of the true nature of *Gothic* architecture, properly so called; not of that of Venice only, but of universal Gothic: for it will be one of the most interesting parts of our subsequent inquiry to find out how far Venetian architecture reached the universal or perfect type of Gothic, and how far it either fell short of it, or assumed foreign and independent forms.

The principal difficulty in doing this arises from the fact that every building of the Gothic period differs in some important respect from every other; and many include features which, if they occurred in other buildings, would not be considered Gothic at all; so that all we have to reason upon is merely, if I may be allowed so to express it, a greater or less degree of *Gothicness* in each building we examine. And it is this Gothicness, – the character which, according as it is found more or less in a building, makes it more or less Gothic, – of which I want to define the nature; and I feel the same kind of difficulty in doing so which would be encountered by any one who undertook to explain, for instance, the nature of Redness, without any actually red thing to point to, but only orange and purple things. Suppose he had only a piece of heather and a dead oak-leaf to do it with. He might say, the colour which is mixed with the yellow in this oak-leaf, and with the blue in this heather, would be red, if you had it separate; but it would be difficult, nevertheless, to make the abstraction perfectly intelligible: and it is so in a far greater degree to make the abstraction of the Gothic character intelligible, because that character itself is made up of many mingled ideas, and can consist only in their union. That is to say, pointed arches do not constitute Gothic, nor vaulted roofs, nor flying buttresses, nor grotesque sculptures; but all or some of these things, and many other things with them, when they come together so as to have life.

Observe also, that, in the definition proposed, I shall only endeavour to analyse the idea which I suppose already to exist in the reader's mind. We all have some notion, most of us a very determined one, of the meaning of the term Gothic, but I know that many persons have this idea in their minds without being able to define it: that is to say, understanding generally that Westminster Abbey is Gothic, and St Paul's is not, that Strasburg Cathedral is Gothic, and St Peter's is not, they have, nevertheless, no clear notion of what it is that they recognize in the one or miss in the other, such as would enable them to say how far the work at Westminster or Strasburg is good and pure of its kind; still less to say of any nondescript building, like St James's Palace or Windsor Castle, how much right Gothic element there is in it, and how much wanting. And I believe this inquiry to be a pleasant and profitable one; and that there will be found something more than usually interesting in tracing out this grey, shadowy, many-pinnacled image of the Gothic spirit within us; and discerning what fellowship there is between it and our Northern hearts. And if, at any point of the inquiry, I should interfere with any of the reader's previously formed conceptions, and use the term Gothic in any sense which he would not willingly attach to it, I do not ask him to accept, but only to examine and understand, my interpretation, as necessary to the intelligibility of what follows in the rest of the work.

We have, then, the Gothic character submitted to our analysis, just as the rough mineral is submitted to that of the chemist, entangled with many other foreign substances, itself perhaps in no place pure, or ever to be obtained or seen in purity for more than an instant; but nevertheless a thing of definite and separate nature, however inextricable or confused in appearance. Now observe: the chemist defines his mineral by two separate kinds of character; one external, its crystalline form, hardness, lustre, etc.; the other internal, the proportions and nature of its constituent atoms. Exactly in the same manner, we shall find that Gothic architecture has external forms and internal elements. Its elements are certain mental tendencies of the builders, legibly expressed in it; as fancifulness, love of variety, love of richness, and such others. Its external forms are pointed arches, vaulted roofs, etc. And unless both the elements and the forms are there, we have no right to call the style Gothic. It is not enough that it has the Form, if it have not also the power and life. It is not enough that it has the Power, if it have not the form. We must therefore inquire into each of these characters successively; and determine first, what is the Mental Expression, and secondly, what the Material Form of Gothic architecture, properly so called.

1st. Mental Power or Expression. What characters, we have to discover, did the Gothic builders love, or instinctively express in their work, as distinguished from all other builders?

Let us go back for a moment to our chemistry, and note that, in defining a mineral by its constituent parts, it is not one nor another of them, that can make up the mineral, but the union of all: for instance, it is neither in charcoal, nor in oxygen, nor in lime, that there is the making of chalk, but in the combination of all three in certain measures; they are all found in very different things from chalk, and there is nothing like chalk either in charcoal or in oxygen, but they are nevertheless necessary to its existence.

So in the various mental characters which make up the soul of Gothic. It is not one nor another that produces it; but their union in certain measures. Each one of them is found in many other architectures beside Gothic; but Gothic cannot exist where they are not found, or, at least, where their place is not in some way supplied. Only there is this great difference between the composition of the mineral and of the architectural style, that if we withdraw one of its elements from the stone, its form is utterly changed, and its existence as such and such a mineral is destroyed; but if we withdraw one of its mental elements from the Gothic style, it is only a little less Gothic than it was before, and the union of two or three of its elements is enough already to bestow a certain Gothicness of character, which gains in intensity as we add the others, and loses as we again withdraw them.

I believe, then, that the characteristic or moral elements of Gothic are the following, placed in the order of their importance:

1. Savageness.
2. Changefulness.
3. Naturalism.
4. Grotesqueness.
5. Rigidity.
6. Redundance.

These characters are here expressed as belonging to the building; as belonging to the builder, they would be expressed thus:— 1. Savageness or Rudeness. 2. Love of Change. 3. Love of Nature. 4. Disturbed Imagination. 5. Obstinacy. 6. Generosity. And I repeat, that the withdrawal of any one, or any two, will not at once destroy the Gothic character of a building, but the removal of a majority of them will. I shall proceed to examine them in their order.

(1.) SAVAGENESS. I am not sure when the word 'Gothic' was first generically applied to the architecture of the North; but

I presume that, whatever the date of its original usage, it was intended to imply reproach, and express the barbaric character of the nations among whom that architecture arose. It never implied that they were literally of Gothic lineage, far less that their architecture had been originally invented by the Goths themselves; but it did imply that they and their buildings together exhibited a degree of sternness and rudeness, which, in contradistinction to the character of Southern and Eastern nations, appeared like a perpetual reflection of the contrast between the Goth and the Roman in their first encounter. And when that fallen Roman, in the utmost impotence of his luxury, and insolence of his guilt, became the model for the imitation of civilized Europe, at the close of the so-called Dark ages, the word Gothic became a term of unmitigated contempt, not unmixed with aversion. From that contempt, by the exertion of the antiquaries and architects of this century, Gothic architecture has been sufficiently vindicated; and perhaps some among us, in our admiration of the magnificent science of its structure, and sacredness of its expression, might desire that the term of ancient reproach should be withdrawn, and some other, of more apparent honourableness, adopted in its place. There is no chance, as there is no need, of such a substitution. As far as the epithet was used scornfully, it was used falsely; but there is no reproach in the word, rightly understood; on the contrary, there is a profound truth, which the instinct of mankind almost unconsciously recognizes. It is true, greatly and deeply true, that the architecture of the North is rude and wild; but it is not true, that, for this reason, we are to condemn it, or despise. Far otherwise: I believe it is in this very character that it deserves our profoundest reverence.

The charts of the world which have been drawn up by modern science have thrown into a narrow space the expression of a vast amount of knowledge, but I have never yet seen any one pictorial enough to enable the spectator to imagine the kind of contrast in physical character which exists between Northern and Southern countries. We know the differences in detail, but we have not that broad glance and grasp which would enable us to feel them in their fulness. We know that gentians grow on the

Alps, and olives on the Apennines; but we do not enough conceive for ourselves that variegated mosaic of the world's surface which a bird sees in its migration, that difference between the district of the gentian and of the olive which the stork and the swallow see far off, as they lean upon the sirocco wind. Let us, for a moment, try to raise ourselves even above the level of their flight, and imagine the Mediterranean lying beneath us like an irregular lake, and all its ancient promontories sleeping in the sun: here and there an angry spot of thunder, a grey stain of storm, moving upon the burning field; and here and there a fixed wreath of white volcano smoke, surrounded by its circle of ashes; but for the most part a great peacefulness of light, Syria and Greece, Italy and Spain, laid like pieces of a golden pavement into the sea-blue, chased, as we stoop nearer to them, with bossy beaten work of mountain chains, and glowing softly with terraced gardens, and flowers heavy with frankincense, mixed among masses of laurel, and orange, and plumy palm, that abate with their grey-green shadows the burning of the marble rocks, and of the ledges of porphyry sloping under lucent sand. Then let us pass farther towards the north, until we see the orient colours change gradually into a vast belt of rainy green, where the pastures of Switzerland, and poplar valleys of France, and dark forests of the Danube and Carpathians stretch from the mouths of the Loire to those of the Volga, seen through clefts in grey swirls of rain-cloud and flaky veils of the mist of the brooks, spreading low along the pasture lands: and then, farther north still, to see the earth heave into mighty masses of leaden rock and heathy moor, bordering with a broad waste of gloomy purple that belt of field and wood, and splintering into irregular and grisly islands amidst the northern seas, beaten by storm, and chilled by ice-drift, and tormented by furious pulses of contending tide, until the roots of the last forests fail from among the hill ravines, and the hunger of the north wind bites their peaks into barrenness; and, at last, the wall of ice, durable like iron, sets, deathlike, its white teeth against us out of the polar twilight. And, having once traversed in thought this gradation of the zoned iris of the earth in all its material vastness, let us go down nearer to it, and watch the parallel change in the belt of animal life; the multitudes of swift and brilliant creatures that glance in the air and sea, or tread the sands of the southern zone; striped zebras and spotted leopards, glistening serpents, and birds arrayed in purple and scarlet. Let us contrast their delicacy and brilliancy of colour, and swiftness of motion, with the frost-cramped strength, and shaggy covering, and dusky plumage of the northern tribes; contrast the Arabian horse with the Shetland, the tiger and leopard with the wolf and bear, the antelope with the elk, the bird of paradise with the osprey; and then, submissively acknowledging the great laws by which the earth and all that it bears are ruled throughout their being, let us not condemn, but rejoice in the expression by man of his own rest in the statutes of the lands that gave him birth. Let us watch him with reverence as he sets side by side the burning gems, and smooths with soft sculpture the jasper pillars, that are to reflect a ceaseless sunshine, and rise into a cloudless sky: but not with less reverence let us stand by him, when, with rough strength and hurried stroke, he smites an uncouth animation out of the rocks which he has torn from among the moss of the moorland, and heaves into the darkened air the pile of iron buttress and rugged wall, instinct with work of an imagination as wild and wayward as the northern sea; creatures of ungainly shape and rigid limb, but full of wolfish life; fierce as the winds that beat, and changeful as the clouds that shade them.

There is, I repeat, no degradation, no reproach in this, but all dignity and honourableness: and we should err grievously in refusing either to recognize as an essential character of the existing architecture of the North, or to admit as a desirable character in that which it yet may be, this wildness of thought, and roughness of work; this look of mountain brotherhood between the cathedral and the Alp; this magnificence of sturdy power, put forth only the more energetically because the fine finger-touch was chilled away by the frosty wind, and the eye dimmed by the moor-mist, or blinded by the hail; this out-speaking of the strong spirit of men who may not gather redundant fruitage from the earth, nor bask in dreamy benignity of sunshine, but must break the rock for bread, and cleave the forest for fire, and show, even in what they did for their delight, some of the hard habits of the arm and heart that grew on them as they swung the axe or pressed the plough.

If, however, the savageness of Gothic architecture, merely as an expression of its origin among Northern nations, may be considered, in some sort, a noble character, it possesses a higher nobility still, when considered as an index, not of climate, but of religious principle.

In the thirteenth and fourteenth paragraphs of Chapter XXI of the first volume of this work, it was noticed that the systems of architectural ornament, properly so called, might be divided into three: 1. Servile ornament, in which the execution or power of the inferior workman is entirely subjected to the intellect of the higher; 2. Constitutional ornament, in which the executive inferior power is, to a certain point, emancipated and independent, having a will of its own, yet confessing its inferiority and rendering obedience to higher powers; and 3. Revolutionary ornament, in which no executive inferiority is admitted at all. I must here explain the nature of these divisions at somewhat greater length.

Of Servile ornament, the principal schools are the Greek, Ninevite, and Egyptian; but their servility is of different kinds. The Greek master-workman was far advanced in knowledge and power above the Assyrian or Egyptian. Neither he nor those for whom he worked could endure the appearance of imperfection in anything; and, therefore, what ornament he appointed to be done by those beneath him was composed of mere geometrical forms – balls, ridges, and perfectly symmetrical foliage – which could be executed with absolute precision by line and rule, and were as perfect in their way, when completed, as his own figure sculpture. The Assyrian and Egyptian, on the contrary, less cognisant of accurate form in anything, were content to allow their figure sculpture to be executed by inferior workmen, but lowered the method of its treatment to a standard which every workman could reach, and then trained him by discipline so rigid, that there was no chance of his falling beneath the standard appointed. The Greek gave to the lower workman no subject which he could not perfectly execute. The

Assyrian gave him subjects which he could only execute imperfectly, but fixed a legal standard for his imperfection. The workman was, in both systems, a slave.*

But in the medieval, or especially Christian, system of ornament, this slavery is done away with altogether; Christianity having recognized, in small things as well as great, the individual value of every soul. But it not only recognizes its value; it confesses its imperfection, in only bestowing dignity upon the acknowledgment of unworthiness. That admission of lost power and fallen nature, which the Greek or Ninevite felt to be intensely painful, and, as far as might be, altogether refused, the Christian makes daily and hourly, contemplating the fact of it without fear, as tending, in the end, to God's greater glory. Therefore, to every spirit which Christianity summons to her service, her exhortation is: Do what you can, and confess frankly what you are unable to do; neither let your effort be shortened for fear of failure, nor your confession silenced for fear of shame. And it is, perhaps, the principal admirableness of the Gothic schools of architecture, that they thus receive the results of the labour of inferior minds; and out of fragments full of imperfection, and betraying that imperfection in every touch, indulgently raise up a stately and unaccusable whole.

But the modern English mind has this much in common with that of the Greek, that it intensely desires, in all things, the utmost completion or perfection compatible with their nature. This is a noble character in the abstract, but becomes ignoble when it causes us to forget the relative dignities of that nature itself, and to prefer the perfectness of the lower nature to the imperfection of the higher; not considering that as, judged by

*The third kind of ornament, the Renaissance, is that in which the inferior detail becomes principal, the executor of every minor portion being required to exhibit skill and possess knowledge as great as that which is possessed by the master of the design; and in the endeavour to endow him with this skill and knowledge, his own original power is overwhelmed, and the whole building becomes a wearisome exhibition of well-educated imbecility. We must fully inquire into the nature of this form of error, when we arrive at the examination of the Renaissance schools.

such a rule, all the brute animals would be preferable to man, because more perfect in their functions and kind, and yet are always held inferior to him, so also in the works of man, those which are more perfect in their kind are always inferior to those which are, in their nature, liable to more faults and shortcomings. For the finer the nature, the more flaws it will show through the clearness of it; and it is a law of this universe, that the best things shall be seldomest seen in their best form. The wild grass grows well and strongly, one year with another; but the wheat is, according to the greater nobleness of its nature, liable to the bitterer blight. And therefore, while in all things that we see or do, we are to desire perfection, and strive for it, we are nevertheless not to set the meaner thing, in its narrow accomplishment, above the nobler thing, in its mighty progress; not to esteem smooth minuteness above shattered majesty; not to prefer mean victory to honourable defeat; not to lower the level of our aim, that we may the more surely enjoy the complacency of success. But, above all, in our dealings with the souls of other men, we are to take care of how we check, by severe requirement or narrow caution, efforts which might otherwise lead to a noble issue; and, still more, how we withhold our admiration from great excellencies, because they are mingled with rough faults. Now, in the make and nature of every man, however rude or simple, whom we employ in manual labour, there are some powers for better things; some tardy imagination, torpid capacity of emotion, tottering steps of thought, there are, even at the worst; and in most cases it is all our own fault that they *are* tardy or torpid. But they cannot be strengthened, unless we are content to take them in their feebleness, and unless we prize and honour them in their imperfection above the best and most perfect manual skill. And this is what we have to do with all our labourers; to look for the *thoughtful* part of them, and get that out of them, whatever we lose for it, whatever faults and errors we are obliged to take with it. For the best that is in them cannot manifest itself, but in company with much error. Understand this clearly: You can teach a man to draw a straight line, and to cut one; to strike a curved line, and to carve it; and to copy and carve any number of given lines or forms, with admirable speed and perfect precision; and you find his work perfect of its kind: but if you ask him to think about any of those forms, to consider if he cannot find any better in his own head, he stops; his execution becomes hesitating; he thinks, and ten to one he thinks wrong; ten to one he makes a mistake in the first touch he gives to his work as a thinking being. But you have made a man of him for all that. He was only a machine before, an animated tool.

And observe, you are put to stern choice in this matter. You must either make a tool of the creature, or a man of him. You cannot make both. Men were not intended to work with the accuracy of tools, to be precise and perfect in all their actions. If you will have that precision out of them, and make their fingers measure degrees like cog-wheels, and their arms strike curves like compasses, you must unhumanize them. All the energy of their spirits must be given to make cogs and compasses of themselves. All their attention and strength must go to the accomplishment of the mean act. The eye of the soul must be bent upon the finger-point, and the soul's force must fill all the invisible nerves that guide it, ten hours a day, that it may not err from its steely precision, and so soul and sight be worn away, and the whole human being be lost at last – a heap of sawdust, so far as its intellectual work in this world is concerned: saved only by its Heart, which cannot go into the form of cogs and compasses, but expands, after the ten hours are over, into fireside humanity. On the other hand, if you will make a man of the working creature, you cannot make a tool. Let him but begin to imagine, to think, to try to do anything worth doing; and the engine-turned precision is lost at once. Out come all his roughness, all his dullness, all his incapability; shame upon shame, failure upon failure, pause after pause: but out comes the whole majesty of him also; and we know the height of it only when we see the clouds settling upon him. And, whether the clouds be bright or dark, there will be transfiguration behind and within them.

And now, reader, look round this English room of yours, about which you have been proud so often, because the work of it was so good and strong, and the ornaments of it so finished.

Examine again all those accurate mouldings, and perfect polishings, and unerring adjustments of the seasoned wood and tempered steel. Many a time you have exulted over them, and thought how great England was, because her slightest work was done so thoroughly. Alas! if read rightly, these perfectnesses are signs of a slavery in our England a thousand times more bitter and more degrading than that of the scourged African, or helot Greek. Men may be beaten, chained, tormented, yoked like cattle, slaughtered like summer flies, and yet remain in one sense, and the best sense, free. But to smother their souls with them, to blight and hew into rotting pollards the suckling branches of their human intelligence, to make the flesh and skin which, after the worm's work on it, is to see God, into leathern thongs to yoke machinery with, – this is to be slave-masters indeed; and there might be more freedom in England, though her feudal lords' lightest words were worth men's lives, and though the blood of the vexed husbandman dropped in the furrows of her fields, than there is while the animation of her multitudes is sent like fuel to feed the factory smoke, and the strength of them is given daily to be wasted into the fineness of a web, or racked into the exactness of a line.

And, on the other hand, go forth again to gaze upon the old cathedral front, where you have smiled so often at the fantastic ignorance of the old sculptors: examine once more those ugly goblins, and formless monsters, and stern statues, anatomiless and rigid; but do not mock at them, for they are signs of the life and liberty of every workman who struck the stone; a freedom of thought, and rank in scale of being, such as no laws, no charters, no charities can secure; but which it must be the first aim of all Europe at this day to regain for her children.

Let me not be thought to speak wildly or extravagantly. It is verily this degradation of the operative into a machine, which, more than any other evil of the times, is leading the mass of the nations everywhere into vain, incoherent, destructive struggling for a freedom of which they cannot explain the nature to themselves. Their universal outcry against wealth, and against nobility, is not forced from them either by the pressure of famine, or the sting of mortified pride. These do much, and have done much in all ages; but the foundations of society were never yet shaken as they are at this day. It is not that men are ill fed, but that they have no pleasure in the work by which they make their bread, and therefore look to wealth as the only means of pleasure. It is not that men are pained by the scorn of the upper classes, but they cannot endure their own; for they feel that the kind of labour to which they are condemned is verily a degrading one, and makes them less than men. Never had the upper classes so much sympathy with the lower, or charity for them, as they have at this day, and yet never were they so much hated by them: for, of old, the separation between the noble and the poor was merely a wall built by law; now it is a veritable difference in level of standing, a precipice between upper and lower grounds in the field of humanity, and there is pestilential air at the bottom of it. I know not if a day is ever to come when the nature of right freedom will be understood, and when men will see that to obey another man, to labour for him, yield reverence to him or to his place, is not slavery. It is often the best kind of liberty, – liberty from care. The man who says to one, Go, and he goeth, and to another, Come, and he cometh, has, in most cases, more sense of restraint and difficulty than the man who obeys him. The movements of the one are hindered by the burden on his shoulder; of the other by the bridle on his lips: there is no way by which the burden may be lightened; but we need not suffer from the bridle if we do not champ at it. To yield reverence to another, to hold ourselves and our likes at his disposal, is not slavery; often it is the noblest state in which a man can live in this world. There is, indeed, a reverence which is servile, that is to say, irrational or selfish: but there is also noble reverence, that is to say, reasonable and loving; and a man is never so noble as when he is reverent in this kind; nay, even if the feeling pass the bounds of mere reason, so that it be loving, a man is raised by it. Which had, in reality, most of the serf nature in him, – the Irish peasant who was lying in wait yesterday for his landlord, with his musket muzzle thrust through the ragged hedge; or that old mountain servant, who two hundred years ago, at Inverkeithing, gave up his own life and the lives of his seven sons for his chief? – as each fell, calling forth his brother to the death, 'Another for Hector!' And therefore, in all ages and all countries, reverence has been paid and sacrifice made by men to each other, not only without complaint, but rejoicingly; and famine, and peril, and sword, and all evil, and all shame, have been borne willingly in the causes of masters and kings; for all these gifts of the heart ennobled the men who gave, not less than the men who received them, and nature prompted, and God rewarded the sacrifice. But to feel their souls withering within them, unthanked, to find their whole being sunk into an unrecognized abyss, to be counted off into a heap of mechanism numbered with its wheels, and weighed with its hammer strokes – this, nature bade not, – this, God blesses not, – this, humanity for no long time is able to endure.

We have much studied and much perfected, of late, the great civilized invention of the division of labour; only we give it a false name. It is not, truly speaking, the labour that is divided; but the men: – Divided into mere segments of men – broken into small fragments and crumbs of life; so that all the little piece of intelligence that is left in a man is not enough to make a pin, or a nail, but exhausts itself in making the point of a pin or the head of a nail. Now it is a good and desirable thing, truly, to make many pins in a day; but if we could only see with what crystal sand their points were polished, – sand of human soil, much to be magnified before it can be discerned for what it is – we should think there might be some loss in it also. And the great cry that rises from all our manufacturing cities, louder than their furnace blast, is all in very deed for this, – that we manufacture everything there except men; we blanch cotton, and strengthen steel, and refine sugar, and shape pottery; but to brighten, to strengthen, to refine, or to form a single living spirit, never enters into our estimate of advantages. And all the evil to which that cry is urging our myriads can be met only in one way: not by teaching nor preaching, for to teach them is but to show them their misery, and to preach to them, if we do nothing more than preach, is to mock at it. It can be met only by a right understanding, on the part of all classes, of what kinds of labour are good for men, raising them, and making them happy; by a determined sacrifice of such convenience, or beauty, or cheapness as is to be got only by the degradation of the workman; and by equally determined demand for the products and results of healthy and ennobling labour.

And how, it will be asked, are these products to be recognized, and this demand to be regulated? Easily: by the observance of three broad and simple rules:

1. Never encourage the manufacture of any article not absolutely necessary, in the production of which *Invention* has no share.

2. Never demand an exact finish for its own sake, but only for some practical or noble end.

3. Never encourage imitation or copying of any kind, except for the sake of preserving records of great works.

The second of these principles is the only one which directly rises out of the consideration of our immediate subject; but I shall briefly explain the meaning and extent of the first also, reserving the enforcement of the third for another place.

1. Never encourage the manufacture of anything not necessary, in the production of which invention has no share.

For instance. Glass beads are utterly unnecessary, and there is no design or thought employed in their manufacture. They are formed by first drawing out the glass into rods; these rods are chopped up into fragments of the size of beads by the human hand, and the fragments are then rounded in the furnace. The men who chop up the rods sit at their work all day, their hands vibrating with a perpetual and exquisitely timed palsy, and the beads dropping beneath their vibration like hail. Neither they, nor the men who draw out the rods or fuse the fragments, have the smallest occasion for the use of any single human faculty; and every young lady, therefore, who buys glass beads is engaged in the slave-trade, and in a much more cruel one than that which we have so long been endeavouring to put down.

But glass cups and vessels may become the subjects of exquisite invention; and if in buying these we pay for the invention, that is to say, for the beautiful form, or colour, or engraving, and not for mere finish of execution, we are doing good to humanity.

So, again, the cutting of precious stones, in all ordinary cases, requires little exertion of any mental faculty; some tact and judgement in avoiding flaws, and so on, but nothing to bring out the whole mind. Every person who wears cut jewels merely for the sake of their value is, therefore, a slave-driver.

But the working of the goldsmith, and the various designing of grouped jewellery and enamel-work, may become the subject of the most noble human intelligence. Therefore, money spent in the purchase of well-designed plate, of precious engraved vases, cameos, or enamels, does good to humanity; and, in work of this kind, jewels may be employed to heighten its splendour; and their cutting is then a price paid for the attainment of a noble end, and thus perfectly allowable.

I shall perhaps press this law farther elsewhere, but our immediate concern is chiefly with the second, namely, never to demand an exact finish, when it does not lead to a noble end. For observe, I have only dwelt upon the rudeness of Gothic, or any other kind of imperfectness, as admirable, where it was impossible to get design or thought without it. If you are to have the thought of a rough and untaught man, you must have it in a rough and untaught way; but from an educated man, who can without effort express his thoughts in an educated way, take the graceful expression, and be thankful. Only *get* the thought, and do not silence the peasant because he cannot speak good grammar, or until you have taught him his grammar. Grammar and refinement are good things, both, only be sure of the better thing first. And thus in art, delicate finish is desirable from the greatest masters, and is always given by them. In some places Michael Angelo, Leonardo, Phidias, Perugino, Turner, all finished with the most exquisite care; and the finish they give always leads to the fuller accomplishment of their noble purposes. But lower men than these cannot finish, for it requires consummate knowledge to finish consummately, and then we must take their thoughts as they are able to give them. So the rule is simple: Always look for invention first, and after that, for such execution as will help the invention, and as the inventor is capable of without painful effort, and *no more*. Above all, demand no refinement of execution where there is no thought, for that is slaves' work, unredeemed. Rather choose rough work than smooth work, so only that the practical purpose be answered, and never imagine there is reason to be proud of anything that may be accomplished by patience and sand-paper.

I shall only give one example, which however will show the reader what I mean, from the manufacture already alluded to, that of glass. Our modern glass is exquisitely clear in its substance, true in its form, accurate in its cutting. We are proud of this. We ought to be ashamed of it. The old Venice glass was muddy, inaccurate in all its forms, and clumsily cut, if at all. And the old Venetian was justly proud of it. For there is this difference between the English and Venetian workman, that the former thinks only of accurately matching his patterns, and getting his curves perfectly true and his edges perfectly sharp, and becomes a mere machine for rounding curves and sharpening edges; while the old Venetian cared not a whit whether his edges were sharp or not, but he invented a new design for every glass that he made, and never moulded a handle or a lip without a new fancy in it. And therefore, though some Venetian glass is ugly and clumsy enough when made by clumsy and uninventive workmen, other Venetian glass is so lovely in its forms that no price is too great for it; and we never see the same form in it twice. Now you cannot have the finish and the varied form too. If the workman is thinking about his edges, he cannot be thinking of his design; if of his design, he cannot think of his edges. Choose whether you will pay for the lovely form or the perfect finish, and choose at the same moment whether you will make the worker a man or a grindstone.

Nay, but the reader interrupts me, 'If the workman can design beautifully, I would not have him kept at the furnace. Let him be taken away and made a gentleman, and have a studio, and design his glass there, and I will have it blown and cut for him by common workmen, and so I will have my design and my finish too.'

All ideas of this kind are founded upon two mistaken suppositions: the first, that one man's thoughts can be, or ought to be, executed by another man's hands; the second, that manual labour is a degradation, when it is governed by intellect.

On a large scale, and in work determinable by line and rule, it is indeed both possible and necessary that the thoughts of one man should be carried out by the labour of others; in this sense I have already defined the best architecture to be the expression of the mind of manhood by the hands of childhood. But on a smaller scale, and in a design which cannot be mathematically defined, one man's thoughts can never be expressed by another: and the difference between the spirit of touch of the man who is inventing, and of the man who is obeying directions, is often all the difference between a great and a common work of art. How wide the separation is between original and second-hand execution, I shall endeavour to show elsewhere; it is not so much to our purpose here as to mark the other and more fatal error of despising manual labour when governed by intellect; for it is no less fatal an error to despise it when thus regulated by intellect, than to value it for its own sake. We are always in these days endeavouring to separate the two; we want one man to be always thinking, and another to be always working, and we call one a gentleman, and the other an operative; whereas the workman ought often to be thinking, and the thinker often to be working, and both should be gentlemen, in the best sense. As it is, we make both ungentle, the one envying, the other despising, his brother; and the mass of society is made up of morbid thinkers, and miserable workers. Now it is only by labour that thought can be made healthy, and only by thought that labour can be made happy, and the two cannot be separated with impunity. It would be well if all of us were good handicraftsmen in some kind, and the dishonour of manual labour done away with altogether; so that though there should still be a trenchant distinction of race between nobles and commoners, there should not, among the latter, be a trenchant distinction of employment, as between idle and working men, or between men of liberal and illiberal professions. All professions should be liberal, and there should be less pride felt in peculiarity of employment, and more in excellence of achievement. And yet more, in each several profession, no master should be too proud to do its hardest work. The painter should grind his own colours; the architect work in the mason's yard with his men; the master-manufacturer be himself a more skilful operative than any man in his mills; and the distinction between one man and another be only in experience and skill, and the authority and wealth which these must naturally and justly obtain.

I should be led far from the matter in hand, if I were to pursue this interesting subject. Enough, I trust, has been said to show the reader that the rudeness or imperfection which at first rendered the term 'Gothic' one of reproach is indeed, when rightly understood, one of the most noble characters of Christian architecture, and not only a noble but an *essential* one. It seems a fantastic paradox, but it is nevertheless a most important truth, that no architecture can be truly noble which is *not* imperfect. And this is easily demonstrable. For since the architect, whom we will suppose capable of doing all in perfection, cannot execute the whole with his own hands, he must either make slaves of his workmen in the old Greek, and present English fashion, and level his work to a slave's capacities, which is to degrade it; or else he must take his workmen as he finds them, and let them show their weaknesses together with their strength, which will involve the Gothic imperfection, but render the whole work as noble as the intellect of the age can make it.

But the principle may be stated more broadly still. I have confined the illustration of it to architecture, but I must not leave it as if true of architecture only. Hitherto I have used the words imperfect and perfect merely to distinguish between work grossly unskilful, and work executed with average precision and science; and I have been pleading that any degree of unskilfulness should be admitted, so only that the labourer's mind had room for expression. But, accurately speaking, no good work whatever can be perfect, and *the demand for perfection is always a sign of a misunderstanding of the ends of art*.

This, for two reasons, both based on everlasting laws. The first, that no great man ever stops working till he has reached his point of failure: that is to say, his mind is always far in advance of his powers of execution, and the latter will now and then give way in trying to follow it; besides that he will always give to the inferior portions of his work only such inferior attention as they require; and according to his greatness he becomes so accustomed to the feeling of dissatisfaction with the best he can do, that in moments of lassitude or anger with himself he will not care though the beholder be dissatisfied also. I believe there has only been one man who would not acknowledge this necessity, and strove always to reach perfection, Leonardo; the end of his vain effort being merely that he would take ten years to a picture and leave it unfinished. And therefore, if we are to have great men working at all, or less men doing their best, the work will be imperfect, however beautiful. Of human work none but what is bad can be perfect, in its own bad way.*

The second reason is, that imperfection is in some sort essential to all that we know of life. It is the sign of life in a mortal body, that is to say, of a state of progress and change. Nothing that lives is, or can be, rigidly perfect; part of it is decaying, part nascent. The foxglove blossom – a third part bud, a third part past, a third part in full bloom, – is a type of the life of this world. And in all things that live there are certain irregularities and deficiencies which are not only signs of life, but sources of beauty. No human face is exactly the same in its lines on each side, no leaf perfect in its lobes, no branch in its symmetry. All admit irregularity as they imply change; and to banish imperfection is to destroy expression, to check exertion, to paralyse vitality. All things are literally better, lovelier, and more beloved for the imperfections which have been divinely appointed, that the law of human life may be Effort, and the law of human judgement, Mercy.

Accept this then for a universal law, that neither architecture nor any other noble work of man can be good unless it be imperfect; and let us be prepared for the otherwise strange fact, which we shall discern clearly as we approach the period of the Renaissance, that the first cause of the fall of the arts of Europe was a relentless requirement of perfection, incapable alike either of being silenced by veneration for greatness, or softened into forgiveness of simplicity.

*The Elgin marbles are supposed by many persons to be 'perfect'. In the most important portions they indeed approach perfection, but only there. The draperies are unfinished, the hair and wool of the animals are unfinished, and the entire bas-reliefs of the frieze are roughly cut.

Thus far then of the Rudeness or Savageness, which is the first mental element of Gothic architecture. It is an element in many other healthy architectures also, as the Byzantine and Romanesque; but true Gothic cannot exist without it.

The second mental element above named was CHANGE-FULNESS, or Variety.

I have already enforced the allowing independent operation to the inferior workman, simply as a duty *to him*, and as ennobling the architecture by rendering it more Christian. We have now to consider what reward we obtain for the performance of this duty, namely, the perpetual variety of every feature of the building.

Wherever the workman is utterly enslaved, the parts of the building must of course be absolutely like each other; for the perfection of his execution can only be reached by exercising him in doing one thing, and giving him nothing else to do. The degree in which the workman is degraded may be thus known at a glance, by observing whether the several parts of the building are similar or not; and if, as in Greek work, all the capitals are alike, and all the mouldings unvaried, then the degradation is complete; if, as in Egyptian or Ninevite work, though the manner of executing certain figures is always the same, the order of design is perpetually varied, the degradation is less total; if, as in Gothic work, there is perpetual change both in design and execution, the workman must have been altogether set free.

How much the beholder gains from the liberty of the labourer may perhaps be questioned in England, where one of the strongest instincts in nearly every mind is that Love of Order which makes us desire that our house windows should pair like our carriage horses, and allows us to yield our faith unhesitatingly to architectural theories which fix a form for everything, and forbid variation from it. I would not impeach love of order: it is one of the most useful elements of the English mind; it helps us in our commerce and in all purely practical matters; and it is in many cases one of the foundation stones of morality. Only do not let us suppose that love of order is love of art. It is true that order, in its highest sense, is one of the necessities of art, just as time is a necessity of music; but love of order has no more to do with our right enjoyment of architecture or painting, than love of punctuality with the appreciation of an opera. Experience, I fear, teaches us that accurate and methodical habits in daily life are seldom characteristic of those who either quickly perceive or richly possess, the creative powers of art; there is, however, nothing inconsistent between the two instincts, and nothing to hinder us from retaining our business habits, and yet fully allowing and enjoying the noblest gifts of Invention. We already do so, in every other branch of art except architecture, and we only do *not* so there because we have been taught that it would be wrong. Our architects gravely inform us that, as there are four rules of arithmetic, there are five orders of architecture; we, in our simplicity, think that this sounds consistent, and believe them. They inform us also that there is one proper form for Corinthian capitals, another for Doric, and another for Ionic. We, considering that there is also a proper form for the letters A, B, and C, think that this also sounds consistent, and accept the proposition. Understanding, therefore, that one form of the said capitals is proper, and no other, and having a conscientious horror of all impropriety, we allow the architect to provide us with the said capitals, of the proper form, in such and such a quantity, and in all other points to take care that the legal forms are observed; which having done, we rest in forced confidence that we are well housed.

But our higher instincts are not deceived. We take no pleasure in the building provided for us, resembling that which we take in a new book or a new picture. We may be proud of its size, complacent in its correctness, and happy in its convenience. We may take the same pleasure in its symmetry and workmanship as in a well-ordered room, or a skilful piece of manufacture. And this we suppose to be all the pleasure that architecture was ever intended to give us. The idea of reading a building as we would read Milton or Dante, and getting the same kind of delight out of the stones as out of the stanzas, never enters our mind for a moment. And for good reason; – There is indeed rhythm in the verses, quite as strict as the symmetries or rhythm of the architecture, and a thousand times more beautiful, but there is something else than rhythm. The verses were neither made to order, nor to match, as the capitals were; and we have therefore a kind of pleasure in them other than a sense of propriety. But it requires a strong effort of common sense to shake ourselves quit of all that we have been taught for the last two centuries, and wake to the perception of a truth just as simple and certain as it is new: that great art, whether expressing itself in words, colours, or stones, does *not* say the same thing over and over again; that the merit of architectural, as of every other art, consists in its saying new and different things; that to repeat itself is no more a characteristic of genius in marble than it is of genius in print; and that we may, without offending any laws of good taste, require of an architect, as we do of a novelist, that he should be not only correct, but entertaining.

Yet all this is true, and self-evident; only hidden from us, as many other self-evident things are, by false teaching. Nothing is a great work of art, for the production of which either rules or models can be given. Exactly so far as architecture works on known rules, and from given models, it is not an art, but a manufacture; and it is, of the two procedures, rather less rational (because more easy) to copy capitals or mouldings from Phidias, and call ourselves architects, than to copy heads and hands from Titian, and call ourselves painters.

Let us then understand at once that change or variety is as much a necessity to the human heart and brain in buildings as in books; that there is no merit, though there is some occasional use, in monotony; and that we must no more expect to derive either pleasure or profit from an architecture whose ornaments are of one pattern, and whose pillars are of one proportion, than we should out of a universe in which the clouds were all of one shape, and the trees all of one size.

And this we confess in deeds, though not in words. All the pleasure which the people of the nineteenth century take in art, is in pictures, sculpture, minor objects of virtù, or medieval architecture, which we enjoy under the term picturesque: no pleasure is taken anywhere in modern buildings, and we find all men of true feeling delighting to escape out of modern cities into natural scenery: hence, as I shall hereafter show, that peculiar love of landscape, which is characteristic of the age. It would be well, if in all other matters, we were as ready to put up with what we dislike, for the sake of compliance with established law, as we are in architecture.

How so debased a law ever came to be established, we shall see when we come to describe the Renaissance schools; here we have only to note, as a second most essential element of the Gothic spirit, that it broke through that law wherever it found it in existence; it not only dared, but delighted in, the infringement of every servile principle; and invented a series of forms of which the merit was, not merely that they were new, but that they were *capable of perpetual novelty*. The pointed arch was not merely a bold variation from the round, but it admitted of millions of variations in itself; for the proportions of a pointed arch are changeable to infinity, while a circular arch is always the same. The grouped shaft was not merely a bold variation from the single one, but it admitted of millions of variations in its grouping, and in the proportions resultant from its grouping. The introduction of tracery was not only a startling change in the treatment of window lights, but admitted endless changes in the interlacement of the tracery bars themselves. So that, while in all living Christian architecture the love of variety exists, the Gothic schools exhibited that love in culminating energy; and their influence, wherever it extended itself, may be sooner and farther traced by this character than by any other; the tendency to the adoption of Gothic types being always first shown by greater irregularity, and richer variation in the forms of architecture it is about to supersede, long before the appearance of the pointed arch or of any other recognizable *outward* sign of the Gothic mind.

We must, however, herein note carefully what distinction there is between a healthy and a diseased love of change; for as it was in healthy love of change that the Gothic architecture rose, it was partly in consequence of diseased love of change that it was destroyed. . . .

From these facts we may gather generally that monotony is, and ought to be, in itself painful to us, just as darkness is; that an architecture which is altogether monotonous is a dark or dead architecture; and of those who love it, it may be truly said, 'they love darkness rather than light'. But monotony in certain measure, used in order to give value to change, and above all, that *transparent* monotony, which, like the shadows of a great painter, suffers all manner of dimly suggested form to be seen through the body of it, is an essential in architectural as in all other composition; and the endurance of monotony has about the same place in a healthy mind that the endurance of darkness has: that is to say, as a strong intellect will have pleasure in the solemnities of storm and twilight, and in the broken and mysterious lights that gleam among them, rather than in mere brilliancy and glare, while a frivolous mind will dread the shadow and the storm; and as a great man will be ready to endure much darkness of fortune in order to reach greater eminence of power or felicity, while an inferior man will not pay the price; exactly in like manner a great mind will accept, or even delight in, monotony which would be wearisome to an inferior intellect, because it has more patience and power of expectation, and is ready to pay the full price for the great future pleasure of change. But in all cases it is not that the noble nature loves monotony, any more than it loves darkness or pain. But it can bear with it, and receive a high pleasure in the endurance or patience, a pleasure necessary to the well-being of this world; while those who will not submit to the temporary sameness, but rush from one change to another, gradually dull the edge of change itself, and bring a shadow and weariness over the whole world from which there is no more escape.

From these general uses of variety in the economy of the world, we may at once understand its use and abuse in architecture. The variety of the Gothic schools is the more healthy and beautiful, because in many cases it is entirely unstudied, and results, not from mere love of change, but from practical necessities. For in one point of view Gothic is not only the best, but the *only rational* architecture, as being that which can fit itself most easily to all services, vulgar or noble. Undefined in its slope of roof, height of shaft, breadth of arch, or disposition of ground plan, it can shrink into a turret, expand into a hall, coil into a staircase, or spring into a spire, with undegraded grace and unexhausted energy; and whenever it finds occasion for change in its form or purpose, it submits to it without the slightest sense of loss either to its unity or majesty, – subtle and flexible like a fiery serpent, but ever attentive to the voice of the charmer. And it is one of the chief virtues of the Gothic builders, that they never suffered ideas of outside symmetries and consistencies to interfere with the real use and value of what they did. If they wanted a window, they opened one; a room, they added one; a buttress, they built one; utterly regardless of any established conventionalities of external appearance, knowing (as indeed it always happened) that such daring interruptions of the formal plan would rather give additional interest to its symmetry than injure it. So that, in the best times of Gothic, a useless window would rather have been opened in an unexpected place for the sake of the surprise, than a useful one forbidden for the sake of symmetry. Every successive architect, employed upon a great work, built the pieces he added in his own way, utterly regardless of the style adopted by his predecessors; and if two towers were raised in nominal correspondence at the sides of a cathedral front, one was nearly sure to be different from the other, and in each the style at the top to be different from the style at the bottom.

These marked variations were, however, only permitted as part of the great system of perpetual change which ran through every member of Gothic design, and rendered it as endless a field for the beholder's inquiry as for the builder's imagination: change, which in the best schools is subtle and delicate, and rendered more delightful by intermingling of a noble monotony; in the more barbaric schools is somewhat fantastic and redundant; but, in all, a necessary and constant condition of the life of the school. Sometimes the variety is in one feature, sometimes in another; it may be in the capitals or crockets, in the niches or the traceries, or in all together, but in some one or other of the features it will be found always. If the mouldings are constant, the surface sculpture will change; if the capitals are of a fixed design, the traceries will change; if the traceries are monotonous, the capitals will change; and if even, as in some fine schools, the early English for example, there is the slightest approximation to an unvarying type of mouldings, capitals, and floral decoration, the variety is found in the disposition of the masses, and in the figure sculpture.

I must now refer for a moment, before we quit the consideration of this, the second mental element of Gothic, to the opening of the third chapter of the *Seven Lamps of Architecture*, in which the distinction was drawn between man gathering and man governing; between his acceptance of the sources of delight from nature, and his development of authoritative or imaginative power in their arrangement: for the two mental elements, not only of Gothic, but of all good architecture, which we have just been examining, belong to it, and are admirable in it, chiefly as it is, more than any other subject of art, the work of man, and the expression of the average power of man. A picture or poem is often little more than a feeble utterance of man's admiration of something out of himself; but architecture approaches more to a creation of his own, born of his necessities, and expressive of his nature. It is also, in some sort, the work of the whole race, while the picture or statue is the work of one only, in most cases more highly gifted than his fellows. And therefore we may expect that the first two elements of good architecture should be expressive of some great truths commonly belonging to the whole race, and necessary to be understood or felt by them in all their work that they do under the sun. And observe what they are: the confession of Imperfection, and the confession of Desire of Change. The building of the bird and the bee needs not express anything like this. It is perfect and unchanging. But just because we are something better than birds or bees, our building must confess that we have not reached the perfection we can imagine, and cannot rest in the condition we have attained. If we pretend to have reached either perfection or satisfaction, we have degraded ourselves and our work. God's work only may express that; but ours may never have that sentence written upon it — 'And behold, it was very good.' And, observe again, it is not merely as it renders the edifice a book of various knowledge, or a mine of precious thought, that variety is essential to its nobleness. The vital principle is not the love of *Knowledge*, but the love of *Change*. It is that strange *disquietude* of the Gothic spirit that is its greatness; that restlessness of the dreaming mind, that wanders hither and thither among the niches, and flickers feverishly around the pinnacles, and frets and fades in labyrinthine knots and shadows along wall and roof, and yet is not satisfied, nor shall be satisfied. The Greek could stay in his triglyph furrow, and be at peace; but the work of the Gothic heart is fretwork still, and it can neither rest in, nor from, its labour, but must pass on, sleeplessly, until its love of change shall be pacified for ever in the change that must come alike on them that wake and them that sleep.

The third constituent element of the Gothic mind was stated to be NATURALISM; that is to say, the love of natural objects for their own sake, and the effort to represent them frankly, unconstrained by artistical laws.

This characteristic of the style partly follows in necessary connection with those named above. For, so soon as the workman is left free to represent what subjects he chooses, he must look to the nature that is round him for material, and will endeavour to represent it as he sees it, with more or less accuracy according to the skill he possesses, and with much play of fancy, but with small respect for law. . . .

I said . . . that Gothic work, when referred to the arrangement of all art, as purist, naturalist, or sensualist, was naturalist. This character follows necessarily on its extreme love of truth, prevailing over the sense of beauty, and causing it to take delight in portraiture of every kind, and to express the various characters of the human countenance and form, as it did the varieties of leaves and the ruggedness of branches. And this tendency is both increased and ennobled by the same Christian humility which we saw expressed in the first character of Gothic work, its rudeness. For as that resulted from a humility which confessed the imperfection of the *workman*, so this naturalist portraiture is rendered more faithful by the humility which confesses the imperfection of the *subject*. The Greek sculptor could neither bear to confess his own feebleness, nor to tell the faults of the forms that he portrayed. But the Christian work-man, believing that all is finally to work together for good, freely confesses both, and neither seeks to disguise his own roughness of work, nor his subject's roughness of make. Yet this frankness being joined, for the most part, with depth of religious feeling in other directions, and especially with charity, there is sometimes a tendency to Purism in the best Gothic sculpture; so that it frequently reaches great dignity of form and tenderness of expression, yet never so as to lose the veracity of portraiture wherever portraiture is possible: not exalting its kings into demi-gods, nor its saints into archangels, but giving what kingliness and sanctity was in them, to the full, mixed with due record of their faults; and this in the most part with a great indifference like that of Scripture history, which sets down, with unmoved and unexcusing resoluteness, the virtues and errors of all men of whom it speaks, often leaving the reader to form his own estimate of them, without an indication of the judgement of the historian. And this veracity is carried out by the Gothic sculptors in the minuteness and generality, as well as the equity, of their delineation: for they do not limit their art to the portraiture of saints and kings, but introduce the most familiar scenes and most simple subjects: filling up the backgrounds of Scripture histories with vivid and curious representations of the commonest incidents of daily life, and availing themselves of every occasion in which, either as a symbol, or an explanation of a scene or time, the things familiar to the eye of the workman could be introduced and made of account. Hence Gothic sculpture and painting are not only full of valuable portraiture of the greatest men, but copious records of all the domestic customs and inferior arts of the ages in which it flourished.*

There is, however, one direction in which the Naturalism of the Gothic workmen is peculiarly manifested; and this direction is even more characteristic of the school than the Naturalism

---

*The best art either represents the facts of its own day, or, if facts of the past, expresses them with accessories of the time in which the work was done. All good art, representing past events, is therefore full of the most frank anachronism, and always *ought* to be. No painter has any business to be an antiquarian. We do not want his impressions or suppositions respecting things that are past. We want his clear assertions respecting things present.

itself; I mean their peculiar fondness for the forms of Vegetation. In rendering the various circumstances of daily life, Egyptian and Ninevite sculpture is as frank and as diffuse as the Gothic. From the highest pomps of state or triumphs of battle, to the most trivial domestic arts and amusements, all is taken advantage of to fill the field of granite with the perpetual interest of a crowded drama; and the early Lombardic and Romanesque sculpture is equally copious in its description of the familiar circumstances of war and the chase. But in all the scenes portrayed by the workmen of these nations, vegetation occurs only as an explanatory accessory; the reed is introduced to mark the course of the river, or the tree to mark the covert of the wild beast, or the ambush of the enemy, but there is no especial interest in the forms of the vegetation strong enough to induce them to make it a subject of separate and accurate study. Again, among the nations who followed the arts of design exclusively, the forms of foliage introduced were meagre and general, and their real intricacy and life were neither admired nor expressed. But to the Gothic workman the living foliage became a subject of intense affection, and he struggled to render all its characters with as much accuracy as was compatible with the laws of his design and the nature of his material, not unfrequently tempted in his enthusiasm to transgress the one and disguise the other.

There is a peculiar significance in this, indicative both of higher civilization and gentler temperament, than had before been manifested in architecture. Rudeness, and the love of change, which we have insisted upon as the first elements of Gothic, are also elements common to all healthy schools. But here is a softer element mingled with them, peculiar to the Gothic itself. The rudeness or ignorance which would have been painfully exposed in the treatment of the human form, are still not so great as to prevent the successful rendering of the wayside herbage; and the love of change, which becomes morbid and feverish in following the haste of the hunter and the rage of the combatant, is at once soothed and satisfied as it watches the wandering of the tendril, and the budding of the flower. Nor is this all: the new direction of mental interest marks an infinite change in the means and the habits of life. The nations whose chief support was in the chase, whose chief interest was in the battle, whose chief pleasure was in the banquet, would take small care respecting the shapes of leaves and flowers; and notice little in the forms of the forest trees which sheltered them, except the signs indicative of the wood which would make the toughest lance, the closest roof, or the clearest fire. The affectionate observation of the grace and outward character of vegetation is the sure sign of a more tranquil and gentle existence, sustained by the gifts, and gladdened by the splendour, of the earth. In that careful distinction of species, and richness of delicate and undisturbed organization, which characterize the Gothic design, there is the history of rural and thoughtful life, influenced by habitual tenderness, and devoted to subtle inquiry; and every discriminating and delicate touch of the chisel, as it rounds the petal or guides the branch, is a prophecy of the development of the entire body of the natural sciences, beginning with that of medicine, of the recovery of literature, and the establishment of the most necessary principles of domestic wisdom and national peace.

I have before alluded to the strange and vain supposition, that the original conception of Gothic architecture had been derived from vegetation, – from the symmetry of avenues, and the interlacing of branches. It is a supposition which never could have existed for a moment in the mind of any person acquainted with early Gothic; but, however idle as a theory, it is most valuable as a testimony to the character of the perfected style. It is precisely because the reverse of this theory is the fact, because the Gothic did not arise out of, but develop itself into, a resemblance to vegetation, that this resemblance is so instructive as an indication of the temper of the builders. It was no chance suggestion of the form of an arch from the bending of a bough, but a gradual and continual discovery of a beauty in natural forms which could be more and more perfectly transferred into those of stone, that influenced at once the heart of the people, and the form of the edifice. The Gothic architecture arose in massy and mountainous strength, axe-hewn, and iron-bound, block heaved upon block by the monk's enthusiasm and the soldier's force; and cramped and stanchioned into such weight of grisly wall, as might bury the anchoret in darkness, and beat back the utmost storm of battle, suffering but by the same narrow crosslet the passing of the sunbeam, or of the arrow. Gradually, as that monkish enthusiasm became more thoughtful, and as the sound of war became more and more intermittent beyond the gates of the convent or the keep, the stony pillar grew slender and the vaulted roof grew light, till they had wreathed themselves into the semblance of the summer woods at their fairest, and of the dead field-flowers, long trodden down in blood, sweet monumental statues were set to bloom for ever, beneath the porch of the temple, or the canopy of the tomb. . . .

The fourth essential element of the Gothic mind was above stated to be the sense of the GROTESQUE; but I shall defer the endeavour to define this most curious and subtle character until we have occasion to examine one of the divisions of the Renaissance schools, which was morbidly influenced by it. It is the less necessary to insist upon it here, because every reader familiar with Gothic architecture must understand what I mean, and will, I believe, have no hesitation in admitting, that the tendency to delight in fantastic and ludicrous, as well as in sublime, images, is a universal instinct of the Gothic imagination.

The fifth element above named was RIGIDITY; and this character I must endeavour carefully to define, for neither the word I have used, nor any other that I can think of, will express it accurately. For I mean, not merely stable, but *active* rigidity; the peculiar energy which gives tension to movement, and stiffness to resistance, which makes the fiercest lightning forked rather than curved, and the stoutest oak-branch angular rather than bending, and is as much seen in the quivering of the lance as in the glittering of the icicle.

I have before had occasion to note some manifestations of this energy or fixedness; but it must be still more attentively considered here, as it shows itself throughout the whole structure and decoration of Gothic work. Egyptian and Greek buildings stand, for the most part, by their own weight and mass, one stone passively incumbent on another; but in the

Gothic vaults and traceries there is a stiffness analogous to that of the bones of a limb, or fibres of a tree; an elastic tension and communication of force from part to part, and also a studious expression of this throughout every visible line of the building. And, in like manner, the Greek and Egyptian ornament is either mere surface engraving, as if the face of the wall had been stamped with a seal, or its lines are flowing, lithe, and luxuriant; in either case, there is no expression of energy in the framework of the ornament itself. But the Gothic ornament stands out in prickly independence, and frosty fortitude, jutting into crockets, and freezing into pinnacles; here starting up into a monster, there germinating into a blossom, anon knitting itself into a branch, alternately thorny, bossy, and bristly, or writhed into every form of nervous entanglement; but, even when most graceful, never for an instant languid, always quickset: erring, if at all, ever on the side of brusquerie.

The feelings or habits in the workman which give rise to this character in the work, are more complicated and various than those indicated by any other sculptural expression hitherto named. There is, first, the habit of hard and rapid working; the industry of the tribes of the North, quickened by the coldness of the climate, and giving an expression of sharp energy to all they do ... as opposed to the languor of the Southern tribes, however much of fire there may be in the heart of that languor, for lava itself may flow languidly. There is also the habit of finding enjoyment in the signs of cold, which is never found, I believe, in the inhabitants of countries south of the Alps. Cold is to them an unredeemed evil, to be suffered and forgotten as soon as may be; but the long winter of the North forces the Goth (I mean the Englishman, Frenchman, Dane, or German), if he would lead a happy life at all, to find sources of happiness in foul weather as well as fair, and to rejoice in the leafless as well as in the shady forest. ...

Last, because the least essential, of the constituent elements of this noble school, was placed that of REDUNDANCE, – the uncalculating bestowal of the wealth of its labour. There is, indeed, much Gothic, and that of the best period, in which this element is hardly traceable, and which depends for its effect almost exclusively on loveliness of simple design and grace of uninvolved proportion; still, in the most characteristic buildings, a certain portion of their effect depends upon accumulation of ornament; and many of those which have most influence on the minds of men, have attained it by means of this attribute alone. And although, by careful study of the school, it is possible to arrive at a condition of taste which shall be better contented by a few perfect lines than by a whole façade covered with fretwork, the building which only satisfies such a taste is not to be considered the best. For the very first requirement of Gothic architecture being, as we saw above, that it shall both admit the aid, and appeal to the admiration, of the rudest as well as the most refined minds, the richness of the work is, paradoxical as the statement may appear, a part of its humility. No architecture is so haughty as that which is simple; which refuses to address the eye, except in a few clear and forceful lines; which implies, in offering so little to our regards, that all it has offered is perfect; and disdains, either by the complexity or the attractiveness of its features, to embarrass our investigation, or betray us into delight. That humility, which is the very life of the Gothic school, is shown not only in the imperfection, but in the accumulation, of ornament. The inferior rank of the workman is often shown as much in the richness, as the roughness, of his work; and if the co-operation of every hand, and the sympathy of every heart, are to be received, we must be content to allow the redundance which disguises the failure of the feeble, and wins the regard of the inattentive. There are, however, far nobler interests mingling, in the Gothic heart, with the rude love of decorative accumulation: a magnificent enthusiasm, which feels as if it never could do enough to reach the fulness of its ideal; an unselfishness of sacrifice, which would rather cast fruitless labour before the altar than stand idle in the market; and, finally, a profound sympathy with the fulness and wealth of the material universe, rising out of that Naturalism whose operation we have already endeavoured to define. The sculptor who sought for his models among the forest leaves, could not but quickly and deeply feel that complexity need not involve the loss of grace, nor richness that of repose; and every hour which he spent in the study of the minute and various work of Nature, made him feel more forcibly the barrenness of what was best in that of man: nor is it to be wondered at, that, seeing her perfect and exquisite creations poured forth in a profusion which conception could not grasp nor calculation sum, he should think that it ill became him to be niggardly of his own rude craftsmanship; and where he saw throughout the universe a faultless beauty lavished on measureless spaces of broidered field and blooming mountain, to grudge his poor and imperfect labour to the few stones that he had raised one upon another, for habitation or memorial. The years of this life passed away before his task was accomplished; but generation succeeded generation with unwearied enthusiasm, and the cathedral front was at last lost in the tapestry of its traceries, like a rock among the thickets and herbage of spring.

We have now, I believe, obtained a view approaching to completeness of the various moral or imaginative elements which composed the inner spirit of Gothic architecture. . . .

Matthew Arnold

Matthew Arnold (1822–88) was the son of Thomas Arnold, a distinguished historian, controversialist and headmaster of Rugby. Arnold was educated at Rugby, Winchester and Oxford. On leaving university he became private secretary to Lord Lansdowne, but in 1851 he was appointed to an Inspectorship of Schools, a post he held until two years before his death. Two volumes of poetry *The Strayed Reveller* (1849) and *Empedocles on Etna* (1852) were quickly followed by *Poems* (1853) for which Arnold wrote a preface expressing his belief that the uncertainties and confusion of modern life made the writing of great poetry virtually impossible. A later reformulation of this view was to appear in 'The Function of Criticism at the Present Time' in *Essays in Criticism* (1865) as the theory of epochs of concentration and expansion. Arnold did not stop writing poetry entirely, but his interests turned increasingly to criticism. In 1857 he was appointed to the Chair of Poetry at Oxford, and from this appointment came a characteristically polemical work, *On Translating Homer* (1861). He also published in 1861 *The Popular Education of France* which was based on an official report he had produced on educational systems in France, Switzerland and Holland. Although constantly arguing for 'sweetness and light' in criticism, Arnold's own work was often fiercely satirical, and his attacks on the provincialism and philistinism of English cultural life provoked angry replies from other critics, but as he wrote in a letter, 'However much I may be attacked, my manner of writing is certainly one that takes hold of people and proves effective.' This was especially true of 'My Countrymen' (1866), *Culture and Anarchy* (1869), and *Friendship's Garland* (1871), his most sustained works of social criticism. *New Poems* (1867) revealed that his earlier poetic inspiration was far from dead, and in the 1870s he seemed to make yet another change of

direction with a series of books on religious topics, notably
Literature and Dogma (1873) and *God and the Bible* (1875). In the
last years of his life he returned to political themes with *Irish
Essays* (1882) and *Discourses in America* (1885). A second series of
Essays in Criticism was published posthumously in 1888.

THE FUNCTION OF CRITICISM AT THE PRESENT TIME

Many objections have been made to a proposition which, in
some remarks of mine on translating Homer, I ventured to put
forth; a proposition about criticism, and its importance at the
present day. I said: 'Of the literature of France and Germany, as
of the intellect of Europe in general, the main effort, for now
many years, has been a critical effort; the endeavour, in all
branches of knowledge, theology, philosophy, history, art,
science, to see the object as in itself it really is.' I added, that
owing to the operation in English literature of certain causes,
'almost the last thing for which one would come to English
literature is just that very thing which now Europe most desires,
– criticism'; and that the power and value of English literature
was thereby impaired. More than one rejoinder declared that the
importance I here assigned to criticism was excessive, and
asserted the inherent superiority of the creative effort of the
human spirit over its critical effort. And the other day, having
been led by an excellent notice of Wordsworth* published in the

---

*I cannot help thinking that a practice, common in England during the
last century, and still followed in France, of printing a notice of this
kind, – a notice by a competent critic, – to serve as an introduction to an
eminent author's works, might be revived among us with advantage.
To introduce all succeeding editions of Wordsworth, Mr Sharp's notice
(it is permitted, I hope, to mention his name) might, it seems to me,
excellently serve; it is written from the point of view of an admirer, nay,
of a disciple, and that is right; but then the disciple must be also, as in
this case he is, a critic, a man of letters, not, as too often happens, some
relation or friend with no qualification for his task except affection for
his author.

North British Review, to turn again to his biography, I found, in the words of this great man, whom I, for one, must always listen to with the profoundest respect, a sentence passed on the critic's business, which seems to justify every possible disparagement of it. Wordsworth says in one of his letters:

'The writers in these publications' (the Reviews), 'while they prosecute their inglorious employment, can not be supposed to be in a state of mind very favourable for being affected by the finer influences of a thing so pure as genuine poetry.'

And a trustworthy reporter of his conversation quotes a more elaborate judgement to the same effect:

'Wordsworth holds the critical power very low, infinitely lower than the inventive; and he said today that if the quantity of time consumed in writing critiques on the works of others were given to original composition, of whatever kind it might be, it would be much better employed; it would make a man find out sooner his own level, and it would do infinitely less mischief. A false or malicious criticism may do much injury to the minds of others; a stupid invention, either in prose or verse, is quite harmless.'

It is almost too much to expect of poor human nature, that a man capable of producing some effect in one line of literature, should, for the greater good of society, voluntarily doom himself to impotence and obscurity in another. Still less is this to be expected from men addicted to the composition of the 'false or malicious criticism,' of which Wordsworth speaks. However, everybody would admit that a false or malicious criticism had better never have been written. Everybody, too, would be willing to admit, as a general proposition, that the critical faculty is lower than the inventive. But is it true that criticism is really, in itself, a baneful and injurious employment; is it true that all time given to writing critiques on the works of others would be much better employed if it were given to original composition, of whatever kind this may be? Is it true that Johnson had better have gone on producing more *Irenes* instead of writing his *Lives of the Poets*; nay, is it certain that Wordsworth himself was better employed in making his Ecclesiastical Sonnets, than when he made his celebrated Preface, so full of criticism, and criticism of the works of others? Wordsworth was himself a great critic, and it is to be sincerely regretted that he has not left us more criticism; Goethe was one of the greatest of critics, and we may sincerely congratulate ourselves that he has left us so much criticism. Without wasting time over the exaggeration which Wordsworth's judgement on criticism clearly contains, or over an attempt to trace the causes, – not difficult I think to be traced, – which may have led Wordsworth to this exaggeration, a critic may with advantage seize an occasion for trying his own conscience, and for asking himself of what real service, at any given moment, the practice of criticism either is, or may be made, to his own mind and spirit, and to the minds and spirits of others.

The critical power is of lower rank than the creative. True; but in assenting to this proposition, one or two things are to be kept in mind. It is undeniable that the exercise of a creative power, that a free creative activity, is the true function of man; it is proved to be so by man's finding in it his true happiness. But it is undeniable, also, that men may have the sense of exercising this free creative activity in other ways than in producing great works of literature or art; if it were not so, all but a very few men would be shut out from the true happiness of all men; they may have it in well-doing, they may have it in learning, they may have it even in criticizing. This is one thing to be kept in mind. Another is, that the exercise of the creative power in the production of great works of literature or art, however high this exercise of it may rank, is not at all epochs and under all conditions possible; and that therefore labour may be vainly spent in attempting it, which might with more fruit be used in preparing for it, in rendering it possible. This creative power works with elements, with materials; what if it has not those materials, those elements, ready for its use? In that case it must surely wait till they are ready. Now in literature, – I will limit myself to literature, for it is about literature that the question arises, the elements with which the creative power works are ideas; the best ideas, on every matter which literature touches, current at the time; at any rate we may lay it down as certain that in modern literature no manifestation of the creative power not working with these can be very important or fruitful. And I say *current* at the time, not merely accessible at the time; for creative literary genius does not principally show itself in discovering new ideas; that is rather the business of the philosopher: the grand work of literary genius is a work of synthesis and exposition, not of analysis and discovery; its gift lies in the faculty of being happily inspired by a certain intellectual and spiritual atmosphere, by a certain order of ideas, when it finds itself in them; of dealing divinely with these ideas, presenting them in the most effective and attractive combinations, – making beautiful works with them, in short. But it must have the atmosphere, it must find itself amidst the order of ideas, in order to work freely; and these it is not so easy to command. This is why great creative epochs in literature are so rare; this is why there is so much that is unsatisfactory in the productions of many men of real genius; because for the creation of a master-work of literature two powers must concur, the power of the man and the power of the moment, and the man is not enough without the moment; the creative power has, for its happy exercise, appointed elements, and those elements are not in its own control.

Nay, they are more within the control of the critical power. It is the business of the critical power, as I said in the words already quoted, 'in all branches of knowledge, theology, philosophy, history, art, science, to see the object as in itself it really is'. Thus it tends, at last, to make an intellectual situation of which the creative power can profitably avail itself. It tends to establish an order of ideas, if not absolutely true, yet true by comparison with that which it displaces; to make the best ideas prevail. Presently these new ideas reach society, the touch of truth is the touch of life, and there is a stir and growth everywhere; out of this stir and growth come the creative epochs of literature.

Or, to narrow our range, and quit these considerations of the general march of genius and of society, considerations which are apt to become too abstract and impalpable – everyone can see that a poet, for instance, ought to know life and the world before dealing with them in poetry; and life and the world being, in modern times, very complex things, the creation of a modern poet, to be worth much, implies a great critical effort behind it; else it must be a comparatively poor, barren, and short-lived affair. This is why Byron's poetry had so little endurance in it, and Goethe's so much; both Byron and Goethe had a great productive power, but Goethe's was nourished by a great critical effort providing the true materials for it, and Byron's was not; Goethe knew life and the world, the poet's necessary subjects, much more comprehensively and thoroughly than Byron. He knew a great deal more of them, and he knew them much more as they really are.

It has long seemed to me that the burst of creative activity in our literature, through the first quarter of this century, had about it, in fact, something premature; and that from this cause its productions are doomed, most of them, in spite of the sanguine hopes which accompanied and do still accompany them, to prove hardly more lasting than do the productions of far less splendid epochs. And this prematureness comes from its having proceeded without having its proper data, without sufficient materials to work with. In other words, the English poetry of the first quarter of this century, with plenty of energy, plenty of creative force, did not know enough. This makes Byron so empty of matter, Shelley so incoherent, Wordsworth even, profound as he is, yet so wanting in completeness and variety. Wordsworth cared little for books, and disparaged Goethe. I admire Wordsworth, as he is, so much that I cannot wish him different; and it is vain, no doubt, to imagine such a man different from what he is, to suppose that he could have been different; but surely the one thing wanting to make Wordsworth an even greater poet than he is, – his thought richer, and his influence of wider application, – was that he should have read more books, among them, no doubt, those of that Goethe whom he disparaged without reading him.

But to speak of books and reading may easily lead to a misunderstanding here. It was not really books and reading that lacked to our poetry, at this epoch; Shelley had plenty of reading, Coleridge had immense reading. Pindar and Sophocles – as we all say so glibly, and often with so little discernment of the real import of what we are saying – had not many books;

Shakespeare was no deep reader. True; but in the Greece of Pindar and Sophocles, in the England of Shakespeare, the poet lived in a current of ideas in the highest degree animating and nourishing to the creative power; society was, in the fullest measure, permeated by fresh thought, intelligent and alive; and this state of things is the true basis for the creative power's exercise, – in this it finds its data, its materials, truly ready for its hand; all the books and reading in the world are only valuable as they are helps to this. Even when this does not actually exist, books and reading may enable a man to construct a kind of semblance of it in his own mind, a world of knowledge and intelligence in which he may live and work: this is by no means an equivalent, to the artist, for the nationally diffused life and thought of the epochs of Sophocles or Shakespeare, but, besides that it may be a means of preparation for such epochs, it does really constitute, if many share in it, a quickening and sustaining atmosphere of great value. Such an atmosphere the many-sided learning and the long and widely-combined critical effort of Germany formed for Goethe, when he lived and worked. There was no national glow of life and thought there, as in the Athens of Pericles, or the England of Elizabeth. That was the poet's weakness. But there was a sort of equivalent for it in the complete culture and unfettered thinking of a large body of Germans. That was his strength. In the England of the first quarter of this century, there was neither a national glow of life and thought, such as we had in the age of Elizabeth, nor yet a culture and a force of learning and criticism, such as were to be found in Germany. Therefore the creative power of poetry wanted, for success in the highest sense, materials and a basis; a thorough interpretation of the world was necessarily denied to it.

At first sight it seems strange that out of the immense stir of the French Revolution and its age should not have come a crop of works of genius equal to that which came out of the stir of the great productive time of Greece, or out of that of the Renaissance, with its powerful episode the Reformation. But the truth is that the stir of the French Revolution took a character which essentially distinguished it from such movements as these. These were, in the main, disinterestedly intellectual and spiritual movements; movements in which the human spirit looked for its satisfaction in itself and in the increased play of its own activity: the French Revolution took a political, practical character. The movement which went on in France under the old *régime*, from 1700 to 1789, was far more really akin than that of the Revolution itself to the movement of the Renaissance; the France of Voltaire and Rousseau told far more powerfully upon the mind of Europe than the France of the Revolution. Goethe reproached this last expressly with having 'thrown quiet culture back'. Nay, and the true key to how much in our Byron, even in our Wordsworth, is this! – that they had their source in a great movement of feeling, not in a great movement of mind. The French Revolution, however, – that object of so much blind love and so much blind hatred, – found undoubtedly its motive-power in the intelligence of men and not in their practical sense; – this is what distinguishes it from the English Revolution of Charles the First's time; this is what makes it a more spiritual event than our Revolution, an event of much more powerful and world-wide interest, though practically less successful, – it appeals to an order of ideas which are universal, certain, permanent. 1789 asked of a thing, Is it rational? 1642 asked of a thing, Is it legal? or, when it went furthest, Is it according to conscience? This is the English fashion; a fashion to be treated, within its own sphere, with the highest respect; for its success, within its own sphere, has been prodigious. But what is law in one place, is not law in another; what is law here today, is not law even here tomorrow; and as for conscience, what is binding on one man's conscience is not binding on another's; the old woman who threw her stool at the head of the surpliced minister in St Giles's Church at Edinburgh obeyed an impulse to which millions of the human race may be permitted to remain strangers. But the prescriptions of reason are absolute, unchanging, of universal validity; *to count by tens is the easiest way of counting*, – that is a proposition of which every one, from here to the Antipodes, feels the force; at least, I should say so, if we did not live in a country where it is not impossible that any morning we may find a letter in the *Times* declaring that a decimal coinage is an absurdity. That a whole nation should have been penetrated with an enthusiasm for pure reason, and with an ardent zeal for making its prescriptions triumph, is a very remarkable thing, when we consider how little of mind, or anything so worthy and quickening as mind, comes into the motives which alone, in general, impel great masses of men. In spite of the extravagant direction given to this enthusiasm, in spite of the crimes and follies in which it lost itself, the French Revolution derives from the force, truth, and universality of the ideas which it took for its law, and from the passion with which it could inspire a multitude for these ideas, a unique and still living power; it is – it will probably long remain – the greatest, the most animating event in history. And, as no sincere passion for the things of the mind, even though it turn out in many respects an unfortunate passion, is ever quite thrown away and quite barren of good, France has reaped from hers one fruit, the natural and legitimate fruit, though not precisely the grand fruit she expected; she is the country in Europe where *the people* is most alive.

But the mania for giving an immediate political and practical application to all these fine ideas of the reason was fatal. Here an Englishman is in his element: on this theme we can all go on for hours. And all we are in the habit of saying on it has undoubtedly a great deal of truth. Ideas cannot be too much prized in and for themselves, cannot be too much lived with; but to transport them abruptly into the world of politics and practice, violently to revolutionize this world to their bidding, – that is quite another thing. There is the world of ideas and there is the world of practice; the French are often for suppressing the one and the English the other; but neither is to be suppressed. A member of the House of Commons said to me the other day: 'That a thing is an anomaly, I consider to be no objection to it whatever.' I venture to think he was wrong; that a thing is an anomaly *is* an objection to it, but absolutely and in the sphere of ideas: it is not necessarily, under such and such circumstances, or at such and such a moment, an objection to it in the sphere of politics and practice. Joubert has said beautifully: 'C'est la force et le droit qui règlent toutes choses dans le monde; la force en attendant le droit.' (Force and right are the governors of this world; force till right is ready.) *Force till right is ready;* and till right is ready, force, the existing order of things, is justified, is the legitimate ruler. But right is something moral, and implies inward recognition, free assent of the will; we are not ready for right, – *right*, so far as we are concerned, *is not ready,* – until we have attained this sense of seeing it and willing it. The way in which for us it may change and transform force, the existing order of things, and become, in its turn, the legitimate ruler of the world, will depend on the way in which, when our time comes, we see it and will it. Therefore for other people enamoured of their own newly-discerned right, to attempt to impose it upon us as ours, and violently to substitute their right for our force, is an act of tyranny, and to be resisted. It sets at nought the second great half of our maxim, *force till right is ready.* This was the grand error of the French Revolution; and its movement of ideas, by quitting the intellectual sphere and rushing furiously into the political sphere, ran, indeed, a prodigious and memorable course, but produced no such intellectual fruit as the movement of ideas of the Renaissance, and created, in opposition to itself, what I may call an *epoch of concentration.* The great force of that epoch of concentration was England; and the great voice of that epoch of concentration was Burke. It is the fashion to treat Burke's writings on the French Revolution as superannuated and conquered by the event; as the eloquent but unphilosophical tirades of bigotry and prejudice. I will not deny that they are often disfigured by the violence and passion of the moment, and that in some directions Burke's view was bounded, and his observation therefore at fault; but on the whole, and for those who can make the needful corrections, what distinguishes these writings is their profound, permanent, fruitful, philosophical truth; they contain the true philosophy of an epoch of concentration, dissipate the heavy atmosphere which its own nature is apt to engender round it, and make its resistance rational instead of mechanical.

But Burke is so great because, almost alone in England, he brings thought to bear upon politics, he saturates politics with thought; it is his accident that his ideas were at the service of an epoch of concentration, not of an epoch of expansion; it is his characteristic that he so lived by ideas, and had such a source of them welling up within him, that he could float even an epoch of concentration and English Tory politics with them. It does not hurt him that Dr Price and the Liberals were enraged with him; it does not even hurt him that George the Third and the Tories were enchanted with him. His greatness is that he lived in a world which neither English Liberalism nor English Toryism is apt to enter, – the world of ideas, not the world of catchwords and party habits. So far is it from being really true of him that he 'to party gave up what was meant for mankind', that at the very end of his fierce struggle with the French Revolution, after all his invectives against its false pretensions, hollowness, and madness, with his sincere conviction of its mischievousness, he can close a memorandum on the best means of combating it, some of the last pages he ever wrote, – the *Thoughts on French Affairs*, in December 1791, – with these striking words:

'The evil is stated, in my opinion, as it exists. The remedy must be where power, wisdom, and information, I hope, are more united with good intentions than they can be with me. I have done with this subject, I believe, for ever. It has given me many anxious moments for the last two years. *If a great change is to be made in human affairs, the minds of men will be fitted to it; the general opinions and feelings will draw that way. Every fear, every hope will forward it; and then they who persist in opposing this mighty current in human affairs, will appear rather to resist the decrees of Providence itself, than the mere designs of men. They will not be resolute and firm, but perverse and obstinate.*'

That return of Burke upon himself has always seemed to me one of the finest things in English literature, or indeed in any literature. That is what I call living by ideas; when one side of a question has long had your earnest support, when all your feelings are engaged, when you hear all round you no language but one, when your party talks this language like a steam-engine and can imagine no other, – still to be able to think, still to be irresistibly carried, if so it be, by the current of thought to the opposite side of the question, and, like Balaam, to be unable to speak anything *but what the Lord has put in your mouth*. I know nothing more striking, and I must add that I know nothing more un-English.

For the Englishman in general is like my friend the Member of Parliament, and believes, point-blank, that for a thing to be an anomaly is absolutely no objection to it whatever. He is like the Lord Auckland of Burke's day, who, in a memorandum on the French Revolution, talks of 'certain miscreants, assuming the name of philosophers, who have presumed themselves capable of establishing a new system of society.' The Englishman has been called a political animal, and he values what is political and practical so much that ideas easily become objects of dislike in his eyes, and thinkers 'miscreants', because ideas and thinkers have rashly meddled with politics and practice. This would be all very well if the dislike and neglect confined themselves to ideas transported out of their own sphere, and meddling rashly with practice; but they are inevitably extended to ideas as such, and to the whole life of intelligence; practice is everything, a free play of the mind is nothing. The notion of the free play of the mind upon all subjects being a pleasure in itself, being an object of desire, being an essential provider of elements without which a nation's spirit, whatever compensations it may have for them, must, in the long run, die of inanition, hardly enters into an Englishman's thoughts. It is noticeable that the word *curiosity*, which in other languages is used in a good sense, to mean, as a high and fine quality of man's nature, just this disinterested love of a free play of the mind on all subjects, for its own sake, – it is noticeable, I say, that this word has in our language no sense of the kind, no sense but a rather bad and disparaging one. But criticism, real criticism, is essentially the exercise of this very quality; it obeys an instinct prompting it to try to know the best that is known and thought in the world, irrespectively of practice, politics, and everything of the kind; and to value knowledge and thought as they approach this best, without the intrusion of any other considerations whatever. This is an instinct for which there is, I think, little original sympathy in the practical English nature, and what there was of it has undergone a long benumbing period of blight and suppression in the epoch of concentration which followed the French Revolution.

But epochs of concentration cannot well endure for ever; epochs of expansion, in the due course of things, follow them. Such an epoch of expansion seems to be opening in this country. In the first place all danger of a hostile forcible pressure of foreign ideas upon our practice has long disappeared; like the traveller in the fable, therefore, we begin to wear our cloak a little more loosely. Then, with a long peace, the ideas of Europe steal gradually and amicably in, and mingle, though in infinitesimally small quantities at a time, with our own notions. Then, too, in spite of all that is said about the absorbing and brutalizing influence of our passionate material progress, it seems to me indisputable that this progress is likely, though not certain, to lead in the end to an apparition of intellectual life; and that man, after he has made himself perfectly comfortable and has now to determine what to do with himself next, may begin to remember that he has a mind, and that the mind may be made the source of great pleasure. I grant it is mainly the privilege of faith, at present, to discern this end to our railways, our business, and our fortune-making; but we shall see if, here as elsewhere, faith is not in the end the true prophet. Our ease, our travelling, and our unbounded liberty to hold just as hard and securely as we please to the practice to which our notions have given birth, all tend to beget an inclination to deal a little more freely with these notions themselves, to canvass them a little, to penetrate a little into their real nature. Flutterings of curiosity, in the foreign sense of the word, appear amongst us, and it is in these that criticism must look to find its account. Criticism first; a time of true creative activity, perhaps, – which, as I have said, must inevitably be preceded amongst us by a time of criticism, – hereafter, when criticism has done its work.

It is of the last importance that English criticism should clearly discern what rule for its course, in order to avail itself of the field now opening to it, and to produce fruit for the future, it ought to take. The rule may be summed up in one word, – *disinterestedness*. And how is criticism to show disinterestedness? By keeping aloof from practice; by resolutely following the law of its own nature. which is to be a free play of the mind on all subjects which it touches; by steadily refusing to lend itself to any of those ulterior, political, practical considerations about ideas which plenty of people will be sure to attach to them, which perhaps ought often to be attached to them, which in this country at any rate are certain to be attached to them quite sufficiently, but which criticism has really nothing to do with. Its business is, as I have said, simply to know the best that is known and thought in the world, and by in its turn making this known, to create a current of true and fresh ideas. Its business is to do this with inflexible honesty, with due ability; but its business is to do no more, and to leave alone all questions of practical consequences and applications, questions which will never fail to have due prominence given to them. Else criticism, besides being really false to its own nature, merely continues in the old rut which it has hitherto followed in this country, and will certainly miss the chance now given to it. For what is at present the bane of criticism in this country? It is that practical considerations cling to it and stifle it; it subserves interests not its own; our organs of criticism are organs of men and parties having practical ends to serve, and with them those practical ends are the first thing and the play of mind the second; so much play of mind as is compatible with the prosecution of those practical ends is all that is wanted. An organ like the *Revue des Deux Mondes*, having for its main function to understand and utter the best that is known and thought in the world, existing, it may be said, as just an organ for a free play of the mind, we have not; but we have the *Edinburgh Review*, existing as an organ of the old Whigs, and for as much play of mind as may suit its being that; we have the *Quarterly Review*, existing as an organ of the Tories, and for as much play of mind as may suit its being that; we have the *British Quarterly Review*, existing as an organ of the political Dissenters, and for as much play of mind as may suit its being that; we have the *Times*, existing as an organ of the common, satisfied, well-to-do Englishman, and for as much play of mind as may suit its being that. And so on through all the various fractions, political and religious, of our society; every fraction has, as such, its organ of criticism, but the notion of combining all fractions in the common pleasure of a free disinterested play of mind meets with no favour. Directly this play of mind wants to have more scope, and to forget the pressure of practical considerations a little, it is checked, it is made to feel the chain; we saw this the other day in the extinction, so much to be regretted, of the *Home and Foreign Review*; perhaps in no organ of criticism in this country was there so much knowledge, so much play of mind; but these could not save it: the *Dublin Review* subordinates play of mind to the practical business of English and Irish Catholicism, and lives. It must needs be that men should act in sects and parties, that each of these sects and parties should have its organ, and should make this organ subserve the interests of its action; but it would be well, too, that there should be a criticism, not the minister of these interests, not their enemy, but absolutely and entirely independent of them. No other criticism will ever attain any real authority or make any real way towards its end, – the creating a current of true and fresh ideas.

It is because criticism has so little kept in the pure intellectual sphere, has so little detached itself from practice, has been so directly polemical and controversial, that it has so ill accomplished, in this country, its best spiritual work; which is to keep man from a self-satisfaction which is retarding and vulgarizing, to lead him towards perfection, by making his mind dwell upon what is excellent in itself, and the absolute beauty and fitness of things. A polemical practical criticism makes men blind even to the ideal imperfection of their practice, makes them willingly assert its ideal perfection, in order the better to secure it against attack; and clearly this is narrowing and baneful for them. If they were reassured on the practical side, speculative considerations of ideal perfection they might be brought to entertain, and their spiritual horizon would thus gradually widen. Mr Adderley says to the Warwickshire farmers:

'Talk of the improvement of breed! Why, the race we ourselves represent, the men and women, the old Anglo-Saxon race, are the best breed in the whole world . . . The absence of a too enervating climate, too unclouded skies, and a too luxurious nature, has produced so vigorous a race of people, and has rendered us so superior to all the world.'

Mr Roebuck says to the Sheffield cutlers:

'I look around me and ask what is the state of England? Is not property safe? Is not every man able to say what he likes? Can you not walk from one end of England to the other in perfect security? I ask you whether, the world over or in past history, there is anything like it? Nothing. I pray that our unrivalled happiness may last.'

Now obviously there is a peril for poor human nature in words and thoughts of such exuberant self-satisfaction, until we find ourselves safe in the streets of the Celestial City.

>   Das wenige verschwindet leicht dem Blicke
>   Der vorwärts sieht, wie viel noch übrig bleibt –

says Goethe; the little that is done seems nothing when we look forward and see how much we have yet to do. Clearly this is a better line of reflection for weak humanity, so long as it remains on this earthly field of labour and trial. But neither Mr Adderley nor Mr Roebuck are by nature inaccessible to considerations of this sort. They only lose sight of them owing to the controversial life we all lead, and the practical form which all speculation takes with us. They have in view opponents whose aim is not ideal, but practical; and in their zeal to uphold their own practice against these innovators, they go so far as even to attribute to this practice an ideal perfection. Somebody has been wanting to introduce a six-pound franchise, or to abolish church-rates, or to collect agricultural statistics by force, or to diminish local self-government. How natural, in reply to such proposals, very likely improper or ill-timed, to go a little beyond the mark, and to say stoutly, 'Such a race of people as we stand, so superior to all the world! The old Anglo-Saxon race, the best breed in the whole world! I pray that our unrivalled happiness may last! I ask you whether, the world over or in past history, there is anything like it!' And so long as criticism answers this dithyramb by insisting that the old Anglo-Saxon race would be still more superior to all others if it had no church-rates, or that our unrivalled happiness would last yet longer with a six-pound franchise, so long will the strain, 'The best breed in the whole world!' swell louder and louder, everything ideal and refining will be lost out of sight, and both the assailed and their critics will remain in a sphere, to say the truth, perfectly unvital, a sphere in which spiritual progression is impossible. But let criticism leave church-rates and the franchise alone, and in the most candid spirit, without a single lurking thought of practical innovation, confront with our dithyramb this paragraph on which I stumbled in a newspaper soon after reading Mr Roebuck:

'A shocking child murder has just been committed at Nottingham. A girl named Wragg left the workhouse there on Saturday morning with her young illegitimate child. The child was soon afterwards found dead on Mapperly Hills, having been strangled. Wragg is in custody.'

Nothing but that; but, in juxtaposition with the absolute eulogies of Mr Adderley and Mr Roebuck, how eloquent, how suggestive are those few lines! 'Our old Anglo-Saxon breed, the best in the whole world!' – how much that is harsh and ill-favoured there is in this best! *Wragg!* If we are to talk of ideal perfection, of 'the best in the whole world', has any one reflected what a touch of grossness in our race, what an original short-coming in the more delicate spiritual perceptions, is shown by the natural growth amongst us of such hideous names – Higginbottom, Stiggins, Bugg! In Ionia and Attica they were luckier in this respect than 'the best race in the world'; by the Ilissus there was no Wragg, poor thing! And 'our unrivalled happiness'; – what an element of grimness, bareness, and hideousness mixes with it and blurs it; the workhouse, the dismal Mapperly Hills, – how dismal those who have seen them will remember; – the gloom, the smoke, the cold, the strangled illegitimate child! 'I ask you whether, the world over or in past history, there is anything like it?' Perhaps not, one is inclined to answer; but at any rate, in that case, the world is very much to be pitied. And the final touch, – short, bleak, and inhuman: *Wragg is in custody.* The sex lost in the confusion of our unrivalled happiness; or (shall I say?) the superfluous Christian name lopped off by the straightforward vigour of our old Anglo-Saxon breed! There is profit for the spirit in such contrasts as this; criticism serves the cause of perfection by establishing them. By eluding sterile conflict, by refusing to remain in the sphere where alone narrow and relative conceptions have any worth and validity, criticism may diminish its momentary importance, but only in this way has it a chance of gaining admittance for those wider and more perfect conceptions to which all its duty is really owed. Mr Roebuck will have a poor opinion of an adversary who replies to his defiant songs of triumph only by murmuring under his breath, *Wragg is in custody*; but in no other way will these songs of triumph be induced gradually to moderate themselves, to get rid of what in them is excessive and offensive, and to fall into a softer and truer key.

It will be said that it is a very subtle and indirect action which I am thus prescribing for criticism, and that by embracing in this manner the Indian virtue of detachment and abandoning the sphere of practical life, it condemns itself to a slow and obscure work. Slow and obscure it may be, but it is the only proper work of criticism. The mass of mankind will never have any ardent zeal for seeing things as they are; very inadequate ideas will always satisfy them. On these inadequate ideas reposes, and must repose, the general practice of the world. That is as much as saying that whoever sets himself to see things as they are will find himself one of a very small circle; but it is only by this small circle resolutely doing its own work that adequate ideas will ever get current at all. The rush and roar of practical life will always have a dizzying and attracting effect upon the most collected spectator, and tend to draw him into its vortex; most of all will this be the case where that life is so powerful as it is in England. But it is only by remaining collected, and refusing to lend himself to the point of view of the practical man, that the critic can do the practical man any service; and it is only by the greatest sincerity in pursuing his own course, and by at last convincing even the practical man of his sincerity, that he can escape misunderstandings which perpetually threaten him.

For the practical man is not apt for fine distinctions, and yet in these distinctions truth and the highest culture greatly find their account. But it is not easy to lead a practical man – unless you reassure him as to your practical intentions, you have no chance of leading him – to see that a thing which he has always been used to look at from one side only, which he greatly values, and which, looked at from that side, more than deserves, perhaps, all the prizing and admiring which he bestows upon it, – that this thing, looked at from another side, may appear much less beneficent and beautiful, and yet retain all its claims to our practical allegiance. Where shall we find language innocent enough, how shall we make the spotless purity of our intentions evident enough, to enable us to say to the political Englishman that the British Constitution itself, which, seen from the practical side, looks such a magnificent organ of progress and virtue, seen from the speculative side, – with its compromises, its love of facts, its horror of theory, its studied avoidance of clear thoughts, – that, seen from this side, our august Constitution sometimes looks, – forgive me, shade of Lord Somers! – a colossal machine for the manufacture of Philistines? How is Cobbett to say this and not be misunderstood, blackened as he is with the smoke of a life-long conflict in the field of political practice? how is Mr Carlyle to say it and not be misunderstood, after his furious raid into this field with his *Latter-day Pamphlets*? how is Mr Ruskin, after his pugnacious political economy? I say, the critic must keep out of the region of immediate practice in the political, social, humanitarian sphere, if he wants to make a beginning for that more free speculative treatment of things, which may perhaps one day make its benefits felt even in this sphere, but in a natural and thence irresistible manner.

Do what he will, however, the critic will still remain exposed to frequent misunderstandings, and nowhere so much as in this country. For here people are particularly indisposed even to comprehend that without this free disinterested treatment of things, truth and the highest culture are out of the question. So immersed are they in practical life, so accustomed to take all their notions from this life and its processes, that they are apt to think that truth and culture themselves can be reached by the processes of this life, and that it is an impertinent singularity to think of reaching them in any other. 'We are all *terrae filii*,' cries their eloquent advocate; 'all Philistines together. Away with the notion of proceeding by any other course than the course dear to the Philistines; let us have a social movement, let us organize and combine a party to pursue truth and new thought, let us call it *the liberal party*, and let us all stick to each other, and back each other up. Let us have no nonsense about independent criticism, and intellectual delicacy, and the few and the many; don't let us trouble ourselves about foreign thought; we shall invent the whole thing for ourselves as we go along: if one of us speaks well, applaud him; if one of us speaks ill, applaud him too; we are all in the same movement, we are all liberals, we are all in pursuit of truth.' In this way the pursuit of truth becomes really a social, practical, pleasurable affair, almost requiring a chairman, a secretary, and advertisements; with the excitement of an occasional scandal, with a little resistance to give the happy sense of difficulty overcome; but, in general, plenty of bustle and very little thought. To act is so easy, as Goethe says; to think is so hard! It is true that the critic has many temptations to go with the stream, to make one of the party of movement, one of these *terrae filii*; it seems ungracious to refuse to be a *terrae filius*, when so many excellent people are; but the critic's duty is to refuse, or, if resistance is vain, at least to cry with Obermann: *Périssons en résistant*.

How serious a matter it is to try and resist, I had ample opportunity of experiencing when I ventured some time ago to criticize the celebrated first volume of Bishop Colenso.* The echoes of the storm which was then raised I still, from time to time, hear grumbling round me. That storm arose out of a

---

*So sincere is my dislike to all personal attack and controversy, that I abstain from reprinting, at this distance of time from the occasion which called them forth, the essays in which I criticized Dr Colenso's book; I feel bound, however, after all that has passed, to make here a final declaration of my sincere impenitence for having published them. Nay, I cannot forbear repeating yet once more, for his benefit and that of his readers, this sentence from my original remarks upon him: *There is truth of science and truth of religion; truth of science does not become truth of religion till it is made religious.* And I will add: Let us have all the science there is from the men of Science; from the men of religion let us have religion.

misunderstanding almost inevitable. It is a result of no little culture to attain to a clear perception that science and religion are two wholly different things; the multitude will for ever confuse them, but happily that is of no great real importance, for while the multitude imagines itself to live by its false science, it does really live by its true religion. Dr Colenso, however, in his first volume did all he could to strengthen the confusion,* and to make it dangerous. He did this with the best intentions, I freely admit, and with the most candid ignorance that this was the natural effect of what he was doing; but, says Joubert, 'Ignorance, which in matters of morals extenuates the crime, is itself, in intellectual matters, a crime of the first order.' I criticized Bishop Colenso's speculative confusion. Immediately there was a cry raised: 'What is this? here is a liberal attacking a liberal. Do not you belong to the movement? are not you a friend of truth? Is not Bishop Colenso in pursuit of truth? then speak with proper respect of his book. Dr Stanley is another friend of truth, and you speak with proper respect of his book; why make these invidious differences? both books are excellent, admirable, liberal; Bishop Colenso's perhaps the most so, because it is the boldest, and will have the best practical consequences for the liberal cause. Do you want to encourage to the attack of a brother liberal his, and your, and our implacable enemies, the *Church and State Review* or the *Record*, – the High Church rhinoceros and the Evangelical hyena? Be silent, therefore; or rather speak as loud as ever you can, and go into ecstacies over the eighty and odd pigeons.'

But criticism cannot follow this coarse and indiscriminate method. It is unfortunately possible for a man in pursuit of truth to write a book which reposes upon a false conception. Even the practical consequences of a book are to genuine criticism no recommendation of it, if the book is, in the highest sense, blundering. I see that a lady who herself, too, is in pursuit of truth, and who writes with great ability, but a little too much,

---

*It has been said I make it 'a crime against literary criticism and the higher culture to attempt to inform the ignorant'. Need I point out that the ignorant are not informed by being confirmed in a confusion?

perhaps, under the influence of the practical spirit of the English liberal movement, classes Bishop Colenso's book and M. Renan's together, in her survey of the religious state of Europe, as facts of the same order, works, both of them, of 'great importance'; 'great ability, power, and skill'; Bishop Colenso's, perhaps, the most powerful; at least, Miss Cobbe gives special expression to her gratitude that to Bishop Colenso 'has been given the strength to grasp, and the courage to teach, truths of such deep import.' In the same way, more than one popular writer has compared him to Luther. Now it is just this kind of false estimate which the critical spirit is, it seems to me, bound to resist. It is really the strongest possible proof of the low ebb at which, in England, the critical spirit is, that while the critical hit in the religious literature of Germany is Dr Strauss's book, in that of France M. Renan's book, the book of Bishop Colenso is the critical hit in the religious literature of England. Bishop Colenso's book reposes on a total misconception of the essential elements of the religious problem, as that problem is now presented for solution. To criticism, therefore, which seeks to have the best that is known and thought on this problem, it is, however well meant, of no importance whatever. M. Renan's book attempts a new synthesis of the elements furnished to us by the Four Gospels. It attempts, in my opinion, a synthesis, perhaps premature, perhaps impossible, certainly not successful. Up to the present time, at any rate, we must acquiesce in Fleury's sentence on such recastings of the Gospel story: *Quiconque s'imagine la pouvoir mieux écrire, ne l'entend pas.* M. Renan had himself passed by anticipation a like sentence on his own work, when he said: 'If a new presentation of the character of Jesus were offered to me, I would not have it; its very clearness would be, in my opinion, the best proof of its insufficiency.' His friends may with perfect justice rejoin that at the sight of the Holy Land, and of the actual scene of the Gospel-story, all the current of M. Renan's thoughts may have naturally changed, and a new casting of that story irresistibly suggested itself to him; and that this is just a case for applying Cicero's maxim: Change of mind is not inconsistency – *nemo doctus unquam mutationem consilii inconstantiam dixit esse.* Nevertheless, for criticism, M. Renan's first thought must still be the truer one, as long as his new casting so fails more fully to commend itself, more fully (to use Coleridge's happy phrase about the Bible) to *find* us. Still M. Renan's attempt is, for criticism, of the most real interest and importance, since, with all its difficulty, a fresh synthesis of the New Testament *data*, – not a making war on them, in Voltaire's fashion, not a leaving them out of mind, in the world's fashion, but the putting a new construction upon them, the taking them from under the old, adoptive, traditional, unspiritual point of view and placing them under a new one, – is the very essence of the religious problem, as now presented; and only by efforts in this direction can it receive a solution.

Again, in the same spirit in which she judges Bishop Colenso, Miss Cobbe, like so many earnest liberals of our practical race, both here and in America, herself sets vigorously about a positive reconstruction of religion, about making a religion of the future out of hand, or at least setting about making it; we must not rest, she and they are always thinking and saying, in negative criticism, we must be creative and constructive; hence we have such works as her recent *Religious Duty*, and works still more considerable, perhaps, by others, which will be in every one's mind. These works often have much ability; they often spring out of sincere convictions, and a sincere wish to do good; and they sometimes, perhaps, do good. Their fault is (if I may be permitted to say so) one which they have in common with the British College of Health, in the New Road. Every one knows the British College of Health; it is that building with the lion and the statue of the Goddess Hygeia before it; at least, I am sure about the lion, though I am not absolutely certain about the Goddess Hygeia. This building does credit, perhaps, to the resources of Dr Morrison and his disciples; but it falls a good deal short of one's idea of what a British College of Health ought to be. In England, where we hate public interference and love individual enterprise, we have a whole crop of places like the British College of Health; the grand name without the grand thing. Unluckily, creditable to individual enterprise as they are, they tend to impair our taste by making us forget what more grandiose, noble, or beautiful character properly belongs to a

public institution. The same may be said of the religions of the
future of Miss Cobbe and others. Creditable, like the British
College of Health, to the resources of their authors, they yet tend
to make us forget what more grandoise, noble, or beautiful
character properly belongs to religious constructions. The
historic religions, with all their faults, have had this; it certainly
belongs to the religious sentiment, when it truly flowers, to have
this; and we impoverish our spirit if we allow a religion of the
future without it. What then is the duty of criticism here? To
take the practical point of view, to applaud the liberal movement
and all its works, – its New Road religions of the future into the
bargain, – for their general utility's sake? By no means; but to be
perpetually dissatisfied with these works, while they perpetually
fall short of a high and perfect ideal.

For criticism, these are elementary laws; but they never can be
popular, and in this country they have been very little followed,
and one meets with immense obstacles in following them. That
is a reason for asserting them again and again. Criticism must
maintain its independence of the practical spirit and its aims.
Even with well-meant efforts of the practical spirit it must
express dissatisfaction, if in the sphere of the ideal they seem
impoverishing and limiting. It must not hurry on to the goal
because of its practical importance. It must be patient, and know
how to wait; and flexible, and know how to attach itself to things
and how to withdraw from them. It must be apt to study and
praise elements that for the fulness of spiritual perfection are
wanted, even though they belong to a power which in the
practical sphere may be maleficent. It must be apt to discern the
spiritual shortcomings or illusions of powers that in the practical
sphere may be beneficent. And this without any notion of
favouring or injuring, in the practical sphere, one power or the
other; without any notion of playing off, in this sphere, one
power against the other. When one looks, for instance, at the
English Divorce Court, – an institution which perhaps has its
practical conveniences, but which in the ideal sphere is so
hideous; an institution which neither makes divorce impossible
nor makes it decent, which allows a man to get rid of his wife, or
a wife of her husband, but makes them drag one another first,

for the public edification, through a mire of unutterable infamy, – when one looks at this charming institution, I say, with its crowded benches, its newspaper-reports, and its money compensations, this institution in which the gross unregenerate British Philistine has indeed stamped an image of himself, – one may be permitted to find the marriage-theory of Catholicism refreshing and elevating. Or when Protestantism, in virtue of its supposed rational and intellectual origin, gives the law to criticism too magisterially, criticism may and must remind it that its pretensions, in this respect, are illusive and do it harm; that the Reformation was a moral rather than an intellectual event; that Luther's theory of grace no more exactly reflects the mind of the spirit than Bossuet's philosophy of history reflects it; and that there is no more antecedent probability of the Bishop of Durham's stock of ideas being agreeable to perfect reason than of Pope Pius the Ninth's. But criticism will not on that account forget the achievements of Protestantism in the practical and moral sphere; nor that, even in the intellectual sphere, Protestantism, though in a blind and stumbling manner, carried forward the Renaissance, while Catholicism threw itself violently across its path.

I lately heard a man of thought and energy contrasting the want of ardour and movement which he now found amongst young men in this country with what he remembered in his own youth, twenty years ago. 'What reformers we were then!' he exclaimed; 'what a zeal we had! how we canvassed every institution in Church and State, and were prepared to remodel them all on first principles!' He was inclined to regret, as a spiritual flagging, the lull which he saw. I am disposed rather to regard it as a pause in which the turn to a new mode of spiritual progress is being accomplished. Everything was long seen, by the young and ardent amongst us, in inseparable connection with politics and practical life; we have pretty well exhausted the benefits of seeing things in this connection, we have got all that can be got by so seeing them. Let us try a more disinterested mode of seeing them; let us betake ourselves more to the serener life of the mind and spirit. This life, too, may have its excesses and dangers; but they are not for us at present. Let us think of quietly enlarging our stock of true and fresh ideas, and not, as soon as we get an idea or half an idea, be running out with it into the street, and trying to make it rule there. Our ideas will, in the end, shape the world all the better for maturing a little. Perhaps in fifty years' time it will in the English House of Commons be an objection to an institution that it is an anomaly, and my friend the Member of Parliament will shudder in his grave. But let us in the meanwhile rather endeavour that in twenty years' time it may, in English literature, be an objection to a proposition that it is absurd. That will be a change so vast, that the imagination almost fails to grasp it. *Ab integro saeclorum nascitur ordo*.

If I have insisted so much on the course which criticism must take where politics and religion are concerned, it is because, where these burning matters are in question, it is most likely to go astray. I have wished, above all, to insist on the attitude which criticism should adopt towards everything; on its right tone and temper of mind. Then comes the question as to the subject-matter which criticism should most seek. Here, in general, its course is determined for it by the idea which is the law of its being; the idea of a disinterested endeavour to learn and propagate the best that is known and thought in the world, and thus to establish a current of fresh and true ideas. By the very nature of things, as England is not all the world, much of the best that is known and thought in the world cannot be of English growth, must be foreign; by the nature of things, again, it is just this that we are least likely to know, while English thought is streaming in upon us from all sides and takes excellent care that we shall not be ignorant of its existence; the English critic, therefore, must dwell much on foreign thought, and with particular heed on any part of it, which, while significant and fruitful in itself, is for any reason specially likely to escape him. Again, judging is often spoken of as the critic's one business; and so in some sense it is; but the judgement which almost insensibly forms itself in a fair and clear mind, along with fresh knowledge, is the valuable one; and thus knowledge, and ever fresh knowledge, must be the critic's great concern for himself; and it is by communicating fresh knowledge, and letting his own judgement pass along with it, – but insensibly, and in the second place not the first, as a sort of companion and clue, not as an abstract lawgiver, – that he will generally do most good to his readers. Sometimes, no doubt, for the sake of establishing an author's place in literature, and his relation to a central standard, (and if this is not done, how are we to get at our *best in the world*?) criticism may have to deal with a subject-matter so familiar that fresh knowledge is out of the question, and then it must be all judgement; an enunciation and detailed application of principles. Here the great safeguard is never to let oneself become abstract, always to retain an intimate and lively consciousness of the truth of what one is saying, and, the moment this fails us, to be sure that something is wrong. Still, under all circumstances, this mere judgement and application of principles is, in itself, not the most satisfactory work to the critic; like mathematics, it is tautological, and cannot well give us, like fresh learning, the sense of creative activity.

But stop, some one will say; all this talk is of no practical use to us whatever; this criticism of yours is not what we have in our minds when we speak of criticism; when we speak of critics and criticism, we mean critics and criticism of the current English literature of the day; when you offer to tell criticism its function, it is to this criticism that we expect you to address yourself. I am sorry for it, for I am afraid I must disappoint these expectations. I am bound by my own definition of criticism: *a disinterested endeavour to learn and propagate the best that is known and thought in the world.* How much of current English literature comes into this 'best that is known and thought in the world'? Not very much, I fear; certainly less, at this moment, than of the current literature of France or Germany. Well, then, am I to alter my definition of criticism, in order to meet the requirements of a number of practising English critics, who, after all, are free in their choice of a business? That would be making criticism lend itself just to one of those alien practical considerations, which, I have said, are so fatal to it. One may say, indeed, to those who have to deal with the mass – so much better disregarded – of current English literature, that they may at all events endeavour, in dealing with this, to try it, so far as they can, by the standard of the best that is known and thought in the world; one may say, that to get anywhere near this standard, every critic should try and possess one great literature, at least, besides his own; and the more unlike his own, the better. But, after all, the criticism I am really concerned with, – the criticism which alone can much help us for the future, the criticism which, throughout Europe, is at the present day meant, when so much stress is laid on the importance of criticism and the critical spirit, – is a criticism which regards Europe as being, for intellectual and spiritual purposes, one great confederation, bound to a joint action and working to a common result; and whose members have, for their proper outfit, a knowledge of Greek, Roman, and Eastern antiquity, and of one another. Special, local, and temporary advantages being put out of account, that modern nation will in the intellectual and spiritual sphere make most progress, which most thoroughly carries out this programme. And what is that but saying that we too, all of us, as individuals, the more thoroughly we carry it out, shall make the more progress?

There is so much inviting us! – what are we to take? what will nourish us in growth towards perfection? That is the question which, with the immense field of life and of literature lying before him, the critic has to answer; for himself first, and afterwards for others. In this idea of the critic's business the essays brought together in the following pages have had their origin; in this idea, widely different as are their subjects, they have, perhaps, their unity.

I conclude with what I said at the beginning: to have the sense of creative activity is the great happiness and the great proof of being alive, and it is not denied to criticism to have it; but then criticism must be sincere, simple, flexible, ardent, ever widening its knowledge. Then it may have, in no contemptible measure, a joyful sense of creative activity; a sense which a man of insight and conscience will prefer to what he might derive from a poor, starved, fragmentary, inadequate creation. And at some epochs no other creation is possible.

Still, in full measure, the sense of creative activity belongs only to genuine creation; in literature we must never forget that. But what true man of letters ever can forget it? It is no such common matter for a gifted nature to come into possession of a current of true and living ideas, and to produce amidst the inspiration of them, that we are likely to underrate it. The epochs of Aeschylus and Shakespeare make us feel their pre-eminence. In an epoch like those is, no doubt, the true life of a literature; there is the promised land, towards which criticism can only beckon. That promised land it will not be ours to enter, and we shall die in the wilderness: but to have desired to enter it, to have saluted it from afar, is already, perhaps, the best distinction among contemporaries; it will certainly be the best title to esteem with posterity.

William Morris

William Morris (1834–96), like Ruskin who was to be such an important influence on him, was the son of a wealthy businessman, though unlike Ruskin his childhood was spent happily, at the family estate on the edge of Epping Forest. He was educated at Marlborough College and Oxford where a friendship with Edward Burne-Jones led to further friendships with the poets and painters who were to form the Pre-Raphaelite Brotherhood. On leaving Oxford, Morris was articled to the architect G. E. Street, but after a year decided to concentrate on painting. No one activity was ever to absorb his artistic energy. In 1858 he published his first book of poems, *The Defence of Guinevere*, and the following year he began, with Philip Webb, to design and build the Red House which was to be a home for himself and Jane Burden whom he married in 1859. His work with Philip Webb led to the formation of a firm specializing in all kinds of house decoration. His interest in Icelandic sagas led him to visit Iceland in 1871, and in 1877 he founded the Society for the Protection of Ancient Buildings. His concern with the relationship between art and society turned into direct political action with the 'Bulgarian Atrocities' agitation in the late 1870s. In 1883 he joined the Democratic Federation – at that time the most 'Marxist' of the various socialist groups in Britain – though he soon left to help form a breakaway group, the Socialist League. During the next ten years he was a tireless campaigner for socialism, giving lectures, writing for the SDF paper *Justice*, joining public demonstrations, acting as editor of *Commonweal*, and uniting the influences of Marx and Ruskin to write a series of tales and novels expressing his socialist beliefs, notably *A Dream of John Ball* (1888) and *News from Nowhere* (1890). 'How We Live and How We Might Live' was written as a lecture in 1884 and published in *Signs of Change* (1888): 'How I

Became a Socialist' was first published in *Justice*, 16 June 1894. In 1890 he left the Socialist League to form the Hammersmith Socialist Society. Although seriously ill for the last five years of his life, he continued to write on socialism, translate Icelandic sagas and to run the Kelmscott Press. The interest in printing was to bring together sharply some of the seemingly contradictory elements in his nature – the love of beauty expressed in expensively-produced books and house furnishings, and his passionate conviction that one day all would share in and appreciate such beauty. One of the first items published by the Kelmscott Press was a special edition of 'The Nature of Gothic' which Morris described in his preface to it as, 'one of the very few necessary and inevitable utterances of the century.'

HOW WE LIVE AND HOW WE MIGHT LIVE

The word Revolution, which we Socialists are so often forced to use, has a terrible sound in most people's ears, even when we have explained to them that it does not necessarily mean a change accompanied by riot and all kinds of violence, and cannot mean a change made mechanically and in the teeth of opinion by a group of men who have somehow managed to seize on the executive power for the moment. Even when we explain that we use the word revolution in its etymological sense, and mean by it a change in the basis of society, people are scared at the idea of such a vast change, and beg that you will speak of reform and not revolution. As, however, we Socialists do not at all mean by our word revolution what these worthy people mean by their word reform, I can't help thinking that it would be a mistake to use it, whatever projects we might conceal beneath its harmless envelope. So we will stick to our word, which means a change of the basis of society; it may frighten people, but it will at least warn them that there is something to be frightened about, which will be no less dangerous for being ignored; and also it may encourage some people, and will mean to them at least not a fear, but a hope.

Fear and Hope – those are the names of the two great passions which rule the race of man, and with which revolutionists have to deal; to give hope to the many oppressed and fear to the few oppressors, that is our business; if we do the first and give hope to the many, the few *must* be frightened by their hope; otherwise we do not want to frighten them; it is not revenge we want for poor people, but happiness; indeed, what revenge can be taken for all the thousands of years of the sufferings of the poor?

However, many of the oppressors of the poor, most of them, we will say, are not conscious of their being oppressors (we shall see why presently); they live in an orderly, quiet way themselves, as far as possible removed from the feelings of a Roman slave-owner or a Legree; they know that the poor exist, but their sufferings do not present themselves to them in a trenchant and dramatic way; they themselves have troubles to bear, and they think doubtless that to bear trouble is the lot of humanity; nor have they any means of comparing the troubles of their lives with those of people lower in the social scale; and if ever the thought of those heavier troubles obtrudes itself upon them, they console themselves with the maxim that people do get used to the troubles they have to bear, whatever they may be.

Indeed, as far as regards individuals at least, that is but too true, so that we have as supporters of the present state of things, however bad it may be, first those comfortable unconscious oppressors who think that they have everything to fear from any change which would involve more than the softest and most gradual of reforms, and secondly those poor people who, living hard and anxiously as they do, can hardly conceive of any change for the better happening to them, and dare not risk one tittle of their poor possessions in taking any action towards a possible bettering of their condition; so that while we can do little with the rich save inspire them with fear, it is hard indeed to give the poor any hope. It is, then, no less than reasonable that those whom we try to involve in the great struggle for a better form of life than that which we now lead should call on us to give them at least some idea of what that life may be like.

A reasonable request, but hard to satisfy, since we are living under a system that makes conscious effort towards reconstruction almost impossible: it is not unreasonable on our part to answer, 'There are certain definite obstacles to the real progress of man; we can tell you what these are; take them away, and then you shall see.'

However, I purpose now to offer myself as a victim for the satisfaction of those who consider that as things now go we have at least got something, and are terrified at the idea of losing their hold of that, lest they should find they are worse off than before, and have nothing. Yet in the course of my endeavour to show how we might live, I must more or less deal in negatives. I mean to say I must point out where in my opinion we fall short in our present attempts at decent life. I must ask the rich and well-to-do what sort of a position it is which they are so anxious to preserve at any cost? and if, after all, it will be such a terrible loss to them to give it up? and I must point out to the poor that they, with capacities for living a dignified and generous life, are in a position which they cannot endure without continued degradation.

How do we live, then, under our present system? Let us look at it a little.

And first, please to understand that our present system of Society is based on a state of perpetual war. Do any of you think that this is as it should be? I know that you have often been told that the competition which is at present the rule of all production, is a good thing, and stimulates the progress of the race; but the people who tell you this should call competition by its shorter name of *war* if they wish to be honest, and you would then be free to consider whether or not war stimulates progress, otherwise than as a mad bull chasing you over your own garden may do. War, or competition, whichever you please to call it, means at the best pursuing your own advantage at the cost of someone else's loss, and in the process of it you must not be sparing of destruction even of your own possessions, or you will certainly come by the worse in the struggle. You understand that perfectly as to the kind of war in which people go out to kill and be killed; that sort of war in which ships are commissioned, for instance, 'to sink, burn, and destroy'; but it appears that you are not so conscious of this waste of goods when you are only carrying on that other war called *commerce*; observe, however, that the waste is there all the same.

Now let us look at this kind of war a little closer, run through some of the forms of it, that we may see how the 'burn, sink, and destroy' is carried on in it.

First, you have that form of it called national rivalry, which in good truth is nowadays the cause of all gunpowder and bayonet wars which civilized nations wage. For years past we English have been rather shy of them, except on those happy occasions when we could carry them on at no sort of risk to ourselves, when the killing was all on one side, or at all events when we hoped it would be. We have been shy of gunpowder war with a respectable enemy for a long while, and I will tell you why: It is because we have had the lion's share of the world-market; we didn't want to fight for it as a nation, for we had got it; but now this is changing in a most significant, and, to a Socialist, a most cheering way; we are losing or have lost that lion's share; it is now a desperate 'competition' between the great nations of civilization for the world-market, and tomorrow it may be a desperate war for that end. As a result, the furthering of war (if it be not on too large a scale) is no longer confined to the honour-and-glory kind of old Tories, who if they meant anything at all by it meant that a Tory war would be a good occasion for damping down democracy; we have changed all that, and now it is quite another kind of politician that is wont to urge us on to 'patriotism' as 'tis called. The leaders of the Progressive Liberals, as they would call themselves, long-headed persons who know well enough that social movements are going on, who are not blind to the fact that the world will move with their help or without it; these have been the Jingoes of these later days. I don't mean to say they know what they are doing: politicians, as you well know, take good care to shut their eyes to everything that may happen six months ahead; but what is being done is this: that the present system, which always must include national rivalry, is pushing us into a desperate scramble for the markets on more or less equal terms with other nations, because, once more, we have lost that command of them which we once had. Desperate is not too strong a word. We shall let this impulse to snatch markets carry us whither it will, whither it must. Today it is successful burglary and disgrace, tomorrow it may be mere defeat and disgrace.

Now this is not a digression, although, in saying this I am nearer to what is generally called politics than I shall be again. I only want to show you what commercial war comes to when it has to do with foreign nations, and that even the dullest can see how mere waste must go with it. That is how we live now with foreign nations, prepared to ruin them without war if possible, with it if necessary, let alone meantime the disgraceful exploiting of savage tribes and barbarous peoples on whom we force at once our shoddy wares and our hypocrisy at the cannon's mouth.

Well, surely Socialism can offer you something in the place of all that. It can; it can offer you peace and friendship instead of war. We might live utterly without national rivalries, acknowledging that while it is best for those who feel that they naturally form a community under one name to govern themselves, yet that no community in civilization should feel that it had interests opposed to any other, their economical condition being at any rate similar; so that any citizen of one community could fall to work and live without disturbance of his life when he was in a foreign country, and would fit into his place quite naturally; so that all civilized nations would form one great community, agreeing together as to the kind and amount of production and distribution needed; working at such and such production where it could be best produced; avoiding waste by all means. Please to think of the amount of waste which they would avoid, how much such a revolution would add to the wealth of the world! What creature on earth would be harmed by such a revolution? Nay, would not everybody be the better for it? And what hinders it? I will tell you presently.

Meantime let us pass from this 'competition' between nations to that between 'the organizers of labour', great firms, joint-stock companies; capitalists in short, and see how competition 'stimulates production' among them: indeed it does do that; but what kind of production? Well, production of something to sell at a profit, or say production of profits: and note how war commercial stimulates that: a certain market is demanding goods; there are, say, a hundred manufacturers who make that kind of goods, and every one of them would if he could keep that market to himself, and struggles desperately to get as much of it as he can, with the obvious result that presently the thing is overdone, and the market is glutted, and all that fury of manufacture has to sink into cold ashes. Doesn't that seem something like war to you? Can't you see the waste of it – waste of labour, skill, cunning, waste of life in short? Well, you may say, but it cheapens the goods. In a sense it does; and yet only apparently, as wages have a tendency to sink for the ordinary workers in proportion as prices sink; and at what a cost do we gain this appearance of cheapness! Plainly speaking, at the cost of cheating the consumer and starving the real producer for the benefit of the gambler, who uses both consumer and producer as his milch cows. I needn't go at length into the subject of adulteration, for everyone knows what kind of a part it plays in this sort of commerce; but remember that it is an absolutely necessary incident to the production of profit out of wares, which is the business of the so-called manufacturer; and this you must understnd, that, taking him in the lump, the consumer is perfectly helpless against the gambler; the goods are forced on him by their cheapness, and with them a certain kind of life which that energetic, that aggressive cheapness determines for him: for so far-reaching is this curse of commercial war that no country is safe from its ravages; the traditions of a thousand years fall before it in a month; it overruns a weak or semi-barbarous country, and whatever romance or pleasure or art existed there, is trodden down into a mire of sordidness and ugliness; the Indian or Javanese craftsman may no longer ply his craft leisurely, working a few hours a day, in producing a maze of strange beauty on a piece of cloth: a steam-engine is set a-going at Manchester, and that victory over Nature and a thousand stubborn difficulties is used for the basework of producing a sort of plaster of china-clay and shoddy, and the Asiatic worker, if he is not starved to death outright, as plentifully happens, is driven himself into a factory to lower the wages of his Manchester brother worker, and nothing of character is left him except, most like, an accumulation of fear and hatred of that to him most unaccountable evil, his English master. The South Sea Islander must leave his canoe-carving, his sweet rest, and his graceful dances, and become the slave of a slave: trousers, shoddy, rum, missionary, and fatal disease – he must swallow all this civilization in the lump, and neither himself nor we can help him now till social order displaces the hideous tyranny of gambling that has ruined him.

Let those be types of the consumer: but now for the producer; I mean the real producer, the worker; how does this scramble for the plunder of the market affect him? The manufacturer, in the eagerness of his war, has had to collect into one neighbourhood a vast army of workers, he has drilled them till they are as fit as may be for his special branch of production, that is, for making a profit out of it, and with the result of their being fit for nothing else: well, when the glut comes in that market he is supplying, what happens to this army, every private in which has been depending on the steady demand in that market, and acting, as he could not choose but act, as if it were to go on for ever? You know well what happens to these men: the factory door is shut on them; on a very large part of them often, and at the best on the reserve army of labour, so busily employed in the time of inflation. What becomes of them? Nay, we know that well enough just now. But what we don't know, or don't choose to know, is, that this reserve army of labour is an absolute necessity for commercial war; if *our* manufacturers had not got these poor devils whom they could draft on to their machines when the demand swelled, other manufacturers in France, or Germany, or America, would step in and take the market from them.

So you see, as we live now, it is necessary that a vast part of the industrial population should be exposed to the danger of periodical semi-starvation, and that, not for the advantage of the people in another part of the world, but for their degradation and enslavement.

Just let your minds run for a moment on the kind of waste which this means, this opening up of new markets among savage and barbarous countries which is the extreme type of the force of the profit-market on the world, and you will surely see what a hideous nightmare that profit-market is: it keeps us sweating and terrified for our livelihood, unable to read a book, or look at a picture, or have pleasant fields to walk in, or to lie in the sun, or to share in the knowledge of our time, to have in short either animal or intellectual pleasure, and for what? that we may go on living the same slavish life till we die, in order to provide for a rich man what is called a life of ease and luxury; that is to say, a life so empty, unwholesome, and degraded, that perhaps, on the whole, he is worse off than we the workers are: and as to the result of all this suffering, it is luckiest when it is nothing at all, when you can say that the wares have done nobody any good; for oftenest they have done many people harm, and we have toiled and groaned and died in making poison and destruction for our fellow-men.

Well, I say all this is war, and the results of war, the war this time, not of competing nations, but of competing firms or capitalist units: and it is this war of the firms which hinders the peace between nations which you surely have agreed with me in thinking is so necessary; for you must know that war is the very breath of the nostrils of these fighting firms, and they have now, in our times, got into their hands nearly all the political power, and they band together in each country in order to make their respective governments fulfil just two functions: the first is at home to act as a strong police force, to keep the ring in which the strong are beating down the weak; the second is to act as a piratical body-guard abroad, a petard to explode the doors which lead to the markets of the world: markets at any price abroad, uninterfered-with privilege, falsely called *laissez-faire*,* at any price at home, to provide these is the sole business of a government such as our industrial captains have been able to conceive of. I must now try to show you the reason of all this, and what it rests on, by trying to answer the question, Why have the profit-makers got all this power, or at least why are they able to keep it?

*Falsely; because the privileged classes have at their back the force of the Executive by means of which to compel the unprivileged to accept their terms; if this is 'free competition' there is no meaning in words.

That takes us to the third form of war commercial: the last, and the one which all the rest is founded on. We have spoken first of the war of rival nations; next of that of rival firms: we have now to speak of rival men. As nations under the present system are driven to compete with one another for the markets of the world, and as firms or the captains of industry have to scramble for their share of the profits of the markets, so also have the workers to compete with each other – for livelihood; and it is this constant competition or war amongst them which enables the profit-grinders to make their profits, and by means of the wealth so acquired to take all the executive power of the country into their hands. But here is the difference between the position of the workers and the profit-makers: to the latter, the profit-grinders, war is necessary; you cannot have profit-making without competition, individual, corporate, and national; but you may work for a livelihood without competing; you may combine instead of competing.

I have said war was the life-breath of the profit-makers; in like manner, combination is the life of the workers. The working-classes or proletariat cannot even exist as a class without combination of some sort. The necessity which forced the profit-grinders to collect their men first into workshops working by the division of labour, and next into great factories worked by machinery, and so gradually to draw them into the great towns and centres of civilization, gave birth to a distinct working-class or proletariat: and this it was which gave them their *mechanical* existence, so to say. But note, that they are indeed combined into social groups for the production of wares, but only as yet mechanically; they do not know what they are working at, nor whom they are working for, because they are combining to produce wares of which the profit of a master forms an essential part, instead of goods for their own use: as long as they do this, and compete with each other for leave to do it, they will be, and will feel themselves to be, simply a part of those competing firms I have been speaking of; they will be in fact just a part of the machinery for the production of profit; and so long as this lasts it will be the aim of the masters or profit-makers to decrease the market value of this human part of the machinery; that is to say, since they already hold in their hands the labour of dead men in the form of capital and machinery, it is their interest, or we will say their necessity, to pay as little as they can help for the labour of living men which they have to buy from day to day: and since the workmen they employ have nothing but their labour-power, they are compelled to underbid one another for employment and wages, and so enable the capitalist to play his game.

I have said that, as things go, the workers are a part of the competing firms, an adjunct of capital. Nevertheless, they are only so by compulsion; and, even without their being conscious of it, they struggle against that compulsion and its immediate results, the lowering of their wages, of their standard of life: and this they do, and must do, both as a class and individually: just as the slave of the great Roman lord, though he distinctly felt himself to be a part of the household, yet collectively was a force in reserve for its destruction, and individually stole from his lord whenever he could safely do so. So, here, you see, is another form of war necessary to the way we live now, the war of class against class, which, when it rises to its height, and it seems to be rising at present, will destroy those other forms of war we have been speaking of; will make the position of the profit-makers, of perpetual commercial war, untenable; will destroy the present system of competitive privilege, or commercial war.

Now observe, I said that to the existence of the workers it was combination, not competition, that was necessary, while to that of the profit-makers combination was impossible, and war necessary. The present position of the workers is that of the machinery of commerce, or in plainer words its slaves; when they change that position and become free, the class of profit-makers must cease to exist; and what will then be the position of the workers? Even as it is they are the one necessary part of society, the life-giving part; the other classes are but hangers-on who live on them. But what should they be, what will they be, when they, once for all, come to know their real power, and cease competing with one another for livelihood? I will tell you: they will be society, they will be the community. And being society — that is, there being no class outside them to contend with — they can then regulate their labour in accordance with their own real needs.

There is much talk about supply and demand, but the supply and demand usually meant is an artificial one; it is under the sway of the gambling-market; the demand is forced, as I hinted above, before it is supplied; nor, as each producer is working against all the rest, can the producers hold their hands, till the market is glutted and the workers, thrown out on the streets, hear that there has been overproduction, amidst which over-plus of unsaleable goods they go ill-supplied with even necessaries, because the wealth which they themselves have created is 'ill-distributed', as we call it — that is, unjustly taken away from them.

When the workers are society they will regulate their labour, so that the supply and demand shall be genuine, not gambling; the two will then be commensurate, for it is the same society which demands that also supplies; there will be no more artificial famines then, no more poverty amidst over-production, amidst too great a stock of the very things which should supply poverty and turn it into well-being. In short, there will be no waste and therefore no tyranny.

Well, now, what Socialism offers you in place of these artificial famines, with their so-called over-production, is, once more, regulation of the markets; supply and demand commensurate; no gambling, and consequently (once more) no waste; not overwork and weariness for the worker one month, and the next no work and terror of starvation, but steady work and plenty of leisure every month; not cheap market wares, that is to say, adulterated wares, with scarcely any *good* in them, mere scaffold-poles for building up profits; no labour would be spent on such things as these, which people would cease to want when they ceased to be slaves. Not these, but such goods as best fulfilled the real uses of the consumers would labour be set to make; for profit being abolished, people could have what they wanted, instead of what the profit-grinders at home and abroad forced them to take.

For what I want you to understand is this: that in every civilized country at least there is plenty for all — is, or at any rate might be. Even with labour so misdirected as it is at present, an equitable distribution of the wealth we have would make all people comparatively comfortable; but that is nothing to the wealth we might have if labour were not misdirected.

Observe, in the early days of the history of man he was the slave of his most immediate necessities; Nature was mighty and he was feeble, and he had to wage constant war with her for his daily food and such shelter as he could get. His life was bound down and limited by this constant struggle; all his morals, laws, religion, are in fact the outcome and the reflection of this ceaseless toil of earning his livelihood. Time passed, and little by little, step by step, he grew stronger, till now after all these ages he has almost completely conquered Nature, and one would think should now have leisure to turn his thoughts towards higher things than procuring tomorrow's dinner. But, alas! his progress has been broken and halting; and though he has indeed conquered Nature and has her forces under his control to do what he will with, he still has himself to conquer, he still has to think how he will best use those forces which he has mastered. At present he uses them blindly, foolishly, as one driven by mere fate. It would almost seem as if some phantom of the ceaseless pursuit of food which was once the master of the savage was still hunting the civilized man; who toils in a dream, as it were, haunted by mere dim unreal hopes, born of vague recollections of the days gone by. Out of that dream he must wake, and face things as they really are. The conquest of Nature is complete, may we not say? and now our business is, and has for long been, the organization of man, who wields the forces of Nature. Nor till this is attempted at least shall we ever be free of that terrible phantom of fear of starvation which, with its brother devil, desire of domination, drives us into injustice, cruelty, and dastardliness of all kinds: to cease to fear our fellows and learn to depend on them, to do away with competition and build up co-operation, is our one necessity.

Now, to get closer to details; you probably know that every man in civilization is worth, so to say, more than his skin; working, as he must work, socially, he can produce more than will keep himself alive and in fair condition; and this has been so for many centuries, from the time, in fact, when warring tribes began to make their conquered enemies slaves instead of killing them; and of course his capacity of producing these extras has gone on increasing faster and faster, till today one man will weave, for instance, as much cloth in a week as will clothe a whole village for years: and the real question of civilization has always been what are we to do with this extra produce of labour – a question which the phantom, fear of starvation, and its fellow, desire of domination, has driven men to answer pretty badly always, and worst of all perhaps in these present days, when the extra produce has grown with such prodigious speed. The practical answer has always been for man to struggle with his fellow for private possession of undue shares of these extras, and all kinds of devices have been employed by those who found themselves in possession of the power of taking them from others to keep those whom they had robbed in perpetual subjection; and these latter, as I have already hinted, had no chance of resisting this fleecing as long as they were few and scattered, and consequently could have little sense of their common oppression. But now that, owing to the very pursuit of these undue shares of profit, or extra earnings, men have become more dependent on each other for production, and have been driven, as I said before, to combine together for that end more completely, the power of the workers – that is to say, of the robbed or fleeced class – has enormously increased, and it only remains for them to understand that they have this power. When they do that they will be able to give the right answer to the question what is to be done with the extra products of labour over and above what will keep the labourer alive to labour: which answer is, that the worker will have all that he produces, and not be fleeced at all: and remember that he produces collectively, and therefore he will do effectively what work is required of him according to his capacity, and of the produce of that work he will have what he needs; because, you see, he cannot *use* more than he needs – he can only *waste* it.

If this arrangement seems to you preposterously ideal, as it well may, looking at our present condition, I must back it up by saying that when men are organized so that their labour is not wasted, they will be relieved from the fear of starvation and the desire of domination, and will have freedom and leisure to look round and see what they really do need.

Now something of that I can conceive for my own self, and I will lay my ideas before you, so that you may compare them with your own, asking you always to remember that the very differences in men's capacities and desires, after the common need of food and shelter is satisfied, will make it easier to deal with their desires in a communal state of things.

What is it that I need, therefore, which my surrounding circumstances can give me – my dealings with my fellow men – setting aside inevitable accidents which co-operation and forethought cannot control, if there be such?

Well, first of all I claim good health; and I say that a vast proportion of people in civilization scarcely even know what that means. To feel mere life a pleasure; to enjoy the moving one's limbs and exercising one's bodily powers; to play, as it were, with sun and wind and rain; to rejoice in satisfying the due bodily appetites of a human animal without fear of degradation or sense of wrong-doing: yes, and therewithal to be well-formed, straight-limbed, strongly knit, expressive of countenance – to be, in a word, beautiful – that also I claim. If we cannot have this claim satisfied, we are but poor creatures after all; and I claim it in the teeth of those terrible doctrines of asceticism, which, born of the despair of the oppressed and degraded, have been for so many ages used as instruments for the continuance of that oppression and degradation.

And I believe that this claim for a healthy body for all of us carries with it all other due claims: for who knows where the seeds of disease which even rich people suffer from were first sown: from the luxury of an ancestor, perhaps; yet often, I suspect, from his poverty. And for the poor: a distinguished physicist has said that the poor suffer always from one disease – hunger; and at least I know this, that if a man is overworked in any degree he cannot enjoy the sort of health I am speaking of; nor can he if he is continually chained to one dull round of mechanical work, with no hope at the other end of it; nor if he lives in continual sordid anxiety for his livelihood, nor if he is ill-housed, nor if he is deprived of all enjoyment of the natural beauty of the world, nor if he has no amusement to quicken the flow of his spirits from time to time: all these things, which touch more or less directly on his bodily condition, are born of the claim I make to live in good health; indeed, I suspect that these good conditions must have been in force for several generations before a population in general will be really healthy, as I have hinted above; but also I doubt not that in the course of time they would, joined to other conditions, of which more hereafter, gradually breed such a population, living in enjoyment of animal life at least, happy therefore, and beautiful according to the beauty of their race. On this point I may note that the very variations in the races of men are caused by the conditions under which they live, and though in these rougher parts of the world we lack some of the advantages of climate and surroundings, yet, if we were working for livelihood and not for profit, we might easily neutralize many of the disadvantages of our climate, at least enough to give due scope to the full development of our race.

Now the next thing I claim is education. And you must not say that every English child is educated now; that sort of education will not answer my claim, though I cheerfully admit it is something: something, and yet after all only class education. What I claim is liberal education; opportunity, that is, to have my share of whatever knowledge there is in the world according to my capacity or bent of mind, historical or scientific; and also to have my share of skill of hand which is about in the world, either in the industrial handicrafts or in the fine arts; picture-painting, sculpture, music, acting, or the like: I claim to be taught, if I can be taught, more than one craft to exercise for the benefit of the community. You may think this a large claim, but I am clear it is not too large a claim if the community is to have any gain out of my special capacities, if we are not all to be beaten down to a dull level of mediocrity as we are now, all but the very strongest and toughest of us.

But also I know that this claim for education involves one for public advantages in the shape of public libraries, schools, and the like, such as no private person, not even the richest, could command: but these I claim very confidently, being sure that no reasonable community could bear to be without such helps to a decent life.

Again, the claim for education involves a claim for abundant leisure, which once more I make with confidence; because when once we have shaken off the slavery of profit, labour would be organized so unwastefully that no heavy burden would be laid on the individual citizens; every one of whom as a matter of course would have to pay his toll of some obviously useful work. At present you must note that all the amazing machinery which we have invented has served only to increase the amount of profit-bearing wares; in other words, to increase the amount of profit pouched by individuals for their own advantage, part of which profit they use as capital for the production of more profit, with ever the same waste attached to it; and part as private riches or means for luxurious living, which again is sheer waste — is in fact to be looked on as a kind of bonfire on which rich men burn up the product of the labour they have fleeced from the workers beyond what they themselves can use. So I say that, in spite of our inventions, no worker works under the present system an hour the less on account of those labour-saving machines, so-called But under a happier state of things they would be used simply for saving labour, with the result of a vast amount of leisure gained for the community to be added to that gained by the avoidance of the waste of useless luxury, and the abolition of the service of commercial war.

And I may say that as to that leisure, as I should in no case do any harm to anyone with it, so I should often do some direct good to the community with it, by practising arts or occupations for my hands or brain which would give pleasure to many of the citizens; in other words, a great deal of the best work done in the leisure time of men relieved from any anxiety as to their livelihood, and eager to exercise their special talent, as all men, nay, all animals are.

Now, again, this leisure would enable me to please myself and expand my mind by travelling if I had a mind to it: because, say, for instance, that I were a shoemaker; if due social order were established, it by no means follows that I should always be obliged to make shoes in one place; a due amount of easily conceivable arrangement would enable me to make shoes in Rome, say, for three months, and to come back with new ideas of building, gathered from the sight of the works of past ages, amongst other things which would perhaps be of service in London.

But now, in order that my leisure might not degenerate into idleness and aimlessness, I must set up a claim for due work to do. Nothing to my mind is more important than this demand, and I must ask your leave to say something about it. I have mentioned that I should probably use my leisure for doing a good deal of what is now called work; but it is clear that if I am a member of a Socialist Community I must do my due share of rougher work than this – my due share of what my capacity enables me to do, that is; no fitting of me to a Procrustean bed; but even that share of work necessary to the existence of the simplest social life must, in the first place, whatever else it is, be reasonable work; that is, it must be such work as a good citizen can see the necessity for; as a member of the community, I must have agreed to do it.

To take two strong instances of the contrary, I won't submit to be dressed up in red and marched off to shoot at my French or German or Arab friend in a quarrel that I don't understand; I will rebel sooner than do that.

Nor will I submit to waste my time and energies in making some trifling toy which I know only a fool can desire; I will rebel sooner than do that.

However, you may be sure that in a state of social order I shall have no need to rebel against any such pieces of unreason; only I am forced to speak from the way we live to the way we might live.

Again, if the necessary reasonable work be of a mechanical kind, I must be helped to do it by a machine, not to cheapen my labour, but so that as little time as possible may be spent upon it, and that I may be able to think of other things while I am tending the machine. And if the work be specially rough or exhausting, you will, I am sure, agree with me in saying that I must take turns in doing it with other people; I mean I mustn't, for instance, be expected to spend my working hours always at the bottom of a coal-pit. I think such work as that ought to be largely volunteer work, and done, as I say, in spells. And what I say of very rough work I say also of nasty work. On the other hand, I should think very little of the manhood of a stout and healthy man who did not feel a pleasure in doing rough work; always supposing him to work under the conditions I have been speaking of – namely, feeling that it was useful (and consequently honoured), and that it was not continuous or hopeless, and that he was really doing it of his own free will.

The last claim I make for my work is that the places I worked in, factories or workshops, should be pleasant, just as the fields where our most necessary work is done are pleasant. Believe me there is nothing in the world to prevent this being done, save the necessity of making profits on all wares; in other words, the wares are cheapened at the expense of people being forced to work in crowded, unwholesome, squalid, noisy dens: that is to say, they are cheapened at the expense of the workman's life.

Well, so much for my claims as to my *necessary* work, my tribute to the community. I believe people would find, as they advanced in their capacity for carrying on social order, that life so lived was much less expensive than we now can have any idea of, and that, after a little, people would rather be anxious to seek work than to avoid it; that our working hours would rather be merry parties of men and maids, young men and old enjoying themselves over their work, than the grumpy weariness it mostly is now. Then would come the time for the new birth of art, so much talked of, so long deferred; people could not help showing their mirth and pleasure in their work, and would be always wishing to express it in a tangible and more or less enduring form, and the workshop would once more be a school of art, whose influence no one could escape from.

And, again, that word art leads me to my last claim, which is that the material surroundings of my life should be pleasant, generous, and beautiful; that I know is a large claim, but this I will say about it, that if it cannot be satisfied, if every civilized community cannot provide such surroundings for all its members, I do not want the world to go on; it is a mere misery that man has ever existed. I do not think it possible under the present circumstances to speak too strongly on this point. I feel sure that the time will come when people will find it difficult to believe that a rich community such as ours, having such command over external Nature, could have submitted to live such a mean, shabby, dirty life as we do.

And once for all, there is nothing in our circumstances save the hunting of profit that drives us into it. It is profit which draws men into enormous unmanageable aggregations called towns, for instance; profit which crowds them up when they are there into quarters without gardens or open spaces; profit which won't take the most ordinary precautions against wrapping a whole district in a cloud of sulphurous smoke; which turns beautiful rivers into filthy sewers; which condemns all but the rich to live in houses idiotically cramped and confined at the best, and at the worst in houses for whose wretchedness there is no name.

I say it is almost incredible that we should bear such crass stupidity as this; nor should we if we could help it. We shall not bear it when the workers get out of their heads that they are but an appendage to profit-grinding, that the more profits that are made the more employment at high wages there will be for them, and that therefore all the incredible filth, disorder, and degradation of modern civilization are signs of their prosperity. So far from that, they are signs of their slavery. When they are no longer slaves they will claim as a matter of course that every man and every family should be generously lodged; that every child should be able to play in a garden close to the place his parents live in; that the houses should by their obvious decency and order be ornaments to Nature, not disfigurements of it; for the decency and order above-mentioned when carried to the due pitch would most assuredly lead to beauty in building. All this, of course, would mean the people – that is, all society – duly organized, having in its own hands the means of production, to be *owned* by no individual, but used by all as occasion called for its use, and can only be done on those terms; on any other terms people will be driven to accumulate private wealth for themselves, and thus, as we have seen, to waste the goods of the community and perpetuate the division into classes, which means continual war and waste.

As to what extent it may be necessary or desirable for people under social order to live in common, we may differ pretty much according to our tendencies towards social life. For my part I can't see why we should think it a hardship to eat with the people we work with; I am sure that as to many things, such as valuable books, pictures, and splendour of surroundings, we shall find it better to club our means together; and I must say that often when I have been sickened by the stupidity of the mean idiotic rabbit-warrens that rich men build for themselves in Bayswater and elsewhere, I console myself with visions of the noble communal hall of the future, unsparing of materials, generous in worthy ornament, alive with the noblest thoughts of our time, and the past, embodied in the best art which a free and manly people could produce; such an abode of man as no private enterprise could come anywhere near for beauty and fitness, because only collective thought and collective life could cherish the aspirations which would give birth to its beauty, or have the skill and leisure to carry them out. I for my part should think it much the reverse of a hardship if I had to read my books and meet my friends in such a place; nor do I think I am better off to live in a vulgar stuccoed house crowded with upholstery that I despise, in all respects degrading to the mind and enervating to the body to live in, simply because I call it my own, or my house.

It is not an original remark, but I make it here, that my home is where I meet people with whom I sympathize, whom I love.

Well, that is my opinion as a middle-class man. Whether a working-class man would think his family possession of his wretched little room better than his share of the palace of which I have spoken, I must leave to his opinion, and to the imaginations of the middle class, who perhaps may sometimes conceive the fact that the said worker is cramped for space and comfort – say on washing-day.

Before I leave this matter of the surroundings of life, I wish to meet a possible objection. I have spoken of machinery being used freely for releasing people from the more mechanical and repulsive part of necessary labour; and I know that to some cultivated people, people of the artistic turn of mind, machinery is particularly distasteful, and they will be apt to say you will never get your surroundings pleasant so long as you are surrounded by machinery. I don't quite admit that; it is the allowing machines to be our masters and not our servants that so injures the beauty of life nowadays. In other words, it is the token of the terrible crime we have fallen into of using our control of the powers of Nature for the purpose of enslaving people, we careless meantime of how much happiness we rob their lives of.

Yet for the consolation of the artists I will say that I believe indeed that a state of social order would probably lead at first to a great development of machinery for really useful purposes, because people will still be anxious about getting through the work necessary to holding society together; but that after a while they will find that there is not so much work to do as they expected, and that then they will have leisure to reconsider the whole subject; and if it seems to them that a certain industry would be carried on more pleasantly as regards the worker, and more effectually as regards the goods, by using hand-work rather than machinery, they will certainly get rid of their machinery, because it will be possible for them to do so. It isn't possible now; we are not at liberty to do so; we are slaves to the monsters which we have created. And I have a kind of hope that the very elaboration of machinery in a society whose purpose is not the multiplication of labour, as it now is, but the carrying on of a pleasant life, as it would be under social order — that the elaboration of machinery, I say, will lead to the simplification of life, and so once more to the limitation of machinery.

Well, I will now let my claims for decent life stand as I have made them. To sum up in brief, they are: first, a healthy body; second, an active mind in sympathy with the past, the present, and the future; thirdly, occupation fit for a healthy body and an active mind; and fourthly, a beautiful world to live in.

These are the conditions of life which the refined man of all ages has set before him as the thing above all others to be attained. Too often he has been so foiled in their pursuit that he has turned longing eyes backwards to the days before civilization, when man's sole business was getting himself food from day to day, and hope was dormant in him, or at least could not be expressed by him.

Indeed, if civilization (as many think) forbids the realization of the hope to obtain such conditions of life, then civilization forbids mankind to be happy; and if that be the case, then let us stifle all aspirations towards progress – nay, all feelings of mutual goodwill and affection between men – and snatch each one of us what we can from the heap of wealth that fools create for rogues to grow fat on; or better still, let us as speedily as possible find some means of dying like men, since we are forbidden to live like men.

Rather, however, take courage, and believe that we of this age, in spite of all its torment and disorder, have been born to a wonderful heritage fashioned of the work of those that have gone before us; and that the day of the organization of man is dawning. It is not we who can build up the new social order; the past ages have done the most of that work for us; but we can clear our eyes to the signs of the times, and we shall then see that the attainment of a good condition of life is being made possible for us, and that it is now our business to stretch out our hands to take it.

And how? Chiefly, I think, by educating people to a sense of their real capacities as men, so that they may be able to use to their own good the political power which is rapidly being thrust upon them; to get them to see that the old system of organizing labour *for individual profit* is becoming unmanageable, and that the whole people have now got to choose between the confusion resulting from the break-up of that system and the determination to take in hand the labour now organized for profit, and use its organization for the livelihood of the community: to get people to see that individual profit-makers are not a necessity for labour but an obstruction to it, and that not only or chiefly because they are the perpetual pensioners of labour, as they are, but rather because of the waste which their existence as a class necessitates. All this we have to teach people, when we have taught ourselves; and I admit that the work is long and burdensome; as

I began by saying, people have been made so timorous of change by the terror of starvation that even the unluckiest of them are stolid and hard to move. Hard as the work is, however, its reward is not doubtful. The mere fact that a body of men, however small, are banded together as Socialist missionaries shows that the change is going on. As the working-classes, the real organic part of society, take in these ideas, hope will arise in them, and they will claim changes in society, many of which doubtless will not tend directly towards their emancipation, because they will be claimed without due knowledge of the one thing necessary to claim, *equality of condition*; but which indirectly will help to break up our rotten sham society, while that claim for equality of condition will be made constantly and with growing loudness till it *must* be listened to, and then at last it will only be a step over the border, and the civilized world will be socialized; and, looking back on what has been, we shall be astonished to think of how long we submitted to live as we live now.

HOW I BECAME A SOCIALIST

I am asked by the editor to give some sort of a history of the above conversion, and I feel that it may be of some use to do so, if my readers will look upon me as a type of a certain group of people but not so easy to do clearly, briefly and truly. Let me, however, try. But first, I will say what I mean by being a Socialist, since I am told that the word no longer expresses defintely and with certainty what it did ten years ago. Well, what I mean by Socialism is a condition of society in which there should be neither rich nor poor, neither master nor master's man, neither idle nor overworked, neither brain-sick brain workers, nor heart-sick hand workers, in a word, in which all men would be living in equality of condition, and would manage their affairs unwastefully, and with the full consciousness that harm to one would mean harm to all – the realization at last of the meaning of the word COMMONWEALTH.

Now this view of Socialism which I hold today, and hope to die holding, is what I began with; I had no transitional period, unless you may call such a brief period of political radicalism during which I saw my ideal clear enough, but had no hope of any realization of it. That came to an end some months before I joined the (then) Democratic Federation, and the meaning of my joining that body was that I had conceived a hope of the realization of my ideal. If you ask me how much of a hope, or what I thought we Socialists then living and working would accomplish towards it, or when there would be effected any change in the face of society, I must say, I do not know. I can only say that I did not measure my hope, nor the joy that it brought me at the time. For the rest, when I took that step I was blankly ignorant of economics; I had never so much as opened Adam Smith, or heard of Ricardo, or of Karl Marx. Oddly enough, I *had* read some of Mill, to wit, those posthumous papers of his (published was it in the *Westminster Review* or the *Fortnightly*?) in which he attacks Socialism in its Fourierist guise. In those papers he put the arguments, as far as they go, clearly and honestly, and the result, so far as I was concerned, was to convince me that Socialism was a necessary change, and that it was possible to bring it about in our own days. Those papers put the finishing touch to my conversion to Socialism. Well, having joined a Socialist body (for the Federation soon became definitely Socialist), I put some conscience into trying to learn the economical side of Socialism, and even tackled Marx, though I must confess that, whereas I thoroughly enjoyed the historical part of 'Capital', I suffered agonies of confusion of the brain over reading the pure economics of that great work. Anyhow, I read what I could, and will hope that some information stuck to me from my reading; but more, I must think, from continuous conversation with such friends as Bax and Hyndman and Scheu, and the brisk course of propaganda meetings which were going on at the time, and in which I took my share. Such finish to what of education in practical Socialism as I am capable of I received afterwards from some of my Anarchist friends, from whom I learned, quite against their intention, that Anarchism was impossible, much as I learned from Mill against *his* intention that Socialism was necessary.

But in this telling how I fell into *practical* Socialism I have begun, as I perceive, in the middle, for in my position of a well-to-do man, not suffering from the disabilities which oppress a working-man at every step, I feel that I might never have been drawn into the practical side of the question if an ideal had not forced me to seek towards it. For politics as politics, i.e., not regarded as a necessary if cumbersome and disgustful means to an end, would never have attracted me, nor when I had become conscious of the wrongs of society as it now is, and the oppression of poor people, could I have ever believed in the possibility of a *partial* setting right of those wrongs. In other words, I could never have been such a fool as to believe in the happy and 'respectable' poor.

If, therefore, my ideal forced me to look for practical Socialism, what was it that forced me to conceive of an ideal? Now, here comes in what I said (in this paper) of my being a type of a certain group of mind.

Before the uprising of *modern* Socialism almost all intelligent people either were, or professed themselves to be, quite contented with the civilization of this century. Again, almost all of these really were thus contented, and saw nothing to do but to perfect the said civilization by getting rid of a few ridiculous survivals of the barbarous ages. To be short, this was the *Whig* frame of mind, natural to the modern prosperous middle-class men, who, in fact, as far as mechanical progress is concerned, have nothing to ask for, if only Socialism would leave them alone to enjoy their plentiful style.

But besides these contented ones there were others who were not really contented, but had a vague sentiment of repulsion to the triumph of civilization, but were coerced into silence by the measureless power of Whiggery. Lastly, there were a few who were in open rebellion against the said Whiggery – a few, say two, Carlyle and Ruskin. The latter, before my days of practical Socialism, was my master towards the ideal aforesaid, and, looking backward, I cannot help saying, by the way, how deadly dull the world would have been twenty years ago but for Ruskin! It was through him that I learned to give form to my discontent, which I must say was not by any means vague. Apart from the desire to produce beautiful things, the leading passion of my life has been and is hatred of modern civilization. What shall I say of it now, when the words are put into my mouth, my hope of its destruction – what shall I say of its supplanting by Socialism?

What shall I say concerning its mastery of and its waste of mechanical power, its commonwealth so poor, its enemies of the commonwealth so rich, its stupendous organization – for the misery of life! Its contempt of simple pleasures which everyone could enjoy but for its folly? Its eyeless vulgarity which has destroyed art, the one certain solace of labour? All this I felt then as now, but I did not know why it was so. The hope of the past times was gone, the struggles of mankind for many ages had produced nothing but this sordid, aimless, ugly confusion; the immediate future seemed to me likely to intensify all the present evils by sweeping away the last survivals of the days before the dull squalor of civilization had settled down on the world. This was a bad look-out indeed, and, if I may mention myself as a personality and not as a mere type, especially so to a man of my disposition, careless of metaphysics and religion, as well as of scientific analysis, but with a deep love of the earth and the life on it, and a passion for the history of the past of mankind. Think of it! Was it all to end in a counting-house on the top of a cinder-heap, with Podsnap's drawing-room in the offing, and a Whig committee dealing out champagne to the rich and margarine to the poor in such convenient proportions as would make all men contented together, though the pleasure of the eyes was gone from the world, and the place of Homer was to be taken by Huxley? Yet, believe me, in my heart, when I really forced myself to look towards the future, that is what I saw in it, and, as far as I could tell, scarce anyone seemed to think it worthwhile to struggle against such a consummation of civilization. So there I was in for a fine pessimistic end of life, if it had not somehow dawned on me that amidst all this filth of civilization the seeds of a great change, what we others call Social Revolution, were beginning to germinate. The whole face of things was changed to me by that discovery, and all I had to do then in order to become a Socialist was to hook myself on to the practical movement, which, as before said, I have tried to do as well as I could.

To sum up, then, the study of history and the love and practice of art forced me into hatred of the civilization which, if things were to stop as they are, would turn history into inconsequent nonsense, and make art a collection of the curiosities of the past which would have no serious relation to the life of the present.

But the consciousness of revolution stirring amidst our hateful modern society prevented me, luckier than many others of artistic perceptions, from crystallizing into a mere railer against 'progress' on the one hand, and on the other from wasting time and energy in any of the numerous schemes by which the quasi-artistic of the middle classes hope to make art grow when it has no longer any root, and thus I became a practical Socialist.

A last word or two. Perhaps some of our friends will say, what have we to do with these matters of history and art? We want by means of Social Democracy to win a decent livelihood, we want in some sort to live, and that at once. Surely anyone who professes to think that the question of art and cultivation must go before that of the knife and fork (and there are some who do propose that) does not understand what art means, or how that its roots must have a soil of a thriving and unanxious life. Yet it must be remembered that civilization has reduced the workman to such a skinny and pitiful existence, that he scarcely knows how to frame a desire for any life much better than that which he now endures perforce. It is the province of art to set the true ideal of a full and reasonable life before him, a life to which the perception and creation of beauty, the enjoyment of real pleasure that is, shall be felt to be as necessary to man as his daily bread, and that no man, and no set of men, can be deprived of this except by mere opposition, which should be resisted to the utmost.

H. G. Wells

H. G. Wells (1866–1946) was born in Bromley, Kent. His father ran a small china shop and played cricket professionally. His mother was a maid, and later housekeeper at Up Park, the country house which Wells was to portray as Bladesover in *Tono-Bungay* (1909). His education was spasmodic: at a local school; a brief spell at Midhurst Grammar School; and then apprenticeships for short periods to a draper and to a chemist. The award of a scholarship to the Normal School of Science at South Kensington gave him the educational break he longed for and the teaching of T. H. Huxley at Kensington strongly influenced his future career. For a while Wells earned his living by teaching and miscellaneous journalism, but the early success of his science-fiction tales allowed him to become a professional writer. *The Time Machine* (1895), was quickly followed by *The Island of Dr Moreau* (1896), *The War of the Worlds* (1898) and many others. *Anticipations* (1901), from which 'The Life-History of Democracy' is taken, consisted of articles first published in the *Fortnightly Review*. It showed Wells moving from futuristic to sociological prophecy, and towards books such as *Mankind in the Making* (1903) and *A Modern Utopia* (1905). It was the success of these books that took Wells into the Fabian Society which he tried unsuccessfully to use as a platform for his own political ideas, but the most productive work of these years went into the novels of lower middle-class life, *Love and Mr Lewisham* (1900), *Kipps* (1905) and *The History of Mr Polly* (1910), and the more deliberately controversial novels such as *Anne Veronica* (1909) and *The New Machiavelli* (1911). A firm believer in the eventual development of a world state, Wells used his considerable fame to travel, meet world leaders, and spread his ideas, through journalism, didactic novels, and encyclopaedic works of popularization such as *A Short History of* the World (1922) and *The Work, Wealth and Happiness of Mankind* (1932). His two-volume *Experiment in Autobiography*, published in 1934, ranks among the very best of his books.

THE LIFE-HISTORY OF DEMOCRACY

In the preceding four chapters there has been developed, in a clumsy laborious way, a smudgy, imperfect picture of the generalized civilized state of the coming century. In terms, vague enough at times, but never absolutely indefinite, the general distribution of the population in this state has been discussed, and its natural development into four great – but in practice intimately interfused – classes. It has been shown – I know not how convincingly – that as the result of forces that are practically irresistible, a world-wide process of social and moral deliquescence is in progress, and that a really functional social body of engineering, managing men, scientifically trained, and having common ideals and interests, is likely to segregate and disentangle itself from our present confusion of aimless and ill-directed lives. It has been pointed out that life is presenting an unprecedented and increasing variety of morals, *ménages*, occupations and types, at present so mingled as to give a general effect of greyness, but containing the promise of local concentration that may presently change that greyness into kaleidoscopic effects. That image of concentrating contrasted colours will be greatly repeated in this present chapter. In the course of these inquiries, we have permitted ourselves to take a few concrete glimpses of households, costumes, conveyances, and conveniences of the coming time, but only as incidental realizations of points in this general thesis. And now, assuming, as we must necessarily do, the soundness of these earlier speculations, we have arrived at a stage when we may consider how the existing arrangements for the ostensible government of the State are likely to develop through their own inherent forces, and how they are likely to be affected by the processes we have forecast.

So far, this has been a speculation upon the probable

development of a civilized society *in vacuo*. Attention has been almost exclusively given to the forces of development, and not to the forces of conflict and restraint. We have ignored the boundaries of language that are flung athwart the great lines of modern communication, we have disregarded the friction of tariffs, the peculiar groups of prejudices and irrational instincts that inspire one miscellany of shareholders, workers, financiers, and superfluous poor such as the English, to hate, exasperate, lie about, and injure another such miscellany as the French or the Germans. Moreover, we have taken very little account of the fact that, quite apart from nationality, each individual case of the new social order is developing within the form of a legal government based on conceptions of a society that has been superseded by the advent of mechanism. It is this last matter that we are about to take into consideration.

Now, this age is being constantly described as a 'Democratic' age; 'Democracy' is alleged to have affected art, literature, trade and religion alike in the most remarkable ways. It is not only tacitly present in the great bulk of contemporary thought that this 'Democracy' is now dominant, but that it is becoming more and more overwhelmingly predominant as the years pass. Allusions to Democracy are so abundant, deductions from its influence so confident and universal, that it is worth while to point out what a very hollow thing the word in most cases really is, a large empty object in thought, of the most vague and faded associations and the most attenuated content, and to inquire just exactly what the original implications and present realities of 'Democracy' may be. The inquiry will leave us with a very different conception of the nature and future of this sort of political arrangement from that generally assumed. We have already seen in the discussion of the growth of great cities that an analytical process may absolutely invert the expectation based on the gross results up-to-date, and I believe it will be equally possible to show cause for believing that the development of Democracy also is, after all, not the opening phase of a world-wide movement going on unbendingly in its present direction, but the first impulse of forces that will finally sweep round into a quite different path. Flying off at a tangent is probably one of the gravest dangers and certainly the one most constantly present, in this enterprise of prophecy.

One may, I suppose, take the Rights of Man as they are embodied in the French Declaration as the ostentations of Democracy; our present Democratic state may be regarded as a practical realization of these claims. As far as the individual goes, the realization takes the form of an untrammelled liberty in matters that have heretofore been considered a part of social procedure, in the lifting of positive religious and moral compulsions, in the recognition of absolute property, and in the abolition of special privileges and special restrictions. Politically modern Democracy takes the form of denying that any specific person or persons shall act as a matter of intrinsic right or capacity on behalf of the community as a whole. Its root idea is representation. Government is based primarily on election, and every ruler is, in theory at least, a delegate and servant of the popular will. It is implicit in the Democratic theory that there *is* such a thing as a popular will, and this is supposed to be the net sum of the wills of all the citizens in the State, so far as public affairs are concerned. In its less perfect and more usual state the democratic theory is advanced either as an ethical theory which postulates an absence of formal acquiescence on the part of the governed as injustice, or else as a convenient political compromise, the least objectionable of all possible methods of public control, because it will permit only the minimum of general unhappiness. . . . I know of no case for the elective Democratic government of modern States that cannot be knocked to pieces in five minutes. It is manifest that upon countless important public issues there is no collective will, and nothing in the mind of the average man except blank indifference; that an electional system simply places power in the hands of the most skilful electioneers; that neither men nor their rights are identically equal, but vary with every individual, and, above all, that the minimum or maximum of general happiness is related only so indirectly to the public control that people will suffer great miseries from their governments unresistingly, and, on the other hand, change their rulers on account of the most trivial irritations. The case against all the prolusions of ostensible Democracy is indeed so strong that it is impossible to consider the present wide establishment of Democratic institutions as being the outcome of any process of intellectual conviction; it arouses suspicion even whether ostensible Democracy may not be a mere rhetorical garment for essentially different facts, and upon that suspicion we will now inquire.

Democracy of the modern type, manhood suffrage and so forth, became a conspicuous phenomenon in the world only in the closing decades of the eighteenth century. Its genesis is so intimately connected with the first expansion of the productive element in the State, through mechanism and a co-operative organization, as to point at once to a causative connection. The more closely one looks into the social and political life of the eighteenth century the more plausible becomes this view. New and potentially influential social factors had begun to appear – the organizing manufacturer, the intelligent worker, the skilled tenant, and the urban abyss, and the traditions of the old land-owning non-progressive aristocratic monarchy that prevailed in Christendom, rendered it incapable – without some destructive shock or convulsion – of any re-organization to incorporate or control these new factors. In the case of the British Empire an additional stress was created by the incapacity of the formal government to assimilate the developing civilization of the American colonies. Everywhere there were new elements, not as yet clearly analyzed or defined, arising as mechanism arose; everywhere the old traditional government and social system, defined and analyzed all too well, appeared increasingly obstructive, irrational, and feeble in its attempts to include and direct these new powers. But now comes a point to which I am inclined to attach very great importance. The new powers were as yet shapeless. It was not the conflict of a new organization with the old. It was the preliminary dwarfing and deliquescence of the mature old beside the embryonic mass of the new. It was impossible then – it is, I believe, only beginning to be possible now – to estimate the proportions, possibilities, and inter-relations of the new social orders out of which a social organization has still to be built in the coming years. No formula of definite re-construction had been evolved, or has even been evolved yet, after a hundred years. And these swelling inchoate new powers, whose very birth condition was the crippling, modification, or destruction of the old order, were almost forced to formulate their proceedings for a time, therefore, in general affirmative propositions that were really in effect not affirmative propositions at all, but propositions of repudiation and denial. 'These kings and nobles and people privileged in relation to obsolescent functions cannot manage our affairs' — that was evident enough, that was the really essential question at that time, and since no other effectual substitute appeared ready-made, the working doctrine of the infallible judgement of humanity in the gross, as distinguished from the quite indisputable incapacity of sample individuals, became, in spite of its inherent absurdity, a convenient and acceptable working hypothesis.

Modern Democracy thus came into being, not, as eloquent persons have pretended, by the sovereign people consciously and definitely assuming power — I imagine the sovereign people in France during the first Revolution, for example, quite amazed and muddle-headed with it all — but by the decline of old ruling classes in the face of the *quasi*-natural growth of mechanism and industrialism, and by the unpreparedness and want of organization in the new intelligent elements in the State. I have compared the human beings in society to a great and increasing variety of colours tumultuously smashed up together, and giving at present a general and quite illusory effect of grey, and I have attempted to show that there is a process in progress that will amount at last to the segregation of these mingled tints into recognizable distinct masses again. It is not a monotony, but an utterly disorderly and confusing variety that makes this grey, but Democracy, for practical purposes, does really assume such a monotony. Like ∞, the Democratic formula is a concrete-looking and negotiable symbol for a negation. It is the aspect in political disputes and contrivances of that social and moral deliquescence the nature and possibilities of which have been discussed in the preceding chapters of this volume.

Modern Democracy first asserted itself in the ancient kingdoms of France and Great Britain (counting the former British colonies in America as part of the latter), and it is in the French and English-speaking communities that Democracy has developed itself most completely. Upon the supposition we have made, democracy broke out first in these States because they were leading the way in material progress, because they were the first States to develop industrialism, wholesale mechanisms, and great masses of insubordinate activity outside the recognized political scheme, and the nature and time and violence of the outbreak was determined by the nature of the superseded government, and the amount of stress between it and the new elements. But the detachment of a great section of the new middle-class from the aristocratic order of England to form the United States of America, and the sudden rejuvenescence of France by the swift and thorough sloughing of its outworn aristocratic monarchy, the consequent wars and the Napoleonic adventure, checked and modified the parallel development that might otherwise have happened in country after country over all Europe west of the Carpathians. The monarchies that would probably have collapsed through internal forces and given place to modern democratic states were smashed from the outside, and a process of political reconstruction, that has probably missed out the complete formal Democratic phase altogether – and which has been enormously complicated through religious, national, and dynastic traditions set in. Throughout America, in England, and, after extraordinary experiments, in France, political democracy has in effect legally established itself – most completely in the United States – and the reflection and influence of its methods upon the methods of all the other countries in intellectual contact with it, have been so considerable as practically to make their monarchies as new in their kind, almost, as democratic republics. In Germany, Austria, and Italy, for example, there is a press nearly as audible as in the more frankly democratic countries, and measurably akin in influence; there are constitutionally established legislative assemblies, and there is the same unofficial development of powerful financial and industrial powers with which the ostensible Government must make terms. In a vast amount of the public discussion of these States, the postulates of Democracy are clearly implicit. Quite as much in reality as the democratic republics of America, are they based not on classes but upon a confusion; they are, in their various degrees and with their various individual differences, just as truly governments of the grey.

It has been argued that the grey is illusory and must sooner or later pass, and that the colour that will emerge to predominance will take its shape as a scientifically-trained middle class of an unprecedented sort, not arising out of the older middle classes, but replacing them. This class will become, I believe, at last consciously *the* State, controlling and restricting very greatly the three non-functional masses with which it is as yet almost indistinguishably mingled. The general nature of its formation within the existing confusion and its emergence may, I think, with a certain degree of confidence, be already forecast, albeit at present its beginnings are singularly unpromising and faint. At present the class of specially-trained and capable people – doctors, engineers, scientific men of all sorts – is quite disproportionally absent from political life, it does not exist as a factor in that life, it is growing up outside that life, and has still to develop, much more to display, a collective intention to come specifically in. But the forces are in active operation to drag it into the centre of the stage for all that.

The modern democracy or democratic quasi-monarchy conducts its affairs as though there was no such thing as special knowledge or practical education. The utmost recognition it affords to the man who has taken the pains to know, and specifically to do, is occasionally to consult him upon specific points and override his counsels in its ampler wisdom, or to entrust to him some otherwise impossible duty under circum-stances of extreme limitation. The man of special equipment is treated always as if he were some sort of curious performing animal. The gunnery specialist, for example, may move and let off guns, but he may not say where they are to be let off – some one a little ignorant of range and trajectory does that; the engineer may move the ship and fire the battery, but only with some man, who does not perfectly understand, shouting instructions down a tube at him. If the cycle is to be adapted to military requirements, the thing is entrusted to Lieutenant-Colonel Balfour. If horses are to be bought for the British Army in India, no specialist goes, but Lord Edward Cecil. These people of the governing class do not understand there is such a thing as special knowledge or an inexorable fact in the world; they have been educated at schools conducted by amateur schoolmasters, whose real aim in life – if such people can be described as having a real aim in life – is the episcopal bench, and they have learnt little or nothing but the extraordinary power of appearances in these democratic times. To look right and to be of good report is to succeed. What else is there? The primarily functional men are ignored in the ostensible political scheme, it operates as though they did not exist, as though nothing, in fact, existed but the irresponsible wealthy, and the manipulators of irresponsible wealth, on the one hand, and a great, grey, politically indifferent community on the other. Having regard only to the present condition of political life, it would seem as though this state of affairs must continue indefinitely, and develop only in accordance with the laws of inter-action between our charlatan governing class on the one hand, and the grey mass of governed on the other. There is no way apparent in the existing political and social order, whereby the class of really educated persons that the continually more complicated mechanical fabric of social life is developing may be expected to come in. And in a very great amount of current political speculation, the development and final emergence of this class is ignored, and attention is concentrated entirely upon the inherent process of development of the political machine. And even in that it is very easy to exaggerate the preponderance of one or other of what are really very evenly-balanced forces in the machine of democratic government.

There are two chief sets of parts in the machine that have a certain antagonistic relation, that play against each other, and one's conception of coming developments is necessarily determined by the relative value one gives to these opposing elements. One may compare these two groups to the Power and the Work, respectively, at the two ends of a lever.[1] On the one hand there is that which pays for the machine, which distributes salaries and rewards, subsidizes newspapers and so forth – the central influence.[2] On the other hand, there is the collectively grey voting mass, with certain prejudices and traditions, and certain laws and limitations of thought upon which the newspapers work, and which, within the confines of its inherent laws, they direct. If one dwell chiefly on the possibilities of the former element, one may conjure up a practical end to democracy in the vision of a State 'run' entirely by a group of highly forcible and intellectual persons – usually the dream takes the shape of financiers and their associates, their perfected mechanism of party control working the elections boldly and capably, and their public policy being directed towards financial ends. One of the common prophecies of the future of the United States is such a domination by a group of trust organizers and political bosses. But a man, or a group of men, so strong and intelligent as would be needed to hold an entire party machine within the confines of his – or their collective – mind and will, could, at the most, be but a very transitory and incidental phenomenon in the history of the world. Either such an exploitation of the central control will have to be covert and subtle beyond any precedent in human disingenuousness, or else its domination will have to be very amply modified indeed, by the requirements of the second factor, and its proceedings made very largely the resultant of that second factor's forces.

[1] The fulcrum, which is generally treated as being absolutely immovable, being the general belief in the theory of democracy.

[2] In the United States, a vast rapidly developing country, with relatively much kinetic wealth, this central influence is the financial support of the Boss, consisting for the most part of active-minded, capable business organizers; in England, the land where irresponsible realized wealth is at a maximum, a public-spirited section of the irresponsible, inspired by the tradition of an aristocratic functional past, qualifies the financial influence with an amateurish, indolent, and publicly unprofitable integrity. In Germany an aggressively functional Court occupies the place and plays the part of a permanently dominant party machine.

Moreover, very subtle men do not aim at things of this sort, or aiming, fail, because subtlety of intelligence involves subtlety of character, a certain fastidiousness and a certain weakness. Now that the garrulous period, when a flow of language and a certain effectiveness of manner was a necessary condition to political pre-eminence, is passing away, political control falls more and more entirely into the hands of a barristerish intriguing sort of person with a tough-wearing, leathery, practical mind. The sort of people who will work the machine are people with 'faith', as the popular preachers say, meaning, in fact, people who do not analyze, people who will take the machine as it is, unquestioningly, shape their ambitions to it, and – saving their vanity – work it as it wants to go. The man who will be boss will be the man who wants to be boss, who finds, in being boss, a complete and final satisfaction, and not the man who complicates things by wanting to be boss in order to be, or do, something else. The machines are governed today, and there is every reason to believe that they will continue to be governed, by masterful-looking resultants, masters of nothing but compromise, and that little fancy of an inner conspiracy of control within the machine and behind ostensible politics is really on all fours with the wonderful Rodin (of the Juif Errant) and as probable as anything else in the romances of Eugene Sue.

If, on the other hand, we direct attention to the antagonistic element in the machine, to Public Opinion, to the alleged collective mind of the grey mass, and consider how it is brought to believe in itself and its possession of certain opinions by the concrete evidence of daily newspapers and eloquent persons saying as much, we may also very readily conjure up a contrasted vision of extraordinary demagogues or newspaper syndicates working the political machine from that direction. So far as the demagogue goes, the increase of population, the multiplication of amusements and interests, the differentiation of social habits, the diffusion of great towns, all militate against that sufficient gathering of masses of voters in meeting-houses which gave him his power in the recent past. It is improbable that ever again will any flushed undignified man with a vast voice, a muscular face in incessant operation, collar crumpled, hair disordered, and arms in wild activity, talking, talking, talking, talking copiously out of the windows of railway carriages, talking on railway platforms, talking from hotel balconies, talking on tubs, barrels, scaffoldings, pulpits – tireless and undammable – rise to be the most powerful thing in any democratic state in the world. Continually the individual vocal demagogue dwindles, and the element of bands and buttons, the organization of the press and procession, the share of the machine, grows.

Mr Harmsworth, of the London *Daily Mail*, in a very interesting article has glanced at certain possibilities of power that may vest in the owners of a great system of world-wide 'simultaneous' newspapers, but he does not analyze the nature of the influence exercised by newspapers during the successive phases of the nineteenth century, nor the probable modifications of that influence in the years to come, and I think, on the whole, he inclines very naturally to over-estimate the amount of intentional direction that may be given by the owner of a paper to the minds and acts of his readers, and to exceed the very definite limits within which that influence is confined. In the earlier Victorian period, the more limited, partly educated, and still very homogeneous enfranchised class, had a certain habit of thinking; its tranquil assurance upon most theological and all moral and aesthetic points left political questions as the chief field of exercise for such thinking as it did, and, as a consequence, the dignified newspapers of that time were able to discuss, and indeed were required to discuss not only specific situations but general principles. That indeed was their principal function, and it fell rather to the eloquent men to misapply these principles according to the necessity of the occasion. The papers did then very much more than they do now to mould opinion, though they did not direct affairs to anything like the extent of their modern successors. They made roads upon which events presently travelled in unexpected fashions. But the often cheaper and always more vivid newspapers that have come with the New Democracy do nothing to mould opinion. Indeed, there is no longer upon most public questions – and as I have tried to make clear in my previous paper, there is not likely to be any longer – a collective opinion to be moulded. Protectionists, for example, are a mere band, Free Traders are a mere band; on all these details we are in chaos. And these modern newspapers simply endeavour to sustain a large circulation and so merit advertisements by being as miscellaneously and vividly interesting as possible, by firing where the crowd seems thickest, by seeking perpetually and without any attempt at consistency, the greatest excitement of the greatest number. It is upon the cultivation and rapid succession of inflammatory topics that the modern newspaper expends its capital and trusts to recover its reward. Its general news sinks steadily to a subordinate position; criticism, discussion, and high responsibility pass out of journalism, and the power of the press comes more and more to be a dramatic and emotional power, the power to cry 'Fire!' in the theatre, the power to give enormous value for a limited time to some personality, some event, some aspect, true or false, without any power of giving a specific direction to the forces this distortion may set going. Directly the press of today passes from that sort of thing to some specific proposal, some implication of principles and beliefs, directly it chooses and selects, then it passes from the miscellaneous to the sectarian, and out of touch with the grey indefiniteness of the general mind. It gives offence here, it perplexes and bores there; no more than the boss politician can the paper of great circulation afford to work consistently for any ulterior aim.

This is the limit of the power of the modern newspaper of large circulation, the newspaper that appeals to the grey element, to the average democratic man, the newspaper of the deliquescence, and if our previous conclusion that human society has ceased to be homogeneous and will presently display new masses segregating from a great confusion, holds good, that will be the limit of its power in the future. It may undergo many remarkable developments and modifications,[1] but none of these tend to give it any greater political importance than it

[1] The nature of these modifications is an interesting side issue. There is every possibility of papers becoming at last papers of world-wide circulation, so far as the language in which they are printed permits, with editions that will follow the sun and change into tomorrow's issue as they go, picking up literary criticism here, financial intelligence

has now. And so, after all, our considerations of the probable developments of the party machine give us only negative results, so long as the grey social confusion continues. Subject to that continuance the party machine will probably continue as it is at present, and Democratic States and governments follow the lines upon which they run at the present time.

Now, how will the emergent class of capable men presently begin to modify the existing form of government in the ostensibly democratic countries and democratic monarchies?

there, here tomorrow's story, and there tomorrow's scandal, and, like some vast intellectual garden-roller, rolling out local provincialism at every revolution. This, for papers in English, at any rate, is merely a question of how long it will be before the price of the best writing (for journalistic purposes) rises actually or relatively above the falling cost of long distance electrical type setting. Each of the local editions of these world travelling papers, in addition to the identical matter that will appear almost simultaneously everywhere, will no doubt have its special matter and its special advertisements. Illustrations will be telegraphed just as well as matter, and probably a much greater use will be made of sketch and diagram than at present. If the theory advanced in this book that democracy is a transitory confusion be sound, there will not be one world paper of this sort only – like Moses' serpent after its miraculous struggle – but several, and as the non-provincial segregation of society goes on, these various great papers will take on more and more decided specific characteristics, and lose more and more their local references. They will come to have not only a distinctive type of matter, a distinctive method of thought and manner of expression, but distinctive fundamental implications, and a distinctive class of writer. This difference in character and tone renders the advent of any Napoleonic master of the newspaper world vastly more improbable than it would otherwise be. These specializing newspapers will, as they find their class, throw out many features that do not belong to that class. It is highly probable that many will restrict the space devoted to news and sham news; that forged and inflated stuff made in offices, that bulks out the foreign intelligence of so many English papers, for example. At present every paper contains a little of everything, inadequate sporting stuff, inadequate financial stuff, vague literary matter, voluminous reports of political vapourings, because no newspaper is quite sure of the sort of readers it has – probably no daily newspaper has yet a distinctive sort of reader.

There will be very many variations and modifications of the methods of this arrival, an infinite complication of detailed incidents, but a general proposition will be found to hold good. The suppression of the party machine in the purely democratic countries and of the official choice of the rich and privileged rulers in the more monarchical ones, by capable operative and administrative men inspired by the belief in a common theory of social order, will come about – peacefully and gradually as a process of change, or violently as a revolution – but inevitably as

Many people, with their minds inspired by the number of editions which evening papers pretend to publish and do not, incline to believe that daily papers may presently give place to hourly papers, each with the last news of the last sixty minutes photographically displayed. As a matter of fact no human being wants that, and very few are so foolish as to think they do; the only kind of news that any sort of people clamours for hot and hot is financial and betting fluctuations, lottery lists and examination results; and the elaborated and cheapened telegraphic and telephonic system of the coming days, with tapes (or phonograph to replace them) in every post-office and nearly every private house, so far from expanding this department, will probably sweep it out of the papers altogether. One will subscribe to a news agency which will wire all the stuff one cares to have so violently fresh, into a phonographic recorder perhaps, in some convenient corner. There the thing will be in every house, beside the barometer, to hear or ignore. With the separation of that function what is left of the newspaper will revert to one daily edition – daily, I think, because of the power of habit to make the newspaper the specific business of some definite moments in the day; the breakfast hour, I suppose, or the 'up-to-town' journey with most Englishmen now. Quite possibly someone will discover some day that there is now machinery for folding and fastening a paper into a form that will not inevitably get into the butter, or lead to bitterness in a railway carriage. This pitch of development reached, I incline to anticipate daily papers much more like the *Spectator* in form than these present mainsails of our public life. They will probably not contain fiction at all, and poetry only rarely, because no one but a partial imbecile wants these things in punctual daily doses, and we are anticipating an escape from a period of partial imbecility. My own culture and turn of mind, which is probably akin to that of a respectable mechanic of the year 2000, inclines me towards a daily paper that will the outcome either of the imminence or else of the disasters of war.

That all these governments of confusion will drift towards war, with a spacious impulse and a final vehemence quite out of comparison greater than the warlike impulses of former times, is a remarkable but by no means inexplicable thing. A tone of public expression, jealous and patriotic to the danger-point, is an unavoidable condition under which democratic governments exist. To be patriotically quarrelsome is imperative upon the party machines that will come to dominate the democratic

have in addition to its concentrated and absolutely trustworthy daily news, full and luminous accounts of new inventions, new theories, and new departures of all sorts (usually illustrated), witty and penetrating comments upon public affairs, criticisms of all sorts of things, representations of newly produced works of art, and an ample amount of ably written controversy upon everything under the sun. The correspondence columns, instead of being an exercising place for bores and conspicuous people who are not mercenary, will be the most ample, the most carefully collected, and the most highly paid of all departments in this paper. Personal paragraphs will be relegated to some obscure and costly corner next to the births, deaths, and marriages. This paper will have, of course, many pages of business advertisements, and these will usually be well worth looking through, for the more intelligent editors of the days to come will edit this department just like any other, and classify their advertisements in a descending scale of freshness and interest that will also be an ascending scale of price. The advertiser who wants to be an indecent bore, and vociferate for the ten millionth time some flatulent falsehood about a pill, for instance, will pay at nuisance rates. Probably many papers will refuse to print nasty and distressful advertisements about people's insides at all. The entire paper will be as free from either greyness or offensive stupidity in its advertisement columns as the shop windows in Bond Street today, and for much the same reason – because the people who go that way do not want that sort of thing.

It has been supposed that, since the real income of the newspaper is derived from advertisements, large advertisers will combine in the future to own papers confined to the advertisements of their specific wares. Some such monopoly is already attempted; several publishing firms own or partially own a number of provincial papers, which they adorn with strange 'Book Chat' columns conspicuously deficient in countries. They will not possess detailed and definite policies and creeds because there are no longer any detailed and definite public opinions, but they will for all that require some ostensible purpose to explain their cohesion, some hold upon the common man that will ensure his appearance in numbers at the polling place sufficient to save the government from the raids of small but determined sects. That hold can be only of one sort. Without moral or religious uniformity, with material interests as involved and confused as a heap of spelicans, there remains only one generality for the politician's purpose, the ampler aspect of a

their information; and a well-known cycle tyre firm supplies 'Cycling' columns that are mere pedestals for the Head-of-King-Charles make of tyre. Many quack firms publish and give away annual almanacks replete with economical illustrations, offensive details, and bad jokes. But I venture to think, in spite of such phenomena, that these suggestions and attempts are made with a certain disregard of the essential conditions of sound advertisement. Sound advertisement consists in perpetual alertness and newness, in appearance in new places and in new aspects, in the constant access to fresh minds. The devotion of a newspaper to the interest of one particular make of a commodity or group of commodities will inevitably rob its advertisement department of most of its interest for the habitual readers of the paper. That is to say, the newspaper will fail in what is one of the chief attractions of a good newspaper. Moreover, such a devotion will react upon all the other matter in the paper, because the editor will need to be constantly alert to exclude seditious reflections upon the Health-Extract-of-Horse-Flesh or Saved-by-Boiling-Jam. His sense of this relation will taint his self-respect and make him a less capable editor than a man whose sole affair is to keep his paper interesting. To these more interesting rival papers the excluded competitor will be driven, and the reader will follow in his wake. There is little more wisdom in the proprietor of an article in popular demand buying or creating a newspaper to contain all his advertisements than in his buying a coal pit for the same purpose. Such a privacy of advertisement will never work, I think, on a large scale; it is probably at or near its maximum development now, and this anticipation of the advertiser-owned paper, like that of hourly papers, and that wonderfully powerful cosmic newspaper syndicate, is simply another instance of prophesying based only on a present trend, an expansion of the obvious, instead of an analysis of determining forces.

man's egotism, his pride in what he imagines to be his particular kind – his patriotism. In every country amenable to democratic influences there emerges, or will emerge, a party machine, vividly and simply patriotic – and indefinite upon the score of any other possible consideration between man and man. This will hold true, not only of the ostensibly democratic states, but also of such reconstituted modern monarchies as Italy and Germany, for they, too, for all their legal difference, rest also on the grey. The party conflicts of the future will turn very largely on the discovery of the true patriot, on the suspicion that the crown or the machine in possession is in some more or less occult way traitorous, and almost all other matters of contention will be shelved and allowed to stagnate, for fear of breaking the unity of the national mechanism.

Now, patriotism is not a thing that flourishes in the void – one needs a foreigner. A national and patriotic party is an anti-foreign party; the altar of the modern god, Democracy, will cry aloud for the stranger men. Simply to keep in power, and out of no love of mischief, the government or the party machine will have to insist upon dangers and national differences, to keep the voter to the polls by alarms, seeking ever to taint the possible nucleus of any competing organization with the scandal of external influence. The party press will play the watch-dog and allay all internal dissensions with its warning bay at some adjacent people, and the adjacent peoples, for reasons to be presently expanded, will be continually more sensitive to such baying. Already one sees country yelping at country all over the modern world, not only in the matter of warlike issues, but with a note of quite furious commercial rivalry – quite furious and, indeed, quite insane, since its ideal of trading enormously with absolutely ruined and tradeless foreigners, exporting everything and importing nothing, is obviously outside reason altogether. The inexorable doom of these governments based on the grey, is to foster enmity between people and people. Even their alliances are but sacrifices to intenser antagonisms. And the phases of the democratic sequence are simple and sure. Forced on by a relentless competition, the tone of the outcries will become fiercer and fiercer; the occasions of excitement, the perilous moments, the ingenuities of annoyance, more and more dramatic – from the mere emptiness and disorder of the general mind! Jealousies and anti-foreign enactments, tariff manipulations and commercial embitterment, destructive, foolish, exasperating obstructions that benefit no human being, will minister to this craving without completely allaying it. Nearer, and ever nearer, the politicians of the coming times will force one another towards the verge, not because they want to go over it, not because anyone wants to go over it, but because they are, by their very nature, compelled to go that way, because to go in any other direction is to break up and lose power. And, consequently, the final development of the democratic system, so far as intrinsic forces go, will be, not the rule of the boss, nor the rule of the trust, nor the rule of the newspaper; no rule, indeed, but international rivalry, international competition, international exasperation and hostility, and at last – irresistible and overwhelming – the definite establishment of the rule of that most stern and educational of all masters – *War*.

At this point there opens a tempting path, and along it historical precedents, like a forest of notice-boards, urge us to go. At the end of the vista poses the figure of Napoleon with 'Caesarism' written beneath it. Disregarding certain alien considerations for a time, assuming the free working out of democracy to its conclusion, we perceive that, in the case of our generalized state, the party machine, together with the nation entrusted to it, must necessarily be forced into passionate national war. But, having blundered into war, the party machine will have an air of having accomplished its destiny. A party machine or a popular government is surely as likely a thing to cause a big disorder of war and as unlikely a thing to conduct it, as the wit of man, working solely to that end, could ever have devised. I have already pointed out why we can never expect an elected government of the modern sort to be guided by any far-reaching designs, it is constructed to get office and keep office, not to do anything in office, the conditions of its survival are to keep appearances up and taxes down,[1] and the care and

[1] One striking illustration of the distinctive possibilities of democratic

management of army and navy is quite outside its possibilities. The military and naval professions in our typical modern State will subsist very largely upon tradition, the ostensible government will interfere with rather than direct them, and there will be no force in the entire scheme to check the corrupting influence of a long peace, to insist upon adequate exercises for the fighting organization or ensure an adequate adaptation to the new and perpetually changing possibilities of untried apparatus. Incapable but confident and energetic persons, having political influence, will have been permitted to tamper with the various arms of the service, the equipment will be largely devised to create an impression of efficiency in times of peace in the minds of the general voting public, and the really efficient soldiers will either have fretted themselves out of the army or have been driven out as political non-effectives, troublesome, innovating persons anxious to spend money upon

government came to light during the last term of office of the present patriotic British Government. As a demonstration of patriotism large sums of money were voted annually for the purpose of building warships, and the patriotic common man paid the taxes gladly with a dream of irresistible naval predominance to sweeten the payment. But the money was not spent on warships; only a portion of it was spent, and the rest remained to make a surplus and warm the heart of the common man in his tax-paying capacity. This artful dodge was repeated for several years; the artful dodger is now a peer, no doubt abjectly respected, and nobody in the most patriotic party so far evolved is a bit the worse for it. In the organizing expedients of all popular governments, as in the prospectus of unsound companies, the disposition is to exaggerate the nominal capital at the expense of the working efficiency. Democratic armies and navies are always short, and probably will always be short, of ammunition, paint, training and reserve stores; battalions and ships, since they count as units, are over-numerous and go short-handed, and democratic army reform almost invariably works out to some device for multiplying units by fission, and counting men three times instead of twice in some ingenious and plausible way. And this must be so, because the sort of men who come inevitably to power under democratic conditions are men trained by all the conditions of their lives to so set appearances before realities as at last to become utterly incapable of realities.

'fads'. So armed, the New Democracy will blunder into war, and the opening stage of the next great war will be the catastrophic breakdown of the formal armies, shame and disasters, and a disorder of conflict between more or less equally matched masses of stupefied, scared, and infuriated people. Just how far the thing may rise from the value of an alarming and edifying incident to a universal catastrophe, depends upon the special nature of the conflict, but it does not alter the fact that any considerable war is bound to be a bitter, appalling, highly educational and constitution-shaking experience for the modern democratic state.

Now, foreseeing this possibility, it is easy to step into the trap of the Napoleonic precedent. One hastens to foretell that either with the pressure of coming war, or in the hour of defeat, there will arise the Man. He will be strong in action, epigrammatic in manner, personally handsome and continually victorious. He will sweep aside parliaments and demagogues, carry the nation to glory, reconstruct it as an empire, and hold it together by circulating his profile and organizing further successes. He will – I gather this from chance lights upon contemporary anticipations – codify everything, rejuvenate the papacy, or, at any rate, galvanize Christianity, organize learning in meek intriguing academies of little men, and prescribe a wonderful educational system. The grateful nations will once more deify a lucky and aggressive egotism. . . . And there the vision loses breath.

Nothing of the sort is going to happen, or, at any rate, if it happens, it will happen as an interlude, as no necessary part in the general progress of the human drama. The world is no more to be recast by chance individuals than a city is to be lit by sky rockets. The purpose of things emerges upon spacious issues, and the day of individual leaders is past. The analogies and precedents that lead one to forecast the coming of military one-man dominions, the coming of such other parodies of Caesar's career as that misapplied, and speedily futile chess champion, Napoleon I, contrived, are false. They are false because they ignore two correlated things; first, the steady development of a new and quite unprecedented educated class as a necessary aspect of the expansion of science and mechanism, and secondly, the absolute revolution in the art of war that science and mechanism are bringing about. This latter consideration the next chapter will expand, but here, in the interests of this discussion, we may in general terms anticipate its gist. War in the past has been a thing entirely different in its nature from what war, with the apparatus of the future, will be – it has been showy, dramatic, emotional, and restricted; war in the future will be none of these things. War in the past was a thing of days and heroisms; battles and campaigns rested in the hand of the great commander, he stood out against the sky, picturesquely on horseback, visibly controlling it all. War in the future will be a question of preparation, of long years of foresight and disciplined imagination, there will be no decisive victory, but a vast diffusion of conflict – it will depend less and less on controlling personalities and driving emotions, and more and more upon the intelligence and personal quality of a great number of skilled men. All this the next chapter will expand. And either before or after, but, at any rate, in the shadow of war, it will become apparent, perhaps even suddenly, that the whole apparatus of power in the country is in the hands of a new class of intelligent and scientifically-educated men. They will probably, under the development of warlike stresses, be discovered – they will discover themselves – almost surprisingly with roads and railways, carts and cities, drains, food supply, electrical supply, and water supply, and with guns and such implements of destruction and intimidation as men scarcely dream of yet, gathered in their hands. And they will be discovered, too, with a growing common consciousness of themselves as distinguished from the grey confusion, a common purpose and implication that the fearless analysis of science is already bringing to light. They will find themselves with bloodshed and horrible disasters ahead, and the material apparatus of control entirely within their power. 'Suppose, after all,' they will say, 'we ignore these very eloquent and showy governing persons above, and this very confused and ineffectual multitude below. Suppose now we put on the brakes and try something a little more stable and orderly. These people in possession have, of course, all sorts of established rights and prescriptions; they have squared the law to their purpose, and the constitution does not know us; they can get at the judges, they can get at the newspapers, they can do all sorts of things except avoid a smash – but, for our part, we have these really most ingenious and subtle guns. Suppose instead of our turning them and our valuable selves in a fool's quarrel against the ingenious and subtle guns of other men akin to ourselves, we use them in the cause of the higher sanity, and clear that jabbering war tumult out of the streets.' . . . There may be no dramatic moment for the expression of this idea, no moment when the new Cromwellism and the new Ironsides will come visibly face to face with talk and baubles, flags and patriotic dinner bells; but, with or without dramatic moments, the idea will be expressed and acted upon. It will be made quite evident then, what is now indeed only a pious opinion, namely, that wealth is, after all, no ultimate Power at all, but only an influence among aimless, police-guarded men. So long as there is peace the class of capable men may be mitigated and gagged and controlled, and the ostensible present order may flourish still in the hands of that other class of men which deals with the appearances of things. But as some super-saturated solution will crystallize out with the mere shaking of its beaker, so must the new order of men come into visibly organized existence through the concussions of war. The charlatans can escape everything except war, but to the cant and violence of nationality, to the sustaining force of international hostility, they are ruthlessly compelled to cling, and what is now their chief support must become at last their destruction. And so it is I infer that, whether violently as a revolution or quietly and slowly, this grey confusion that is Democracy must pass away inevitably by its own inherent conditions, as the twilight passes, as the embryonic confusion of the cocoon creature passes, into the higher stage, into the higher organism, the world-state of the coming years.

Further Reading

There is now a vast literature on the authors contained in this anthology. Details of much of it can be found in *The New Cambridge Bibliography of English Literature*. Volume III (1969), edited by George Watson, covers Carlyle, Arnold, Ruskin and Mill; Volume IV (1972), edited by I. R. Willison, covers Wells. *Victorian Prose: A Guide to Research* (New York, 1973), edited by David DeLaura, has chapters on Carlyle, Mill, Arnold and Ruskin. There is no equivalent readily available bibliography for Marx and Engels, but David McLellan's *Karl Marx: His Life and Thought* (1973), in addition to being an excellent biography of Marx, contains a substantial descriptive listing of secondary material.

Of the more general or wide-ranging books on the Victorian prophets, John Holloway's *The Victorian Sage* (1953) is a valuable stylistic and philosophical study of Carlyle, Disraeli, George Eliot, Newman, Arnold and Hardy. *The Art of Victorian Prose* (1968), edited by George Levine and William Madden, includes essays on Carlyle, Mill, Arnold and Ruskin, which are also largely stylistic in emphasis. Raymond Williams's *Culture and Society 1780–1950* (1958) is the outstanding, pioneering study of literature and social change in the nineteenth century and Williams's own views of that book, twenty years on, in *Politics and Letters* (1979), make fascinating reading. In *The Idea of the Clerisy in the Nineteenth Century* (1978), Ben Knights traces the idea of the clerisy from Coleridge through Carlyle, Arnold, Mill and Newman to the twentieth century, and is particularly interesting on the role of universities. A far less sympathetic interpretation of 'the Sages' is advanced by George Watson in *The English Ideology* (1973). I. F. Clarke's *The Pattern of Expectation 1644–2001* (1979), though not dealing directly with the Victorian 'prophets' discussed here, contains a good deal of relevant material on futuristic predictions and the rise of 'futurology'

INTO UNKNOWN ENGLAND 1866-1913

SELECTIONS FROM THE SOCIAL EXPLORERS

Edited by Peter Keating

How did the poor live in late Victorian and Edwardian England? In the slums of London and Birmingham? In the iron-town of Middlesbrough? In a Devon fishing village? In rural Essex?

This is a fascinating sequence of extracts from the writings of those individuals, journalists and wealthy businessmen, a minister's wife, and a popular novelist, who temporarily left the comfort of their middle-class homes to find out how the other half lived. Peter Keating includes material from Charles Booth, Jack London, B. S. Rowntree and C. F. G. Masterman as well as by such lesser-known figures as George Sims, Andrew Mearns and Stephen Reynolds.

'. . . a brilliant and compelling anthology . . . *Into Unknown England* is not only an education in itself, throwing into three-dimensional chiaroscuro the flat statistics of "scientific" history, but a splendid example of prose which is always immediate and alive.'
Alan Brien, *Spectator*

'The writers collected here used all the techniques they could to solicit sympathy. Their descendants are a thousand television documentaries.'
Paul Barker, *The Times*

'. . . a rich collection of passages, intelligently presented.'
The Guardian

Language Made Plain

Anthony Burgess

In this book Anthony Burgess, well known through his novels as a master and lover of language, looks at the basic elements of which literature is made. By approaching semantics, the science of linguistics, phonetics and the development of language in simple and entertaining terms, he provides a perfect basis for his second theme: the learning of languages, which is so vital and so often unnecessarily neglected through misunderstanding and mistrust.

'An enthralling study of how languages are related to one another, how they have grown apart, how and why they change.'

Daily Mirror

'. . . the pithy forcefulness of his style should win many a timid traveller to the confident and successful study of a whole range of languages.' *Times Educational Supplement*

Illuminations

Walter Benjamin

'From the evidence of this book I would suggest that Benjamin was one of the great European writers of this century.'
Philip Toynbee, *Observer*

Only since his death have Benjamin's works – literary essays, general reflections, aphorisms and probings into cultural phenomena – achieved fame outside his native Germany, where a discerning audience had already recognised him as one of the most acute and original minds of his time.

This aptly named collection includes Benjamin's views on Kafka, Baudelaire and Proust, essays on Leskov and Brecht's Epic Theatre, and discussions on art, technology and mass society, translation as a literary mode, and the philosophy of history.

In her introduction Hannah Arendt presents the critic's personality and intellectual development as well as placing his life and work in the context of Hitler's Germany.

Keywords

Raymond Williams

Alienation, creative, family, media, radical, structural, taste: these are seven of the hundred or so words whose derivation, development and contemporary meaning Raymond Williams explores in this unique study of the language in which we discuss 'culture' and 'Society'.

A series of connecting essays investigate how these 'keywords' have been formed, redefined, confused and reinforced as the historical contexts in which they were applied changed to give us their current meaning and significance.

'This is a book which everyone who is still capable of being educated should read.' Christopher Hill, *New Society*

'. . . for the first time we have some of the materials for constructing a genuinely historical and a genuinely social semantics . . . Williams's book is unique in its kind so far and it provides a model as well as a resource for us all.'
Alasdair MacIntyre, *New Statesman*

Course in General Linguistics

Ferdinand de Saussure

Ferdinand de Saussure died in 1913 with his masterpiece, *Cours de linguistique générale* still unwritten. Only in 1916 was a text reconstructed and published from his students' notes. But since then Saussure has been recognized as not only the founder of modern linguistics, but a formative influence on the development of twentieth-century thought.

In *Course in General Linguistics* Saussure defines those distinctions that have provided the basis for all subsequent linguistic studies. The book is a classic of intellectual discovery, whose more general implications are only now being widely recognized. As Jonathan Culler writes in his introduction: 'Saussure helps us to understand the role played by distinctions which structure our world and the systems of convention by which man becomes *homo significans*, a creature who gives things meaning.'

Fontana Paperbacks

Fontana is a leading paperback publisher of fiction and non-fiction, with authors ranging from Alistair MacLean, Agatha Christie and Desmond Bagley to Solzhenitsyn and Pasternak, from Gerald Durrell and Joy Adamson to the famous Modern Masters series.

In addition to a wide-ranging collection of internationally popular writers of fiction, Fontana also has an outstanding reputation for history, natural history, military history, psychology, psychiatry, politics, economics, religion and the social sciences.

All Fontana books are available at your bookshop or newsagent; or can be ordered direct. Just fill in the form and list the titles you want.

FONTANA BOOKS, Cash Sales Department, G.P.O. Box 29, Douglas, Isle of Man, British Isles. Please send purchase price, plus 8p per book. Customers outside the U.K. send purchase price, plus 10p per book. Cheque, postal or money order. No currency.

NAME (Block letters)

ADDRESS

While every effort is made to keep prices low, it is sometimes necessary to increase prices on short notice. Fontana Books reserve the right to show new retail prices on covers which may differ from those previously advertised in the text or elsewhere.